Student Engagement in Neoliberal Times

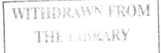

Nick Zepke

Student Engagement in Neoliberal Times

Theories and Practices for Learning and Teaching in Higher Education

 Springer

Nick Zepke
Institute of Education
Massey University Manawatu
Palmerston North
New Zealand

ISBN 978-981-10-9815-4   ISBN 978-981-10-3200-4   (eBook)
DOI 10.1007/978-981-10-3200-4

Printed on acid-free paper

This Springer imprint is published by Springer Nature
The registered company is Springer Nature Singapore Pte Ltd.
The registered company address is: 152 Beach Road, #22-06/08 Gateway East, Singapore 189721, Singapore

For Linda Leach, co-researcher and life companion with respect, gratitude and love.

Preface

Over the last 30 years or so, *student engagement* has become an all-round good thing in higher education. A very large and far-reaching research literature has inspired claims for its great value as an enabler of learning. These include that student engagement encourages persistence, assures quality learning, enables success, prepares graduates for the job market and helps them as active citizens to individual and social well-being. This literature offers many practical, yet varied, ideas for teachers in higher education to implement in their classrooms. The sheer number and diversity of ideas about engagement have led me to ask the following questions which inspire and organize this book.

- How can the rich and diverse engagement research be synthesized into useful strategies for use by higher education teachers to improve learning and teaching?
- Why have the outputs from this complex and varied body of work become a standard bearer for improving learning and teaching in higher education?
- What is missing from engagement research and how can this be addressed?

As a teacher of adults in undergraduate and postgraduate education, I have always wanted to become a more effective enabler of learning. The student engagement literature came to my notice while colleagues and I were researching student retention and persistence in a funded project. As it became clearer that student engagement and persistence are connected, I transferred my research attention toward engagement. This has been the focus of my work over the last decade and gave rise to the first question about organizing the book which is addressed in Chaps. 1–3. The second question emerged when I became intrigued by the reasons engagement was so popular. I was struck by the way engagement research seemed to focus on practical 'how to' questions while skimming more lightly over 'why' questions. With a background in politics and history I became aware that student engagement research and practice flourished in a political and economic climate dominated by neoliberalism, a way of thinking that forms the dominant mainstream of ideas in higher education today. This question is discussed in Chaps. 4–6. The third question followed because my response to the second question suggested that there was more to student engagement than has been aired in the engagement literature. Chapters 7–11 argue that ideas from critical theory could supplement what is missing in mainstream student education praxis.

Each of my original questions gave rise to a tentative answer. These in turn generated three propositions which underpin the argument in the book. The propositions are:

- There is a mainstream view of student engagement that makes a considerable contribution to understanding what works in learning and teaching in higher education to enable students to achieve success in a quality focused learning environment. This proposition draws heavily on articles I published with research partners from a funded Teaching and Learning Research Initiative (TLRI) project in New Zealand. These publications are listed in Appendix B.
- Student engagement research has achieved its importance in higher education at a time when dominant neoliberal political ideas and practices aligned with mainstream engagement research. While not caused by neoliberalism, student engagement has an elective affinity with it. This limits its potential. This proposition owes much to independent research I did between 2000 and 2015. Relevant publications in forming Chaps. 4–6 are listed in the Appendix.
- To reach its potential, student engagement needs to develop another dimension in research and practice. This dimension moves it away from neoliberal thinking and towards enabling learners to engage in a holistic, critical way in order to work for greater social justice. This proposition is supported by work I published between 2013 and 2015.

While the book does mine mainstream engagement research for practical ways to improve learning in higher education, this is not intended as a *how to do engagement* book. It rejects the notion that learning in classrooms is somehow divorced from the world of politics. Instead the book recognizes the symbiotic relationship between education and politics. Dominant ideas about learning and teaching such as those about student engagement are produced and supported within a congenial political climate. Consequently, this book is a work of critical scholarship. It values mainstream engagement research but also critiques its accepted understandings as limiting. This critique results in fresh insights about student engagement in higher education. It employs ideas from critical theory to develop a more holistic view of student engagement; one that distances it from the influence of neoliberal ideas and policies. The book is designed primarily for teachers and postgraduate students in higher education who wish to develop their own engagement pedagogy without being captured by its affinity with neoliberalism. It will also appeal to readers interested in critical analyses of education that seek to find ways to achieve a fairer society.

This preface hints at but does not acknowledge explicitly my own viewpoints. To discuss them at length would undoubtedly be extremely boring. However, you are entitled to know where I generally stand on topics addressed in the book. As a teacher, I see myself as problem poser and enabler of learning rather than as a transmitter of knowledge; as a learner I find myself to be a questioner rather than a believer in received truths; as a theorist I am of a critical disposition and as a citizen I am firmly aligned to the left of centre in politics and opposed to neoliberalism.

Palmerston North, New Zealand   Nick Zepke

Acknowledgments

As I progressed this book I increasingly became aware of the debt I owed others. Formal citations and references of course formally acknowledge the information, backing and general assistance I gained from published works. But the ideas, inspiration and insights gained by personal interactions with many others go largely unacknowledged. I want to go some way to acknowledge such a variety of personal debts.

A project funded by the New Zealand *Teaching and Learning Research Initiative* (TLRI) gave early support to my interest in student engagement. I acknowledge Robyn Baker, the then Director of the New Zealand Institute of Educational Research (NZIER), for her support of this work and Linda Leach who led the project with me. Linda was also a co-author of numerous articles (see Appendix B) inspired by the project. I also thank our research partners in the project for their important contributions: Helen Anderson, Alison Ayrton, Philippa Butler, Judy Henderson, Jerry Hoffman, Peter Isaacs, Jill Moseley, Catherine Ross, Barbara Russell, Gloria Slater, Kiri Solomon, Stewart Wilson and Adelle Wiseley.

I owe a considerable debt to a number of people active in researching teaching and learning in higher education for their contribution to my understanding of student engagement: Airini, Tom Angelo, Sally Brown, Colin Bryson, John Clarke, Peter Coolbear, Brian Findsen, Cedric Hall, Tony Harland, Richard James, Sally Kift, Luke Millard, Karen Nelson, Guyon Neutze, Dean Nugent, Phil Race, Ian Solomonides, Sumalee Sungsri, Vincent Tinto and Alison Viskovic.

To yet another group of people I am grateful for helping me get to grips with the politics in higher education and student engagement. These include John Codd, Aroha Dahm, Bernie Clarke, Shane Edwards, marg gilling, Tina Olsen-Ratana, Anne-Marie O'Neill, John O'Neill, Anania Randall, Huhana Reihana, Peter Roberts, Martin Stirling and Lynn Tett.

Last but not least, doctoral students investigating learning and teaching I have worked with have contributed in major ways to my learning about engagement.

Thank you Kirsty Farrant, Eva Heinrich, Zoe Jordens, Ella Kahu, Brian Marsh, Bridget Percy, Christine Pritchard, Catherine Ross, Murray Simons, Paora Stucki.

Thank you all and I acknowledge your contributions to this book. But of course you carry no responsibility for my errors or misinterpretations.

Contents

Part II   Questioning the Mainstream View

List of Tables

Part I
Exploring Mainstream Views
of Student Engagement

Chapter 1
Glimpsing Student Engagement

Abstract There is a very large body of research on student engagement in higher education. This book summarizes and builds on that literature by exploring a new direction for student engagement. This first chapter overviews the book by introducing some of its key features. It summarizes the main ideas informing the engagement construct, identifies shortcomings with it and argues for the need of new thinking. It grapples with the thorny issue of defining student engagement, discusses theoretical assumptions supporting it and details the purposes, assumptions and structure of the book. The chapter makes clear that this is not an empirically driven 'how to do' engagement book. While it does not ignore practice, the book is developed as a result of an ongoing and in depth engagement with theory.

Student engagement is a major area of research about student success and quality learning and teaching in higher education. Maiers (2008) identified it as a hot topic; Weimer (2012) called it a popular buzz phrase; Reschly and Christensen (2012) see it as a burgeoning construct. Kuh (2009) saw engagement as pervasive in conversations about higher education policy, in research, and even in the general media. This view of engagement as ever-present in the learning and teaching literature is supported by the amount of engagement research published between, say 2000 and 2010. For example, Wimpenny and Savin-Baden (2013) found 2530 articles published on the subject in these years. Trowler (2010) identified more than 1000 items. In their review of Australasian research on the first year experience, Nelson et al. (2011) found almost 400 empirical and conceptual studies. Linda Leach and I (2010) included almost 300 research reports in our synthesis of the engagement literature. Foci and methods in these reviews varied. Wimpenny and Savin-Baden's review used qualitative studies about learners' experiences. Trowler (2010) on the other hand, excluded most qualitative and 'grey' studies as lacking robustness. Nelson et al. (2011) were interested in any studies dealing with engagement and learning that contributed to a successful first year experience. Our own review synthesized both quantitative and qualitative studies that focused on engaging teaching.

© Springer Nature Singapore Pte Ltd. 2017
N. Zepke, *Student Engagement in Neoliberal Times*,
DOI 10.1007/978-981-10-3200-4_1

These four literature reviews synthesize what I consider to be mainstream research on student engagement. Such research attempts to meet the world-wide higher education community's expectation of evidence based, practical and largely uncritical research into how to facilitate learning that achieves student success. Governments, institutions and teachers are keen to accept and implement its findings. They consider engagement research useful in helping higher education achieve its mission of quality learning and teaching that helps learners into productive employment. In this chapter 1 introduce some key aspects of mainstream engagement research. I first unpack some of its features and complexities before attempting to find a suitable definition. I then précis some theoretical assumptions underpinning engagement research and finally discuss the purposes, processes and content of the book.

A Snapshot of Mainstream Engagement

Mainstream student engagement is not a simple construct. Its meaning is more glimpsed than clear-cut. It is interpreted in different ways. Fredricks et al. (2004) considered it a meta-construct, one that draws on a wide variety of intellectual traditions and views. These multiple faces are partly responsible for its widespread acceptance. In higher education research it divides into three broad strands. One, originating in the United States, focuses on learning behaviours identified and turned into quantifiable and generic indicators of engagement. Examples of such indicators are found in 'variable based' empirical research (Lawson and Lawson 2013) such as that found in the National Survey of Student Engagement (NSSE) used in the United States and its cousins in Australasia (Australia and New Zealand), China, Canada, South Africa and now the United Kingdom. In a recently revised version of the NSSE students are asked to respond to questions about five engagement measures—academic challenge, learning with peers, experiences with faculty (teachers) campus environment and participation in high impact practices (McCormick et al. 2013). Likert style questions ask students to indicate how often or how much they have engaged with, for example, reaching conclusions based on their own analysis of numerical information, or asking another student to help with an academic problem (McCormick et al. 2013). Four of the engagement measures investigate classroom behaviours. The fifth—participation in high impact practices—ask students to relate the extent of their participation in out of class activities such as learning communities, service learning, research with staff, and study abroad. The underpinning design of NSSE and similar engagement approaches conceives of engagement as identifiable and quantifiable student, teacher and institutional behaviours.

Another strand is focussed more on students' feelings of emotional belonging and agency (Thomas 2012). This view owes much to work originated by Vincent Tinto in the United States on academic and social integration (Tinto 1987). Originally associated with retention, academic and social integration have also been linked with student engagement. Tinto (2010, p. 73) suggested that a "key concept is that of educational community and the capacity of institutions to establish supportive social and academic communities, especially in the classroom, that actively involve all students as equal members". In a project linking student engagement with success, Thomas (2012) reframed academic and social integration as students having a sense of belonging. Students who do not feel they belong are more likely to be disengaged. Bryson and Hardy (2012) offer a framework comprising influences on feelings of belonging. These include students feeling a sense of relevance in what they learn; of suitable challenges; of a balance of choice, autonomy, risk, growth and enjoyability; of appropriate trust relationships with teachers and of ongoing dialogue with them; of a strong sense of purpose and strong social networks. Trowler (2010) operationalizes this by characterizing engaged learners as co-producers of learning in the classroom while also emphasizing their involvement in structure, processes and identity building in the wider community.

A third strand, 'approaches to learning', had diverse origins in Europe, the United Kingdom, South Africa and Australia. Some may consider it a bit of a stretch to label it an approach to engagement as at first researchers employing this approach did not use the word engagement. But it investigates learners' cognitive involvement in learning and so can be included as a part of the engagement construct (Solomonides et al. 2012). Rooted in phenomenology the 'approaches to learning' strand identifies what learning means to students and how they perceive and tackle it. This change of perspective leads to learning being seen as an individual construction of meaning not as a set of behaviours (Solomonides et al. 2012). Marton and Säljö (1976) identified two approaches to learning: one deep the other more superficial. Biggs (1978) confirmed the deep and surface approaches identified by Marton and Säljö. But he considered them to be *congruent motive packages* with each package comprising a motive connected to the approach chosen. He suggested that the motives for using the surface approach were extrinsic to the real purpose of the task. The motives for students engaging in deep learning were to engage for intrinsic reasons. Meyer (1991) developed the term *study orchestration* to capture an emphasis on self-direction that "focuses on the different ways students direct their resources in specific learning contexts" (Meyer 1991, p. 67).

Overarching these mainstream strands is engagement's strong association with quality teaching and learning and student success. Krause (2012) regards engagement as a key indicator of the quality of the student experience and of teaching and institutional performance. Kuh (2009) argues that student engagement is an important predictor of retention in higher education. It is positively correlated with a range of student outcomes such as critical thinking, cognitive development, self-esteem, student satisfaction and improved grades and persistence (Pascarella et al. 2010). Engagement researchers not associated with variable-centred quantitative research also recognize the close association of engagement with quality. In their case it is often engagement developed through positive relationships and emotion (Bryson and Hand 2007; Wimpenny and Savin-Baden 2013). As noted above, engagement is also associated with student success. This comes in different guises. Outcomes such as retention, completion and productive employment often feature as indicators of success influenced by engagement (Kuh 2009). While Hagel et al. (2011) and Krause (2012) have challenged such findings, McCormick (2009) and Kuh (2009) found some evidence that a high level of engagement predicts student success. Bryson and Hardy (2012) suggest that by engaging in a variety of educationally productive activities students can develop the foundation of skills and dispositions people need to live a productive, satisfying life after graduation.

The many versions of mainstream engagement all offer a very sunny understanding of what teaching and engaged learning can achieve. With good teaching student engagement is possible for all students. It encourages retention, assures quality learning, enables success, prepares graduates for the job market and insures that students are valued as consumers of good teaching. Such understandings reveal two underlying concerns. The first is that such attributes align student engagement with neoliberalism, the dominant ideology of our times (Carey 2013; Macfarlane 2016). Neoliberal ideas seem aligned to mainstream student engagement and student engagement seems to support a neoliberal agenda. I will argue that this affinity is what makes student engagement such a powerful influence in learning and teaching today. The second concern is that not all students are engaged. In a seminal paper Mann (2001) offers a darker glimpse of engagement from the mainstream literature. Here, engagement is a matter of compliance with externally set expectations, rules and procedures. Student success is defined by criteria set by others rather than students themselves. She suggests that this can lead to alienation, the opposite to engagement. She identifies seven reasons that can lead to alienation: needing to conform to expectations of performativity, accountability and practicality; perceiving their powerlessness with what to many are alien discourses; feeling strange in a foreign culture; needing to be compliant rather than creative; losing ownership of learning goals; being made docile by the evaluation process; and seeking safety and release from the other reasons for being alienated.

Mann (2001) does not claim that feelings of alienation are inevitable. Nor does Carey (2013) suggest that the neoliberal ideas feeding mainstream student engagement are always bad. He suggests that there is a possible nested hierarchy of engagement approaches enabling a variety of versions of student engagement to coexist. Fielding (2001) offers such a hierarchy. He suggests it has four stages: (i) students conform to expectations and make few decisions; (ii) are consulted by teachers but have no guaranteed influence; (iii) are partners in the engagement process but do not lead; and (iv) have a leadership role. Every stage is valuable in student engagement. The first two dominate the mainstream literature; the third appears occasionally; the fourth barely. To mitigate Mann's conditions for alienation requires that the third and fourth stages are represented more abundantly in the classroom. They represent another dimension of student engagement that gets much less attention. In this book I develop this dimension. I use the work of Freire, Habermas, hooks, Smith and Brameld among other to develop a critical theory of student engagement, one that impacts each of Bernstein's (1996) three educational message systems: curriculum, pedagogy and evaluation. Engagement here builds consciousness of self, others and society at large, critiques the mainstream, involves dialogue among equals, strives for communicative action, recognizes and acts to achieve social justice for others, especially 'the other' and exercises leadership in the production of knowledge. To do this requires reader engagement with both mainstream research and critical theory in order to glimpse a different way to practice. So, this is not a 'how to do engagement' book. While it offers practical ideas, it is more focused on asking critical questions about mainstream engagement and developing alternative theoretical approaches.

Defining Engagement?

Many researchers have tried to define this diverse and complex construct. Kuh et al. (2008, p. 542) considered engagement "both the time and energy students invest in educationally purposeful activities and the effort institutions devote to effective educational practices". Responsibility for student engagement here is bounded within the learning institution. It is achieved by the actions of learners who are supported by peers, teachers and institutions. Right behaviours by students and teachers enable engagement. This bounded view of engagement is questioned by researchers who envisage a more holistic process. For example, Fredricks et al. (2004) suggested that engagement is not only about right behaviours but also involves students' cognitive investment in and emotional commitment to their learning. Cognitive engagement points to investment in deep learning of concepts and skills, of individual construction of meaning and of transforming meanings (Marton and Säljö 1976). Emotional engagement results from feelings of psychological well-being such as a sense of belonging and security in relationships both inside and outside the classroom (Wimpenny and Savin-Baden 2013). Solomonides et al. (2012) offered a relational framework to identify some of the factors helping learners to make sense of their experiences. Engagement emerges when students gain a sense of being and transformation in mastering professional and discipline knowledge.

Such definitions generally view engagement through a classroom focused lens. Increasingly though researchers recognize the importance of external influences. Carey (2013) views engagement as an expansive idea that in addition to active student participation in learning includes a sense of identity and belonging and involvement in institutional structures and processes. Lawson and Lawson (2013) go wider still with a multi- dimensional view of engagement. They synthesize student engagement using a sociocultural ecological lens tracing student, teacher, institutional and external environment perspectives. Kahu (2013) suggested that while engagement occurs in the classroom, it has positive proximal and distal consequences for people, such as satisfaction and well-being, citizenship and personal growth, thus highlighting a connection between well-being, citizenship, education and engagement both inside and outside the classroom. Leach (2014) endorses Kahu's holistic model of engagement with the following definition:

> Student engagement is understood as the time and effort students invest in educational activities. The consequences of their engagement - their success in their study, their personal growth and the contribution they make to society through active citizenship - are affected by personal and contextual antecedents as well as the actions taken by teachers, institutions, families and friends to facilitate their engagement in an active partnership.

Such wide ranging views no longer confine engagement to higher education classroom settings, but involve engaged learners in the affairs of wider cultural, social and political community contexts. Engagement becomes part of lifewide experiences that feed into and out of the classroom environment.

Such varied and abundant attempts to grasp student engagement lead to a number of questions about the actual meaning of engagement in education. With the varied definitions offered by researchers, can we consider engagement as a single construct at all or is it a multi-hued rainbow of concepts grouped under the same label for convenience? While definitions are expected in academic work, are they useful in understanding complex and diverse constructs like engagement? Krause (2012), in discussing quality in higher education, suggested that the meaning of quality posed a 'wicked problem'. She cites Rittel as the originator of the idea of wicked problems who explains that such problems are ill defined, suffer from confusing information, are based on conflicting perspectives and are unlikely to lead to either tidy or permanent solutions. The same must be said of student engagement. In this book, answers to the two questions above would be: yes, student engagement can be treated as a single construct as purposeful and active involvement in lifewide and lifelong learning; but no, a single definition is not useful in grasping the full scope of such engagement.

With these answers I offer a perspective on, not a definition of engagement. In my view it is holistic not atomistic, inclusive not exclusive, lifewide and lifelong not confined to involvement in the tasks set by the teacher delivering a set curriculum or the agenda determined by an institution or even the government. Engagement is about agency; students are agents determining their own learning goals that will often include challenges of what is and also lead to actions for change. Certainly, a single definition cannot capture the many faceted contribution that engagement makes to our understanding of learning and teaching in higher education. Such a definition would be generic and limit engagement, have all the properties of a wicked problem, and potentially be blind to individual, contextual and historical differences. In short, a definition confines student engagement to predetermined processes and outcomes and inhibits change.

So I am reluctant to define engagement in any formal way. Yet when reading this book you are entitled to know how I understand the term. I consider engagement to be a metaphor; a prism through which we can discover diverse understandings of what can lead to effective learning and teaching. In short, the book examines effective education seen through the student engagement lens (Krause and Coates 2008) and its multiple supporting factors such as personal motivation and energy, critically reflective learning in an agentic curriculum, supportive yet challenging pedagogy, institutional and community support, affirming learning experiences in diverse communities and positive outcomes for learners. Engagement is not limited to what occurs face-to-face in classrooms, laboratories and workshops. It includes the interactions and relationships in using new technologies. It also applies to learning in the world outside the classroom. Engaging students requires similar attributes and processes in classrooms, online learning at a distance and in communities. I do not consider that engagement in new technology is so different to other forms of teaching that special mention must be made of it. However, while we can synthesize engagement research to develop practical propositions leading to more effective learning and teaching, such propositions are not intended to be generic. They draw on specific disciplines and are shaped by different and often unique contexts. They are also developed in a specific political and intellectual climate that helps shape how engagement is perceived in different cultures and at different times.

Theoretical Assumptions?

Kahn (2014) observed that student engagement research is weakly theorized. Certainly, given the diversity of definitions and perspectives which emphasize the 'doing' of student engagement, it is perhaps surprising that it has theoretical underpinnings at all. While I agree that extensive theoretical discussions of student engagement are hard to find, there are some overarching theoretical understandings generally shared by engagement researchers. First among these is a constructionist theory of knowledge. In this view knowledge of reality is neither given nor discovered, but constructed. Crotty (1998, p. 42) suggests that "all knowledge, and therefore all meaningful reality as such, is contingent upon human practices, being constructed in and out of interaction between human beings and their world, and developed and transmitted within an essentially social context". This theory of knowledge has been applied in the work of researchers such as Piaget and Papert to children's learning (Ackerman 2004). To them knowledge and the world are both constructed and interpreted through action, and explained through the use of symbols. Knowledge, to a constructionist, is not a commodity to be transmitted, encoded, retained, and re-applied. It is gained through experience and is actively built, both individually and collectively. Similarly, the world is not just waiting to be discovered, but gets progressively shaped and formed through people's interactions (Ackerman 2004). Piaget's and especially Papert's ideas about knowledge and learning live in higher education engagement research. Krause and Coates (2008), for example, affirm that learning in higher education is constructed by individuals who actively participate in educationally purposeful activities.

The constructionist understanding of knowledge is reflected in the assumption that engagement research is learner centred. This can be illustrated by reference to the work of Barr and Tagg (1995) and adult learning theory. Barr and Tagg introduced what they called a learning paradigm. This has a focus on individual learning with the learner achieving positive outcomes for them, society and the economy. Rather than a receptacle for the words of teachers, students are co-producers of knowledge who take shared responsibility for their learning with their teachers and institutions. This joint endeavour leads to powerful results through engagement. Theoretical assumptions from research into adult learning echo those in the learning paradigm. Rooted in humanism and pragmatism, adult learning theories emphasize self-directed, experiential and transformative learning. Self-directed learning is based on the view that adults are autonomous decision-making learners. According to Knowles (1983), self-directed learners require significant control over the learning process to achieve their own goals. Experiential learning "has been accorded a privileged place as the source of learning in a learner-centred pedagogy and at the very centre of knowledge production and knowledge acquisition" (Usher et al. 1997, p. 100). Writers such as Dewey, Lewin, Piaget and Kolb place great store in experiential learning as a "process whereby knowledge is created through the transformation of experience" (Kolb 1984, p. 38). In this process people reflect on, analyze and reconstruct their experiences in order to engage with their world. It is teachers' responsibility to facilitate this process.

But this apparently straightforward interpretation of engagement research as constructionist and learner centred is misleading. Student engagement fits Krause's (2012) description of a wicked problem: ill defined, imbued with confusing information, conflicting points of view and lacking either a tidy or permanent explanation. To make sense of engagement requires a theoretical perspective that accommodates such complexity. Cohen et al. (2011) identify complexity theory as an emerging educational research paradigm that is capable of making sense of the similarities and differences embedded in engagement research through a process of emergent order. Cohen et al. describe education and engagement as complex adaptive systems that break with linear cause and effect models of research and replace these with organic, nonlinear and holistic approaches. Complexity involves many simultaneously interacting variables that enable emergence of order and understanding from feedback, adaptation, self-organization and the interactions between learners and their environments. It is an interpretative perspective and accommodates both qualitative and quantitative research designs. New understandings that emerge are generated from within the system and do not use linear cause and effect reasoning. Researching student engagement, then, relies on researchers appreciating that it is holistic, relational, dynamic, an ever changing ecosystem from which understandings about learning and teaching emerge in a nonlinear fashion.

This interpretative approach to engagement is captured by Lawson and Lawson (2013) who echo the observation that engagement is a meta-construct researched from three primary perspectives: emotional engagement, cognitive engagement, and behavioural engagement. They add a fourth to these, a socioecological perspective, which focuses on classroom, institutional and community influences shaped in a specific but possibly fleeting political climate. Lawson and Lawson's eclectic understanding of engagement methodologies derives from research in the school sector. It is supported by Pascarella and Terenzini (1991, 2005) who in their stocktaking syntheses of learning research in higher education identify two primary orientations that underpin engagement research methodologies. One orientation, they suggest, contains theories that focus on personal growth generated from within individuals. Psychological factors such as cognitive development, motivation and identity formation are examples of what interests this family of researchers. The other orientation focuses more on factors generated from without the individual. Sociological factors such as social practices associated with culture, class and politics are seen as impacting student learning. The two orientations are not completely separate though. Pascarella and Terenzini acknowledge overlaps between them when they discuss, for example, research into the impact of students' family and other background factors on learning. Such person-environment influences can be conceived as ecological.

One important methodology in engagement research focuses on motivation as a necessary but not sufficient orientation for engagement research (Wentzel 2012). There are many motivational theories. Self-determination theory, achievement goal theory, achievement motivation theory, attribution theory, self-efficacy theory, and expectancy-value theory of achievement have all been used to research motivation for engagement (Eccles and Wang 2012). Self-belief seems to be a very important motivator as Schuetz (2008) found in her attempt to construct a coherent theoretical framework for motivation in engagement. She also found that Self-Determination Theory (SDT) (Ryan and Deci 2000) was an excellent fit for her research data drawn from a survey of American Community College students. Self-determination is an important feature of engagement and is enhanced where supportive social-contextual conditions exist to promote feelings of competence or self-efficacy. Such feelings in turn encourage the exercise of choice and self-direction, leading to a greater feeling of autonomy. Ryan and Deci (2000) refer to strong links between motivation and autonomy and competence. They also suggest that relatedness, at least in a distal sense, is important in motivation, particularly intrinsic motivation. This may be secure relations with others, a sense of social, cultural belonging, or identification with ideas. Self-determination enables individuals to meet such competence, autonomy and relational motivational needs. SDT is well supported by large-scale empirical studies and seems well suited to explain the motivation and agency needed for engagement. It is a valuable perspective for researching student engagement.

But the theoretical approaches used in engagement research are not restricted to the psychological. Engagement with learning happens simultaneously in a context, be it an individual or group learning activity, a classroom discussion, a climate of institutional values, culture and norms, or events involving families and communities. Engagement processes are seen as relational and dynamic; as involving ongoing relationships between individuals and their contexts (Eccles and Wang 2012). Some contexts such as classrooms are focused explicitly on learning, others are more indirectly situated in politics and policy. For example, institutions, teachers and students work in a policy context built on assumptions about student success, often understood as increasing or widening participation, achieving high levels of course completions and attaining a passport to employment with a positive attitude to lifelong learning (Yorke 2006). According to Wentzel (2012) the context within which engagement occurs or not is just as important for understanding engagement as motivational states. But contexts are diverse and learners and teachers require social competence to engage successfully with others. According to Lawson and Lawson (2013) socially competent students collaborate with others to achieve desired group as well as individual outcomes. They establish constructive relationships with diverse peers—mature students, part-time students, economically disadvantaged students, students from ethnic minorities, students with disabilities and students with family responsibilities—as well as teachers and administrators. Socially competent students act as partners with others in research and governance of classroom and institutional structures (Janosz 2012). This more sociological dimension has become another important focus for engagement research.

The role of engagement outside formal higher education was somewhat neglected in the past. But increasingly researchers have recognized that engagement is holistic. Research designs now include family and community life as important contexts and motivators for engagement (Wentzel 2012). Two important theoretical assumptions about engagement emerge. The first depicts engagement as conceptual glue that connects students' activity in classrooms to their surrounding social contexts. The second situates engagement within the ecology of social relations (Lawson and Lawson 2013). These assumptions about ecological dimensions of engagement have been researched widely in higher education methodologies. McInnis (2003), for example, recognized a new engagement reality in higher education as students increasingly study part-time. In Australia, James et al. (2010) found that more than half the students surveyed thought that paid work interfered with their academic performance. Such students expected study to fit their lives; not fit their lives around study. McInnis (2003) suggested that engagement can no longer be assumed; it must be negotiated. Yorke and Longden (2008) found that seven factors explained dis-engagement and early departure. While five of these factors related mainly to institutional issues such as poor quality teaching, and to personal considerations such as choosing the wrong course, two factors originated outside the institution: problems with finance and employment; and problems with social integration into aspects of institutional life due to background. James et al. (2010) found that over half of the students in part-time employment offered family reasons for seeking employment. Some wanted to gain greater financial independence from their family; others, and this was particularly so for indigenous students, were supporting their families.

Purposes, Structures and Processes

I came to research student engagement on the back of a longstanding interest in quality teaching in post-compulsory education. A funded research project on how to improve student retention led me to student engagement. Another funded research project led to a rich vein of data which I reported in numerous journal articles that in turn contribute to the book (see Appendix B for details). However, writing these articles led to many questions about the complex nature of student engagement:

how to characterize and then improve it; why it should have become such a diverse, complex and popular construct; and what ideas about engagement might be found beyond the current mainstream. These questions scaffold this book. They are:

- How can the rich and diverse mainstream engagement research be synthesized into manageable, verifiable and practical strategies for use by higher education teachers?
- Why have the outputs from this complex and varied body of work become a standard bearer for improving learning and teaching in higher education?
- What is missing from engagement research and how can this be addressed?

These questions are addressed within a constructionist theory of knowledge and an interpretive/subjectivist theoretical framework (Crotty 1998). They employ hermeneutic, critical and postmodern perspectives. The method used to construct my arguments in the book is relatively new and seems to have been used so far mainly in the health sciences (Walsh and Downe 2005). It is labelled 'meta-synthesis' by Schreiber et al. (1997) who consider it as a qualitative equivalent to the quantitative use of meta-analyses. Erwin et al. (2011, p. 186) describe it as

> an intentional and coherent approach to analyzing data across qualitative studies. It is a process that enables researchers to identify a specific research question and then search for, select, appraise, summarize, and combine qualitative evidence to address the research question.

Its goal is to tap into complex largely qualitative data to foster the emergence of new conceptualizations and interpretations of a research field. I use this literature to address each of the questions. I have selected the material from peer reviewed journal articles, books published by respected publishers, official reports published by named research agencies such as the British Higher Education Academy and other government agencies. Some grey media was used to inform the argument where the author of blogs or conference papers was a recognized expert in the field.

The meta-synthesis generated three propositions in response to the questions. Each proposition addresses one of the questions in a series of chapters. The propositions are:

- There is a mainstream view of student engagement that makes a considerable contribution to understanding what works in learning and teaching in higher education to enable students to achieve success in a quality focused learning environment.
- Student engagement research has achieved its importance in higher education at a time when dominant neoliberal political ideas and practices align with mainstream engagement research. While not caused by neoliberalism, student engagement has an elective affinity with it. This limits its potential.
- To reach its potential, student engagement needs to develop another dimension in research and practice. This dimension moves it away from neoliberal thinking and towards enabling learners to engage in a holistic, critical way in order to work for greater social justice.

Part 1: Exploring Mainstream Views of Student Engagement

1. *Glimpsing student engagement*

This chapter sets the scene for the book by addressing the question "what is important to know about mainstream research on student engagement in higher education". It introduces some key aspects of mainstream engagement research. It unpacks some of its features and complexities before attempting to find (and avoiding) a formal definition. It then discusses key theoretical assumptions underpinning engagement research and finally explains the purposes, processes and content of the book.

2. *Mainstream perspectives and frameworks*

Underpinning this chapter is an enquiry about what research perspectives and conceptual frameworks inform research in the mainstream student engagement enterprise. It begins with a long list of diverse characteristics assigned to student engagement. It attempts to make sense of this diversity by constructing a broad sketch of student engagement research that outlines different ways engagement is conceived and investigated. It then constructs a more detailed map of the various conceptual frameworks that have been employed.

3. *Towards an emergent mainstream engagement framework*

This chapter asks how we might make sense of the complexities of student engagement revealed in Chap. 2. It uses complexity thinking as a way of identifying practical, evidence-based and useful propositions to inform learning and teaching in higher education. The chapter uses a key attribute of complexity, 'emergence', as a way of identifying 10 generic propositions for engagement that can be applied to higher education's unique contexts and students.

Part 2: Questioning the Mainstream View

4. *Higher education in neoliberal times*

What is the ideological climate that informs and influences student engagement? This question focuses the chapter. It identifies neoliberalism as a hegemonic ideology that is very important in explaining the appeal of student engagement theory and practice in higher education. It examines key features of neoliberalism and a selected number of contributing policy discourses and how they impact on educational policy using a New Zealand case study before finally briefly outlining the relationship between student engagement and neoliberalism.

5. *Student engagement and neoliberalism: An elective affinity?*

This chapter turns the spotlight more specifically on student engagement and its relationship with neoliberalism. It asks whether there is a distinguishing feature to the relationship. It argues that Weber's idea of an elective affinity is suitable for understanding the relationship. This means that theory, research and practices of student engagement are allied to neoliberalism. But the chapter is careful not to suggest that student engagement is a creature of neoliberalism.

6. *A critique of mainstream student engagement*

What are the advantages and disadvantages of this elective affinity for student learning? This chapter explores how the mainstream view of student engagement might be critiqued. It questions various aspects of the four conceptual frameworks introduced in Chap. 2 and in particular questions the overwhelming positivity in engagement research, its generic reading of effective teaching and learning, its prioritizing of pedagogy over curriculum, its reliance on psychology and its elective affinity with neoliberalism.

Part 3: Student Engagement Beyond the Mainstream

7. *Student engagement beyond the mainstream*

This chapter asks whether it is possible to retain mainstream conceptual frameworks and propositions while reducing the influence of neoliberalism. It answers affirmatively and acknowledges that mainstream engagement research has great value in spite of the influence of neoliberalism. This influence can be weakened by drawing on ideas from critical thinkers such as Foucault, hooks, Smith, Habermas, Freire and Brameld.

8. *Towards a critical pedagogy of engagement*

What would student engagement be like with less neoliberalism? This chapter acknowledges that while neoliberalism will retain influence, this can be offset by the more critical orientations discussed in Chap. 8. It offers a view of practice beyond the mainstream by synthesizing research from a wide variety of sources such as positive psychology, sociology and political science. An emergent holistic view suggests that student engagement must include critical and emotional dimensions.

9. *Towards a critical curriculum for engagement*

This chapter discusses one of what Bernstein considered to be three interdependent educational message systems: pedagogy, curriculum and evaluation. Chapters 1–9 focused on pedagogy. This chapter considers how curriculum can foster a critical engagement. Because pedagogy is but a subset of curriculum and therefore offers only a partial understanding of students' learning, this chapter explores how curriculum can help create a critical form of engagement.

10. *Supporting engagement through critical evaluation*

How can evaluation, the third of Bernstein's message systems, contribute to a more critical student engagement? This chapter explores how evaluation can enhance student engagement by involving students directly in accountability systems, enabling them to participate in institutional evaluations beyond filling out survey questionnaires as well as sharing decision-making powers in the way assessment processes are conducted.

11. *Through distributive leadership to critical engagement*

This chapter addresses two questions: how can critical engagement be grafted into the mainstream engagement discourse; and what might a critical engagement look like? It draws on a radical vision of distributive leadership to argue that this can graft critical engagement into the mainstream. It offers three case studies as working examples.

12. *Achieving change: opportunities, challenges and limits*

What are the opportunities for achieving the kind of changes canvassed in the book? This chapter explores opportunities and challenges for student engagement in an education system in which critical practices must coexist within a neoliberal ideology. It points out challenges to and limits of achieving change. The chapter will provide case studies of what change may look like in practice.

References

Ackermann, E. (2004). Constructing knowledge and transforming the world. In M. Tokoro & L. Steels (Eds.), *A learning zone of one's own: Sharing representations and flow in collaborative learning environments* (pp. 15–37). Amsterdam: IOS Press.

Barr, R., & Tagg, J. (1995). From teaching to learning: A new paradigm for undergraduate education. *Change, 26*(6), 13–25.

Bernstein, B. (1996). *Pedagogy, symbolic control and identity: Theory, research, critique.* London, UK: Taylor and Francis.

Biggs, J. (1978). Individual and group differences in study processes. *British Journal of Educational Psychology, 48*(3), 266–297. Doi:10.1111/j.2044-8279.1978.tb03013.x

Bryson, C., & Hand, L. (2007). The role of engagement in inspiring teaching and learning. *Innovations in Education and Teaching International, 44*(4), 349–362.

Bryson, C., & Hardy, C. (2012). The nature of academic engagement: What the students tell us. In I. Solomonides, A. Reid, & P. Petocz (Eds.), *Engaging with learning in higher education.* Faringdon, UK: Libri Publishing.

Carey, P. (2013). *Student engagement in university decision-making: Policies, processes and the student voice.* (Doctoral), Lancaster University, Lancaster, UK.

Cohen, L., Manion, L., & Morrison, K. (2011). *Research methods in education* (7th ed.). London, UK: Routledge.

Crotty, M. (1998). *The foundations of social research: Meanings and perspectives in the research process.* Crows Nest, NSW, Australia: Allen & Unwin.

Eccles, J., & Wang, M.-T. (2012). So what is student engagement anyway? In S. Christenson, A. Reschly, & C. Wylie (Eds.), *Handbook of research on student engagement* (pp. 133–148). New York, NY: Springer.

Erwin, J., Brotherson, M., & Summers, J. (2011). Understanding qualitative meta-synthesis: Issues and opportunities in early childhood intervention research. *Journal of Early Intervention, 33* (3), 186–200. Doi:10.1177/1053815111425493

Fielding, M. (2001). Students as radical agents of change. *Journal of Educational Change, 2,* 123–141.

Fredricks, J., Blumenfeld, P., & Paris, A. (2004). School engagement: Potential of the concept, state of the evidence. *Review of Educational Research, 74*(1), 59–109.

Hagel, P., Carr, R., & Devlin, M. (2011). Conceptualizing and measuring student engagement through the Australasian Survey of Student Engagement (AUSSE): A critique. *Assessment and Evaluation in Higher Education, 37*(4), 475–486.

James, R., Krause, K.-L., & Jennings, C. (2010). *The first year experience in Australian universities: Findings from 1994 to 2009.* Australia: Centre for the Study of Higher Education, University of Melbourne.

Janosz, M. (2012). Outcomes of engagement and engagement as an outcome: Some consensus, divergences, and unanswered questions. In S. Christenson, A. Reschly, & C. Wylie (Eds.), *Handbook of research on student engagement* (pp. 695–703). New York, NY: Springer.

Kahn, P. (2014). Theorising student engagement in higher education. *British Educational Research Journal, 40*(6), 1005–1018.

Kahu, E. (2013). Framing student engagement in higher education. *Studies in Higher Education, 38*(5), 758–773. Doi:10.1080/03075079.2011.598505

Knowles, M. (1983). Andragogy: An emerging technology for adult learning. In M. Tight (Ed.), *Adult learning and education* (Vol. 1, pp. 53–70). Abingdon, UK: Routledge.

Kolb, D. (1984). *Experiential learning: Experience as the source of learning and development.* Englewood Cliffs, NJ: Prentice Hall.

Krause, K.-L. (2012). Addressing the wicked problem of quality in higher education. *Higher Education Research & Development, 31*(3), 285–297. Doi:10.1080/07294360.2011.634381

Krause, K.-L., & Coates, H. (2008). Students' engagement in first-year university. *Assessment and Evaluation in Higher Education, 33*(5), 493–505. Doi:10.1080/02602930701698892

Kuh, G. (2009). The national survey of student engagement: Conceptual and empirical foundations. *New Directions for Institutional Research, 141,* 5–20. Doi:10.1002/ir.v2009: 141/issuetoc

Kuh, G., Cruce, T., Shoup, R., Kinzie, J., & Gonyea, R. (2008). Unmasking the effects of student engagement on first-year college grades and persistence. *Journal of Higher Education, 79,* 540–563. Doi:10.1080/01421590701721721

Lawson, M., & Lawson, H. (2013). New conceptual frameworks for student engagement research, policy and practice. *Review of Educational Research, 83*(3), 432–479.

Leach, L. (2014). *Exploring discipline differences in student engagement in one institution.* Unpublished paper.

Macfarlane, B. (2016). The performative turn in the assessment of student learning: A rights perspective. *Teaching in Higher Education.* Retrieved from http://dx.doi.org/10.1080/13562517.2016.1183623

Maiers, A. (2008). 26 keys to student engagement. Retrieved from http://www.angelamaiers.com/2008/04/engagement-alph.html

Mann, S. (2001). Alternative perspectives on the student experience: Alienation and engagement. *Studies in Higher Education, 26*(1), 7–19. Doi:10.1080/03075070020030689

Marton, F., & Säljö, R. (1976). On qualitative differences in learning: Outcome and process. *British Journal of Educational Psychology, 46*(1), 4–11.

McCormick, A. (2009). Toward reflective accountability: Using NSSE for accountability and transparency. *New Directions for Institutional Research, 141,* 97–106. Doi:10.1002/ir.v2009: 141/issuetoc

McCormick, A., Gonyea, R., & Kinzie, J. (2013). Refreshing engagement: NSSE at 13. *Change: The Magazine of Higher Learning, 45*(3), 6–15. Doi:10.1080/00091383.2013.786985.

McInnis, C. (2003). *New realities of the student experience: How should universities respond?* Paper presented at the European Association for Institutional Research, Limerick, Ireland.

Meyer, J. (1991). Study orchestration: The manifestation, interpretation and consequences of contextualised approaches to studying. *Higher Education, 22*(3), 297–316.

Nelson, K., Clarke, J., Kift, S., & Creagh, T. (2011). *Trends in policies, programs and practices in the Australasian first year experience literature 2000-2010.* The First Year in Higher Education Research Series on Evidence-based Practice. Queensland University of Technology, Brisbane, Australia.

Pascarella, E., Seifert, T., & Blaich, C. (2010). How effective are the NSSE benchmarks in predicting important educational outcomes? *Change: The Magazine of Higher Learning, 42*(1), 16–22.

Pascarella, E., & Terenzini, P. (1991). *How college affects students: Findings and insights from twenty years of research.* San Francisco: Jossey Bass.

Pascarella, E., & Terenzini, P. (2005). *How college affects students: A third decade of research.* San Francisco, CA: Jossey Bass.

Reschly, A., & Christenson, S. (2012). Jingle, jangle and conceptual haziness: Evolution and future directions of the engagement construct. In S. Christenson, A. Reschly, & C. Wylie (Eds.), *Handbook of research on student engagement* (pp. 3–20). New York, NY: Springer.

Ryan, R., & Deci, E. (2000). Intrinsic and extrinsic motivations: Classic definitions and new directions. *Contemporary Educational Psychology, 25*(1), 54–67.

Schreiber, R., Crooks, D., & Stern, P. (1997). Qualitative meta-synthesis: Issues and techniques. In J. Morse (Ed.), *Completing a qualitative project: Details and dialogue.* Thousand Oaks, CA: Sage.

Schuetz, P. (2008). A theory-driven model of community college student engagement. *Community College Journal of Research and Practice, 32*(4–6), 305–324.

Solomonides, I., Reid, A., & Petocz, P. (2012). A relational model of student engagement. In I. Solomonides, A. Reid, & P. Petocz (Eds.), *Engaging with learning in higher education.* Faringdon, UK: Libri Publishing.

Thomas, L. (2012). *Building student engagement and belonging in higher education at a time of change: Final report from the what works? Student retention and success project.*

Tinto, V. (1987). *The principles of effective retention.* Paper presented at the Maryland College Personnel Association, Prince George's Community College, Largo, MD. http://files.eric.ed.govt/fulltext/ED301267.pdf

Tinto, V. (2010). From theory to action: Exploring the institutional conditions for student retention. In J. Smart (Ed.), *Higher education: Handbook of theory and research* (pp. 51–89). New York, NY: Springer.

Trowler, V. (2010). *Student engagement literature review.* Retrieved from http://www.heacademy.ac.uk/assets/documents/studentengagement/StudentEngagementLiteratureReview.pdf

Usher, R., Bryant, I., & Johnston, R. (1997). *Adult education and the postmodern challenge: Learning beyond the limits.* London, UK: Routledge.

Walsh, D., & Downe, S. (2005). Meta-synthesis method for qualitative research: A literature review. *Journal of Advanced Nursing, 5*(2), 204–211.

Weimer, M. (2012). 10 ways to promote student engagement. Retrieved from http://www/facultyfocus.com/articles/effective-teaching-strategies/10-ways-to-promote-student-engagement

Wentzel, K. (2012). Socio-cultural contexts, social competence, and engagement at school. In S. Christenson, A. Reschly, & C. Wylie (Eds.), *Handbook of research on student engagement* (pp. 479–488). New York, NY: Springer.

Wimpenny, K., & Savin-Baden, M. (2013). Alienation, agency and authenticity: A synthesis of the literature on student engagement. *Teaching in Higher Education, 18*(3), 311–326. Doi:10.1080/13562517.2012.725223

Yorke, M. (2006). *Student engagement: Deep, surface or strategic?* Paper presented at the Pacific Rim First Year in Higher Education Conference, Griffith University, Gold Coast Campus, Australia.

Yorke, M., & Longden, B. (2008). *The first year experience of higher education in the UK: Final report.* Retrieved from https://www.heacademy.ac.uk/sites/default/files/fyefinalreport_1.pdf

Zepke, N., & Leach, L. (2010). Improving student engagement: Ten proposals for action. *Active Learning in Higher Education, 11*(3), 167–179. Doi:10.1177/1469787410379680

Chapter 2
Mainstream Perspectives and Frameworks

Abstract This chapter digs more deeply into the multiple views about student engagement introduced in Chap. 1. Three different meaning perspectives are discussed: a quantitative generic pedagogical perspective; a cognitive learning focused perspective and a holistic lifewide experience perspective. Together, these perspectives provide a historical account of the development of student engagement. But this account focuses on theoretical developments and does not offer a clear view of possible practical differences between perspectives. To offer a more practice orientated overview of student engagement, the chapter identifies four practice frameworks derived from the three broad perspectives. The quantitative generic pedagogical perspective and the cognitive learning focused perspective are retained as separate practice frameworks. The holistic lifewide experience perspective divides into psychocultural and sociopolitical frameworks. Four variables —how learning agency and motivation are stimulated; what key learning and teaching processes are practised; how learner wellbeing is promoted; and how active citizenship is conceived—reveal differences between them.

Student engagement may be a popular buzz phrase, but perhaps because of this popularity, it also suffers from conceptual complexity and uncertainty, even indigestion. Ramsden and Callender (2014, p. 28) bring this home with their description of student engagement as a convenient expression for almost any appealing form of teaching that encourages learning. They note that the following characteristics have all been noted in the research literature as leading to engagement.

- A component of quality enhancement and assurance: engaging students more effectively in shaping their learning experiences;
- The 'student voice';
- Participating in activities that lead to learning and development gains;
- Feeling a sense of belonging to (rather than disjunction from) an institution;
- Learning with and from other students;
- Learning on campus in a social community;

© Springer Nature Singapore Pte Ltd. 2017
N. Zepke, *Student Engagement in Neoliberal Times*,
DOI 10.1007/978-981-10-3200-4_2

- A sense of accomplishment from successful academic learning;
- Adopting a deep approach to learning when undertaking academic tasks;
- Self-efficacy in learning; intrinsic motivation;
- Not being alienated through academic power and culture or market-driven changes to HE (especially non-traditional students);
- "Engaging the whole person";
- Emotional attachment to learning deriving from good teaching, curriculum, assessment, resources and support;
- 'Student-centred' education (teaching that focuses on students' needs);
- Involvement in learning, including time on task, participation in extracurricular activities, enjoyment and interest.

This profusion of understandings makes a singular and definitive definition difficult to construct, and we may be better served by a more detailed examination of some of the diverse perspectives given to engagement in research and practice.

The diversity of meaning and perspectives may be because conceptually student engagement has different roots in American and European (including the United Kingdom) traditions of researching learning and teaching. American researchers used the term *student engagement* early to research student learning behaviours. European researchers did not generally use the term until much later than the Americans. They preferred to focus on students' approaches to, patterns of and intentions for learning. These two traditions of student engagement resulted in engagement research running along different lines. In Europe and United Kingdom the emphasis is more on understanding a student's own sense of what learning is in a constructivist framework; the Americans view engagement more within a pre-determined and generic pedagogical framework (Solomonides et al. 2012). However, this geographical distinction can be overstated. Engagement researchers have constructed quite diverse meanings of and perspectives on engagement across and within such geographic boundaries. For example, in higher education in the United States, the generic pedagogical conceptual framework was constructed around a quantitative research instrument that measures quantitatively student and institutional behaviours. But in the American school sector more holistic perspectives emerged that include cognitive and emotional attributes in addition to the behavioural ones favoured in the National Survey of Student Engagement (NSSE). In Europe (including the United Kingdom) and Australia conceptual frameworks have been built around phenomenographic perspectives of student learning; building students' sense of belonging; and providing space for student agency and voice.

This chapter offers first a broad sketch of what I consider to be important meanings and perspectives on mainstream student engagement research. Second, it constructs a more detailed map of the various mainstream practice frameworks that have been developed and activated.

Major Meaning Perspectives in Mainstream Student Engagement

A Quantitative Generic Pedagogical Perspective

In the United States the term student engagement has been used for more than 70 years (Axelson and Flick 2010). Work by Tyler in the 1930s, Pace in the 1960s and Astin in the 1980s laid the groundwork for combining involvement in active learning with student success. Students would be more likely to achieve their learning goals if they invested quality effort and energy into learning activities. Tyler, in developing his curriculum principles, found that time spent on learning tasks had positive effects. Pace developed the College Student Experiences Questionnaire (CSEQ) which focused on students' quality of effort. He found that what matters most in learning is what students do well. He showed that learning was most gainful when learners spent time and energy on purposeful learning tasks by studying individually, interacting with peers and teachers and applying what they learnt in practical situations. Alexander Astin studied undergraduates in the 1960s and 70s to identify and specify university impact on student success. He developed a 'theory of involvement' which advanced and publicized the time on task and quality of effort concepts. He was a major contributor to the influential report *Involvement in Learning* which popularized the ideas of time on task and quality of effort. Like the work of Tyler and Pace, Astin's work takes the focus off disciplines and transmission of content. All were clear that the theory of student involvement puts the spotlight on generic learning and teaching behaviours leading to success (Kuh 2009; Solomonides et al. 2012).

Vincent Tinto is another major figure in the American tradition of engagement research. This is at first glance surprising as most of his pioneering work in the late 1980s and early 1990s focused on early departure. But a strong link has been found between retention and engagement leading to acceptance that the chances of retention are enhanced when students are engaged in their learning (Kuh 2009). Moreover, Tinto developed a model of retention that is easily transferable to engagement. The model has six progressive phases. Two focus on students' social and academic integration into their institution. Much student retention research is based on these two integrative constructs and engagement research builds on this. Tinto (1987) suggested that students who enrol in tertiary study leave their culture of origin and enter a different, academic, culture. Students who leave early may not have sufficiently integrated socially or academically into their institution and courses. This can be translated as students who don't sufficiently engage socially or academically with their learning may not taste success. Institutions, therefore, must act to facilitate the transition by helping students to integrate, and thereby optimize their retention, engagement and success. Tinto (2010, p. 73) suggested that a "key concept is that of educational community and the capacity of institutions to establish supportive social and academic communities, especially in the classroom, that actively involve all students as equal members". Other indicators are perhaps more surprising. Tinto (1987) found that intellectual, social and emotional well-being was a vital factor in student participation (engagement) and success.

The work of Arthur Chickering and Zelda Gamson also contributes heavily to the development of the American engagement perspective. They confirmed that student success requires quality and intensity of effort from students that are socially and academically integrated into their programmes. They added that teacher work and institutional support also make critical contributions. In 1987 they published their well-known seven principles for good practice in undergraduate education: nurture positive student–teacher relationships, foster cooperation among students, promote active learning, provide prompt and constructive feedback on student work; ensure students have sufficient time to do set tasks, communicate that they have high expectations of students, and respect diverse talents and ways of learning. These are well accepted today as valuable guidelines for engaging teaching practice (Kuh 2009). Their list was based on many years of research on how teachers teach, students learn and on how students and teachers relate to each other. They suggested that each principle is important in its own right but when applied together their effects multiply. Chickering and Gamson (1987) suggested that together the principles release six powerful forces in the learning process: activity, high expectations, cooperative behaviour, interaction, diversity, and responsibility. While their principles are expressed in generic terms, Chickering and Gamson warn that the application of the principles will vary depending on the needs of students and how they are seen by different institutions.

Over the full 70 years of interest in student engagement American researchers developed surveys to identify and measure various behaviours associated with quality of effort and involvement in productive learning activities. By far the most influential of these surveys became the NSSE. Kuh (2009) discussed the political and economic stimulants that gave birth to NSSE and its Community College sibling, the Community College Survey of Student Engagement (CCSSE). Kuh identified a growing emphasis on assessment, accountability and transparency in the work of a variety of commissions and academic groups. They sought a generic indicator of educational quality in student and institutional performance. Student engagement was the chosen indicator and this has been used to define quality learning and teaching in education policy circles, research literature, and the popular media. NSSE was not new and used many items from other surveys. According to Kuh its main purposes were threefold: to provide data institutions could use to improve the undergraduate experience; to learn more about effective educational practice in higher education settings; and to promote engagement and NSSE to the public to increase public acceptance and use of statistically driven conceptions of quality. Together, these purposes were conceived to establish in the public mind through repeated and well publicized reporting of survey results the validity and value of the survey's process indicators as proxies for learning success (Kuh 2009).

Individual items used in the NSSE have changed over time. In its original form the survey was organized around six benchmarks, each containing a variable number of behavioural and experiential items. The benchmarks were: level of academic challenge; active and collaborative learning; student–teacher interactions; supportive campus environment; and enriching educational experiences. In 2013, after 13 years, the NSSE changed in response to research findings elsewhere and the needs of institutions (McCormick et al. 2013). The benchmarks are now called themes and students are asked to respond to questions about their experiences of higher order learning, reflective and integrative learning, quantitative reasoning, collaborative learning, effective teaching practices, and supportive environment and their participation in high impact practices such as learning communities, service learning, research with staff, and study abroad. Changes illustrate a search to find student experiences involving deeper forms of learning such as analysis, synthesis and evaluation. Introduced into this new version is specific recognition of engagement involving such behaviours. Likert style questions ask students to indicate how often or how much they have engaged with, for example, reaching conclusions based on their own analysis of numerical information, or asking another student to help them with an academic problem. Despite these changes NSSE's underpinning design still conceives of engagement as identifiable and quantifiable student, teacher and institutional behaviours. NSSE has spread its influence around the world having parented similar surveys in Canada, Australasia, China, South Africa, Ireland and latterly in the United Kingdom.

A More Qualitative Learning Focused Perspective

In Sweden, the United Kingdom and Australia a different research tradition for student engagement emerged over the last four decades. Instead of using generic surveys to identify how students behaved on predetermined indicators, these researchers focused more on discovering how students approached learning tasks through interviews, observations and inventories to gauge perceptions of learning. This gave rise to phenomenography, the research process developed to identify different approaches to learning. This change of perspective led to learning being seen as an individual construction of meaning not as a set of behaviours. Swedish, British and Australian researchers led the way in developing the methods and findings of this emerging tradition. In Sweden Marton and Säljö (1976) explored how students approached a particular learning task. Students were asked to read an academic text and to answer questions about this learning experience. From answers the researchers identified two approaches to learning. One group of students tried to understand and make meaning of the whole text. These students were identified as adopting a deep approach to learning. The second group focused on memory and tried to retain facts they thought they might be asked about after the reading. The researchers labelled theirs as a superficial or surface approach. Deep and surface approaches to learning are terms most teachers in higher education recognize. They connect to engagement in that they reveal the degree to which learners actively involve themselves in finding meaning in what they learn. Deep learning is seen as transformative; surface learning as reproducing.

Entwistle (2005) was also interested in approaches to learning in authentic, often subject specific, learning contexts and worked with Swedish and UK colleagues to refine the approaches to learning perspective. He and Ramsden (1983) developed the Approaches to Studying Inventory (ASI) to help better identify surface and deep learning approaches. The use of this inventory identified a third approach to learning. The strategic approach was used by students who had very high academic goals and mixed deep and surface approaches to achieve them. The approaches to learning construct now had three components—deep, surface and strategic. Entwistle (2005) suggested that learners using the deep transforming approach wanted to understand ideas for themselves. Key aspects included linking new ideas to previous knowledge and experiences; looking for underlying principles; checking evidence and relating it to conclusions; examining logic and arguments critically; and becoming actively interested in course content. The key intention of learners adopting a surface or reproducing approach was to cope with course requirements. This resulted in studying without reflecting on either purpose or learning strategy; treating the course as unrelated bits of knowledge; memorizing facts and procedures; finding it difficult to make sense of new ideas; and feeling undue pressure about assessments. The intention of students using the strategic or organizing approach was to achieve the highest possible grades by putting consistent effort into studying; finding the right conditions and materials for study; managing time and effort effectively; being alert to assessment requirements and criteria; and producing work to meet the perceived preferences of lecturers.

Researchers working outside Europe also contributed to the development of the approaches to learning perspective. In Australia Biggs (1978) used the Study Process Questionnaire (SPQ) to develop similar understandings to the approaches to learning construct identified by Marton and Säljö and Entwistle. But he considered the approaches to learning to be *congruent motive packages* with each package comprising a motive connected to learning strategies to realize them. He suggested that the motives for using the surface approach were external to the real purpose of the task. The motives for students engaging in deep learning were to engage with the task on its own terms. This was founded on an intrinsic interest in the task. This enables students to find a suitable strategy to realize their deep learning goal. In South Africa Jan (Erik) Meyer (1991) developed the term *study orchestration* to describe the learning process that students use in different contexts. The term orchestration captures an emphasis on self-direction in higher education and "focuses on the different ways students direct their resources in specific learning contexts (Meyer 1991, p. 67). It captures the unique nature of individual approaches to studying. Study orchestration is a qualitative approach to a qualitatively perceived context. Orchestration recognizes three features of student learning; the existence of qualitative individual differences in how students engage in learning tasks; the contextual influences on such engagement; and different conceptions of learning among individuals.

Just as the NSSE survey in the United States encapsulates key interests of American engagement researchers, so have 'approaches to learning' researchers developed inventories that offer a bird's eye view of surface, deep and strategic approaches. The Approaches and Study Skills Inventory for Students (ASSIST) (Entwistle et al. 2013) incorporates ideas from prior inventories. It uses a Likert scale to generate an overall score that identifies whether a student is a deep, strategic or surface learner. The deep approach contains five subscales: seeking meaning; relating ideas; using evidence; and interest in ideas. Seeking meaning probes understanding, author intent, reflection and problem analysis. Relating ideas investigates how ideas are connected and independent thinking. Use of evidence includes drawing conclusions, questioning, considering details and finding reasons. Interest in ideas probes intrinsic motivation—excitement, getting hooked and thinking about ideas, events and influences outside of class. Monitoring effectiveness includes revision, objective setting, planning and evaluation. The strategic approach has four subscales around organizing study, time management, identifying and achieving assessment demands. Organizing study involves study conditions, work systems, following up on suggestions and advance planning. Time management revolves around organizing time, keeping to schedules and making efficient use of time. Achieving is about motivation to do well. Alertness to assessment demands focuses on keeping on side with the marker, using assessment comments effectively, and mirroring teachers' expectations. The surface approach also has four subscales: lack of purpose; unrelated memorizing, fear of failure and boundedness. Lack of purpose includes questioning value, interest and relevance of study. Unrelated memorizing focuses on developing techniques, sense-making and judging importance. Fear of failure is about motivation for learning—coping with work load, making sense of the whole picture and just generally worrying. Boundedness probes situations where students stay strictly within course boundaries and expectations.

A Holistic Lifewide Experience Perspective

Without question the behaviourist (NSSE) and cognitive (approaches to learning) research perspectives provide the most influential source of ideas about student engagement in higher education. The behaviourist tradition provides indictors derived from quantitative research, while the cognitive perspective focuses more on indicators that draw on qualitative differences in approaches to learning that can be supported by more quantitative inventories. But these perspectives are not the only ones about student engagement. In the United States, school based researchers have provided further insights. Lam et al. (2012) attempted to conceptualize student engagement as a fusion of two elements. The first focuses on the learner. They support Fredricks et al. (2004) behavioural, emotional, and cognitive characteristics of engagement. Here behavioural engagement relates to active involvement in academic and social activities leading to positive academic outcomes. Emotional engagement is about reactions to and relationships with teachers, classmates and administrators that encourage a love of learning. Cognitive engagement points to investment in deep learning of concepts and skills. Lam et al.'s (2012) second element focuses on facilitators of engagement, actors in the educational landscape that support engagement in a wide variety of ways. They include students themselves, teachers, institutions and external influences such as the background of students.

Such researchers generally built a more holistic view of student engagement. They bring together the American behavioural and European cognitive traditions and add an emotional dimension. Lawson and Lawson's (2013) sociocultural ecological perspective on student engagement situates student engagement within an ecology of social relations. "Guided in part by social–ecological analysis and social–cultural theory, engagement is conceptualized as a dynamic system of social and psychological constructs as well as a synergistic process" (Lawson and Lawson 2013, p. 432). In this perspective the focus moves off the individual learner and teacher and their behaviours to a wider social context. A sociocultural ecological perspective moves engagement beyond the boundaries of classrooms and institutions to acknowledge the contributions of significant others in their varied contextual ecologies. This broadens the scope of their learning from a narrow prescribed curriculum and technical pedagogy to one that engages learners in the cultural politics that provide the context for higher education (McLaren 2003). Engagement is now lifewide as it includes learning about individual and critical social wellbeing and active citizenship across the lifespan. Lawson and Lawson's (2013) socio-cultural ecological perspective explores relationships between people, but is mute about relationships between them and natural environmental ecologies. Furman and Gruenewald (2004) address this limitation by emphasizing that a critical engagement with the lived conflicts in diverse human and non-human communities is equally important.

Intuitively it makes sense that wellbeing is linked with engagement which, particularly in its holistic lifewide guise, requires cognitive, behavioural and emotional energy, a positive outlook on life, social connection, self-confidence and self-regulation. These indicators of engagement share some common features with research from positive psychology about subjective wellbeing which is often interpreted to mean experiencing a high level of positive affect, a low level of negative affect, and a high degree of satisfaction with one's life. Personal well-being requires autonomy, competence, engagement and self-esteem, and social well-being involves social engagement, sound interpersonal relationships and social competence. Field (2009) observes that learning impacts positively on these by stimulating employability and earnings, social participation and engagement and a sense of agency. With a sense of well-being, individuals are able to develop their potential, work productively, build positive relationships, engage in and contribute to their communities as active citizens (Field 2009; Seligman 2011). According to Forgeard et al. (2011), engagement for well-being occurs when individuals are absorbed by and focus on what they are doing. High levels of engagement are present when the individual has clear goals and is intrinsically interested in the task at hand; the task presents challenges that meet the skill level of the individual; the task provides direct and immediate feedback to the individual; the individual retains a sense of personal control over the activity; and action and awareness become merged, such that the individual becomes completely immersed in what he or she is doing. This view of engagement echoes that found in student engagement research.

Another feature of the varied engagement landscape is worth considering. It emerges from critiques of the way engagement is generally constructed in the research literature (Báez 2011). McMahon and Portelli (2004, 2012), for example, view engagement research as too conservative and/or student centred. Conservative views interpret engagement as psychological dispositions and academic achievement leading to learning that lacks social context. They concede that student-centred conceptions of engagement do recognize context, require engagement by teachers as well as learners and are nested in the relationships they share. But both views, they argue, are too narrowly focused on operational matters. What is needed is a democratic–critical conception of engagement that goes beyond strategies, techniques or behaviours; a conception in which engagement is participatory and dialogic, leading not only to academic achievement but success as active citizens. Barnett and Coate (2005) expand this critique by distinguishing between operational engagement and ontological engagement. The former encompasses conservative and student-centred engagement; the latter reflects a level of commitment aligned to active citizenship in which the student commits herself, seizes opportunities and tries to extend the boundaries of the curriculum. They see three curriculum projects in ontological engagement for active citizenship. The first is the project of knowing—how students can learn to make legitimate claims in a world of uncertainty and how to negotiate challenges to such claims. The second is the project of acting—how students can learn to act constructively in the world. The third project involves students becoming aware of themselves and their potential in a world that is open, fluid, contested and in need of courageous knowledge acts.

On first sight, these perspectives in engagement research seem to sort themselves quite neatly into the quantitative 'generic pedagogical' and more qualitative 'approaches to learning' perspectives focused on the classroom on the one hand and the holistic perceptions which have a lifewide focus on learning across a student's whole lifeworld (Barnett 2010) on the other. But such first impressions are hasty. The updated 2013 version of the NSSE, for example, includes items on out of class learning such as experiences of students with people unlike themselves and in public service activities (McCormick et al. 2013). The 'approaches to learning' work, while focused on *inner* teaching–learning environments in the classroom (Entwistle et al. 2002), also acknowledges that deep learning involves thinking about ideas, events and influences from outside the classroom. Additionally, it recognizes the importance of *outer* teaching-learning environments such as individual learning histories and supports, orientations, beliefs, norms and values. In short, motivation, learning and teaching processes, an interest in student wellbeing and engagement in active citizenship are lenses that provide important insights about student engagement in all mainstream perspectives.

From Meaning Perspectives to Practice

So far I have sketched three broad meaning perspectives in engagement research. These outline broad historical and theoretical developments but do not pinpoint potential differences in practice between these perspectives. So a more thorough mapping is needed to tease out differences in practice between the perspectives. In this section I extract four distinct practice-focused conceptual engagement frameworks from the three broad perspectives. Miles and Huberman (1994, p. 18) define a conceptual framework as a description that "explains, either graphically or in narrative form, the main things to be studied—the key factors, concepts, or variables—and the presumed relationships among them". In this instance the conceptual frameworks comprise variables that focus on practice. Two of the perspectives, the quantitative generic behavioural and the mixed method cognitive perspectives, translate neatly into distinct frameworks. The diverse ecological and lifewide perspective conceptually divides into two frameworks: one offering a more psychocultural viewpoint, the other a more sociopolitical standpoint. The four resulting conceptual frameworks are discussed through the work of an author who is considered to be representative of that framework. The representatives used are George Kuh and colleagues to represent the perspective encapsulated by NSSE; Noel Entwistle and colleagues to represent the 'approaches to learning' perspective; Ella Kahu to stand for the psychocultural perspective; and Ronald Barnett and Kelly Coate represent the sociopolitical views of the holistic lifewide perspective. Four variables will be used to view key similarities and differences between the frameworks. These are: how learning agency and motivation can be stimulated; what key learning and teaching processes are engaging; how learner wellbeing is associated with engagement; and how active citizenship is nurtured.

Kuh and colleagues (2006) acknowledge that there are numerous pathways into and out of education, but argue that institutions have relatively little influence on these. So their framework focuses on the learning experience itself. This is made up of two central features: student behaviours and institutional conditions. They locate student engagement where these intersect. In a 2008 paper Kuh and colleagues summarize this framework; a summary that could also be used as a definition. Engagement is "both the time and energy students invest in educationally purposeful activities and the effort institutions devote to effective educational practices" (Kuh et al. 2008, p. 542). Questions asked in the NSSE 2013 survey provide a very good overview of practices valued in this conceptual framework. It pictures engaged students as active learners inside and outside the classroom. Assumptions about *student agency and motivation* are revealed in questions about what they are willing to do to be successful, and how long they spend on tasks individually and with others. A variety of *Learning and teaching processes* are indicated in NSSE but overwhelmingly involve specific and predetermined learning behaviours. Behaviours resulting in success include completion of set work, meeting learning task challenges and participating in out of class events. Cognitive successes focus on memorizing, analysing, synthesizing, evaluating and forming opinions, for example, about numerical problems and discussion with diverse others. Appreciating others' points of view can be associated with emotional engagement. Questions about *wellbeing* are indirect. They ask about services such as health care, learning support and management of out of course responsibilities provided by the institution. *Active citizenship* is considered in questions about attending meetings, taking leadership roles and activities in learning communities.

The 'approaches to learning' perspective also focuses on actual learning activities. But rather than students reporting how they perform on specific and generic items, researchers analyse how students approach academic tasks cognitively, such as in subject related readings. Researchers used interviews and inventories to sort learning into the two primary deep and surface groups and later also into the strategic category. The word 'engagement' did not feature in their work although both Meyer (1991) and Entwistle et al. (2002) use it. Depth of learning is the major yardstick for judging whether a learner is engaged. The conceptual framework is represented in Entwistle and colleagues Approaches and Study Skills Inventory for Students (ASSIST) (Entwistle et al. 2013) to identify learners engaged in this way. *Learning agency and motivation* are features of engagement in this tradition. Deep learners are intrinsically motivated which is evidenced by student interest and emotions like excitement, getting hooked and behaviours like thinking about ideas outside of class. *Learning and teaching processes* aim to generate deep or strategic learning. Success for deep learners lies in seeking meaning, connecting ideas, using evidence and being interested in ideas, events and influences, even when they originate from outside the classroom. For strategic learners' success is achieved by effectively organizing study, time management, identifying and achieving assessment demands. Surface learning is not associated with learning success, being couched in largely negative feelings like lack of purpose, unrelated memorizing, fear of failure and boundedness. *Wellbeing* in this conceptual framework is an implied rather than explicit variable, but it can be associated with deep and strategic learning. *Active citizenship* is not part of this framework with the research focussing largely on learning in specific and variable contexts.

The psychocultural holistic tradition reaches beyond the classroom into personal, family and community life. Holistic frameworks connect lifewide experiences (Barnett 2010). These are framed as antecedents to and consequences of engagement as part of an engagement algorithm. Kahu's (2013) engagement framework is an example of such a holistic and lifewide framework. It is pictured as a psychocultural process involving institutional and personal factors that are embedded in a wider social context that connects cultural, psychological and behavioural views (Ramsden and Callender 2014). Kahu offers a three-phase framework of engagement. At its centre is a narrowly conceived state of engagement resulting from learning activities, often in a classroom setting. But engagement does not happen just as a result of events in this setting. It is influenced by structural and psychosocial antecedents and is followed by personal and social consequences. Antecedents include influences such as institutional culture and curriculum; student background, peer relations and community influences; teaching, personal skills, identity and self-efficacy. *Student agency and motivation* is extrinsic or intrinsic and applied in the state of engagement and its consequences. *Learning and teaching processes* are activated with students' cognitive, emotional and behavioural involvement in educational activities. Cognitive engagement involves deep learning and self-regulation; emotional engagement motivation and belonging; behavioural engagement involves time and effort on tasks and participation in learning activities. A sense of *wellbeing* is associated with the state of engagement through feelings of belonging but is most evident in immediate and distal consequences of engagement, where personal satisfaction contributes to a sense of personal growth and wellbeing. *Active citizenship* is mentioned in Kahu's model as a consequence of engagement but its nature is not explored.

A sociopolitical perspective leads to another holistic and lifewide conceptual framework. This emerges from the notion that student engagement is more than just a generic set of behaviours or context bound deep learning experiences. It focuses on a conception of engagement that goes beyond strategies, techniques and behaviours; a conception that leads to success as active citizens (McMahon and Portelli 2004). Barnett and Coate (2005) suggest a three level framework to give substance to engagement for active citizenship. Their framework is based on the higher education curriculum. It suggests that engagement for active citizenship is first about reproductive knowing. It involves learners knowing about prevailing structures and cultures and how they operate on their and other's behalf. Second, it is about acting constructively in uncertain times. Students apply what they learnt about the system and its operation. At the third level active citizenship is a socially critical perspective. This enables engaged learners to challenge the status quo and be prepared to pursue a greater level of social justice in classroom and wider society. *Student agency and motivation* at the first level is readiness to engage with knowledge outside the usual vocational curriculum; at the second level it is about acting on such knowledge; and at the third it is being willing to critique and change the status quo. Trowler (2010) operationalizes active citizenship in higher education by suggesting that the *learning process* enables engaged students to be co-producers of knowledge in classrooms while also emphasizing working within structures and processes to build identity in the classroom, institutional and wider community. Individual and social *wellbeing* is enhanced when students engage in these ways in curriculum, classroom and community.

These four conceptual frameworks are not all that are on offer. For example, in Australasia Nelson et al. (2012) adapted Biggs' Presage–Process–Product (3P) model to suggest a transition pedagogy that serves also as a model for student engagement. Their version of the 3P model recognizes the major factors involved in engagement within institutions and classrooms. They propose input factors such as what students, institutions and teachers contribute to engagement. These enable transforming learning experiences which in turn result in output or success factors such as completion and employment. Coates (2007) constructed a four cell matrix that recognizes the importance of academic and social factors for engagement applicable to online and face-to-face learning. He maps student attitudes to engagement as collaborative, intense, independent or passive. Solomonides et al.

(2012) offer a relational framework to identify some of the factors helping learners to make sense of their experiences. A feeling of engagement emerges when students gain a sense of being and transformation by being professional and commanding discipline knowledge. They also summarize a variety of other frameworks. For example frameworks where engagement is a measured quantity and either more or less than a desired state; where it is made up of different categories; and a multi-dimensional view that combines diverse aspects of the student experience.

Engagement: One Word, Many Meanings and Applications

These conceptual frameworks highlight considerable similarities and differences in how student engagement is understood. Overarching the frameworks is a shared view that engagement contributes to success, be it academic, personal or lifewide. All accept the importance of a learning centred pedagogy in which learners actively construct their own meanings. They concur that quality learning experiences, often provided by teachers, contribute to engagement. Indeed, there is a consensus that learning occurs in partnership between teachers, students and institutions. They also agree that learning experiences are shaped by behavioural, cognitive and emotional effort. Each framework considers questions about motivation and agency, learning and teaching processes, how engagement furthers student wellbeing and that student action can promote a healthy classroom climate. In short, there is considerable agreement with Kuh et al.'s (2008, p. 542) conclusion that engagement is "both the time and energy students invest in educationally purposeful activities and the effort institutions devote to effective educational practices".

But there are also considerable differences in focus, emphasis and nuances between the frameworks. These emerge, for example, when considering the four practice variables: agency and motivation; learning processes; subjective wellbeing and active citizenship. Kuh's work, for example seems to make no explicit distinction between extrinsic and intrinsic motivation; for Entwistle and the 'approaches to learning' researchers' engagement is the result of intrinsic motivation; for the psycho-cultural group of scholars represented here by Kahu, motivation precedes engagement. Learning processes according to Kuh et al. do involve behavioural, cognitive and affective engagement, but the emphasis is on the behavioural whereas to Entwistle and colleagues engagement is largely cognitive and the holistic group of researchers focus on lifewide learners' experiences. Subjective wellbeing is implied rather than explicit in the work of Kuh and Entwistle but a specific and important aspect in the work of both holistic/lifewide frameworks. Kuh et al. recognize that leadership in, for example, learning communities is valuable for engagement whereas the 'approaches to learning' group are largely silent on citizenship, something recognized by both holistic/lifewide groups as an important consequence of engagement.

Each of the lenses affords a similar overview of engagement, while detailed analysis also shows up differences. The focus on learning behaviours is brought into strong focus by the lenses used by Kuh et al.; cognitive processes are highlighted in the 'approaches to learning' framework represented by Entwistle et al.; emotional engagement is visible in the sociocultural framework offered by Kahu; and political activism both inside and outside the classroom can be recognized in the framework built around the work of Barnett and Coate et al. Another key difference is the orientation of the frameworks. The 'approaches to learning' framework is focused almost totally on the classroom and in the institution. The Kuh et al. and Kahu frameworks are centred there but with greater reference to the learners' environments. The Barnett and Coate framework is ontological and leads to engaging with knowledge generating political action.

The practice variables used in this analysis are of course only the tip of the iceberg of possibilities in constructing a coherent view of student engagement. They do, however, lay a foundation for understanding the difficulties of constructing a singular representation of mainstream student engagement; something attempted in the next chapter.

References

Axelson, R., & Flick, A. (2010). Defining student engagement. *Change: The Magazine of Higher Learning, 43*(1), 38–43. Doi:10.1080/00091383.2011.533096

Báez, C. (2011). *Crafting programs to stimulate student engagement and persistence in higher education.* Paper Presented at the 15th Biennial of the International Study Association on Teachers and Teaching (ISATT), University of Minho, Braga, Portugal.

Barnett, R. (2010). Life-wide education: A new and transformative concept for higher education? *Enabling a More Complete Education e-Proceedings On-line.* Retrieved from http://lifewidelearningconference.pbworks.com/w/page/24285296/E%20proceedings

Barnett, R., & Coate, K. (2005). *Engaging the curriculum in higher education.* Maidenhead, UK: Society for Research into Higher Education and Open University Press.

Biggs, J. (1978). Individual and group differences in study processes. *British Journal of Educational Psychology, 48*(3), 266–297. Doi:10.1111/j.2044-8279.1978.tb03013.x

Chickering, A., & Gamson, Z. (1987). Seven principles for good practice in undergraduate education. *American Association for Higher Education Bulletin, 39*(7), 3–7.

Coates, H. (2007). A model of online and general campus-based student engagement. *Assessment and Evaluation in Higher Education, 32*(2), 121–141.

Entwistle, N. (2005). Contrasting perspectives on learning. In F. Marton, D. Hounsell, & N. Entwistle (Eds.), *The experience of learning: Implications for teaching and studying in higher education* (3rd (Internet) ed., pp. 3–22). Edinburgh, UK: Centre for Teaching, Learning and Assessment, University of Edinburgh.

Entwistle, N., McCune, V., & Hounsell, J. (2002). *Approaches to studying and perceptions of university teaching-learning environments: Concepts, measures and preliminary findings. Occasional Report 1.* Enhancing Teaching-Learning Environments (ETL) Project.

Entwistle, N., McCune, V., & Tait, H. (2013). Approaches and study skills inventories for students (ASSIST) incorporating the revised approaches to studying inventory. Report of the development and use of the inventories. Retrieved from https://www.mededportal.org/publication/9404

Entwistle, N., & Ramsden, P. (1983). *Understanding student learning.* London, UK: Croom Helm.

Field, J. (2009). *Well-being and happiness: Inquiry into the future for lifelong learning. Thematic Article 4.* Retrieved from Leicester, UK

Forgeard, M., Jayawickreme, E., Kern, M., & Seligman, M. (2011). Doing the right thing: Measuring wellbeing for public policy. *International Journal of Wellbeing, 1*(1), 79–106.

Fredricks, J., Blumenfeld, P., & Paris, A. (2004). School engagement: Potential of the concept, state of the evidence. *Review of Educational Research, 74*(1), 59–109.

Furman, G., & Gruenewald, D. (2004). Expanding the landscape of social justice: A critical ecological analysis. *Educational Administration Quarterly, 40*(1), 47–76.

Kahu, E. (2013). Framing student engagement in higher education. *Studies in Higher Education, 38*(5), 758–773. Doi:10.1080/03075079.2011.598505

Kuh, G. (2009). The national survey of student engagement: Conceptual and empirical foundations. *New Directions for Institutional Research, 141*, 5–20. Doi:10.1002/ir.v2009: 141/issuetoc

Kuh, G., Cruce, T., Shoup, R., Kinzie, J., & Gonyea, R. (2008). Unmasking the effects of student engagement on first-year college grades and persistence. *Journal of Higher Education, 79*, 540–563. Doi:10.1080/01421590701721721

Kuh, G., Kinzie, J., Buckley, J., Bridges, B., & Hayek, J. (2006). *What matters to student success; A review of the literature.* Retrieved from http://nces.ed.gov/IPEDS/research/pdf/Kuh_Team_Report.pdf

Lam, S., Wong, B., Yang, H., & Liu, M. (2012). Understanding student engagement with a conceptual model. In S. Christenson, A. Reschly, & C. Wylie (Eds.), *Handbook of research on student engagement* (pp. 403–420). New York, NY: Springer.

Lawson, M., & Lawson, H. (2013). New conceptual frameworks for student engagement research, policy and practice. *Review of Educational Research, 83*(3), 432–479.

Marton, F., & Säljö, R. (1976). On qualitative differences in learning: Outcome and process. *British Journal of Educational Psychology, 46*(1), 4–11.

McCormick, A., Gonyea, R., & Kinzie, J. (2013). Refreshing engagement: NSSE at 13. *Change: The Magazine of Higher Learning, 45*(3), 6–15. Doi:10.1080/00091383.2013.786985

McLaren, P. (2003). *Life in schools: An introduction to critical pedagogy in the foundations of education* (4th ed.). New York, NY: Allyn and Bacon.

McMahon, B., & Portelli, J. (2004). Engagement for what? Beyond popular discourses of student engagement. *Leadership and Policy in Schools, 3*(1), 59–76.

McMahon, B., & Portelli, J. (2012). The challenges of neoliberalism in education: Implications for student engagement. In B. McMahon & J. Portelli (Eds.), *Student engagement in urban school: Beyond neoliberal discourses* (pp. 1–10). Charlotte, NC: Information Age Publishing.

Meyer, J. (1991). Study orchestration: The manifestation, interpretation and consequences of contextualised approaches to studying. *Higher Education, 22*(3), 297–316.

Miles, M., & Huberman, M. (1994). *Qualitative data analysis: An expanded source book* (2nd ed.). Thousand Oaks, CA: Sage Publications.

Nelson, K., Kift, S., & Clarke, J. (2012). A transition pedagogy for student engagement and first-year learning, success and retention. In I. Solomonides, A. Reid, & P. Petocz (Eds.), Engaging with learning in higher education (pp. 117–144). Faringdon, UK: Libri Publishing.

Ramsden, P., & Callender, C. (2014). *Review of the national student survey: Appendix A: Literature review.* Retrieved from London, UK: http://www.hefce.ac.uk/pubs/rereports/year/2014/nssreview/#alldownloads

Seligman, M. (2011). *Flourish.* New York, NY: Simon & Schuster.

Solomonides, I., Reid, A., & Petocz, P. (2012). A relational model of student engagement. In I. Solomonides, A. Reid, & P. Petocz (Eds.), *Engaging with learning in higher education* (pp. 11–24). Faringdon, UK: Libri Publishing.

Tinto, V. (1987). *The principles of effective retention.* Paper Presented at the Maryland College Personnel Association, Prince George's Community College, Largo, MD. http://files.eric.ed.govt/fulltext/ED301267.pdf

Tinto, V. (2010). From theory to action: Exploring the institutional conditions for student retention. In J. Smart (Ed.), *Higher education: Handbook of theory and research* (pp. 51–89). New York, NY: Springer.

Trowler, V. (2010). Student engagement literature review. Retrieved from http://www.heacademy.ac.uk/assets/documents/studentengagement/StudentEngagementLiteratureReview.pdf

Chapter 3
Towards an Emergent Mainstream Engagement Framework

Abstract This chapter offers 10 propositions of what teachers can do to engage their students. The propositions are synthesized from the mainstream research literature discussed in Chap. 2. The synthesis is informed by complexity theory and its by-product 'emergence' which enables clear proposals for action to be developed from diverse perspectives and practice frameworks. Each proposition is intended for both students and teachers. They are arranged under three headings: students invest in their own learning, teachers and institutions are vital enablers of engagement, and engagement is assisted by enabling external environments. Emergence is captured by a conceptual organizer for mainstream student engagement practice. An appendix (Appendix A) investigates whether there is any empirical support for the organizer.

The perspectives and practice frameworks discussed in Chap. 2 highlight both differences and similarities in student engagement research. They reveal student engagement as complex with features that have strong connections to each other while also being distinct. For example, engagement researchers working in all conceptual frameworks share the view that engagement is learner centred and constructionist but differ about whether it is primarily behavioural, cognitive, affective or all three, and if the latter in what proportions. Complexity is a feature of a system in which connection and distinction operate simultaneously. Connection offers system continuity and stability by opening possibilities for definition, a necessary condition for system maintenance; distinction enables diverse ideas to flourish, for change in the system to occur and for multiple definitions. Heylighen (1999) goes back to the original Latin word 'complexus' meaning 'entwined' to describe complex systems that are closely connected while simultaneously being distinct. Aspects of such systems are entwined in unpredictable ways leading to the similar yet diverse practice frameworks identified in Chap. 2.

However, merely labelling a system complex does not get us closer to understanding what engagement looks like in practice. It is very difficult to obtain a coherent and defensible view of how we might practice engagement when confronted by the complex array of conceptual frameworks discussed so far, as

© Springer Nature Singapore Pte Ltd. 2017
N. Zepke, *Student Engagement in Neoliberal Times*,
DOI 10.1007/978-981-10-3200-4_3

engagement is "a system that is comprised of a large number of entities that display a high level of nonlinear interactivity" (Richardson and Cilliers 2001, p. 8). It is this nonlinear interactivity that offers the opportunity to gain a more cohesive view of engagement. Complexity researchers like Davis and Sumara (2008) observe that complex systems are able to address the question 'how should we act?' This question enables new practices and understandings to emerge. Emergence is a feature of complex systems. It often happens at the margins of a complex network, is not lineally derived from data and so is not usually predictable. This chapter identifies the emergence of possible strategies from the many nonlinear activities revealed in the mainstream conceptual engagement frameworks discussed so far.

Emergence: Ten Propositions for Enabling Student Engagement

A key emergent property of the frameworks is that the student engagement construct is made up of separate yet intertwining organizing ideas. Three such organizing ideas emerge from the perspectives and frameworks: engaged students invest in learning; institution and classroom practices support learning; and engaging features of external environments sustain learning. An important understanding about emergence is that emergent properties are not necessarily traceable to or lineally derived from any particular framework, but might be evident in a number or even all. Each property is important for engagement as it is essential to know about the generic, the connected ideas offered by the frameworks and other engagement research. But it is even more critical to understand that these properties apply to our own contexts, how they can be adapted to suit our own students, our teaching philosophies and content areas. They are both generic and unique at the same time. The aim of the chapter is to trace the emergence of generic propositions for engagement that can be applied to our unique contexts and students. These propositions will help learners to engage in learning but with the understanding that they have to be shaped to suit diverse individuals and contexts. They are like items on supermarket shelves that have yet to be prepared in our own kitchen for our own consumption.

I have abstracted 10 emergent and generic propositions from the perspectives and frameworks identified in Chap. 2. They address 'how research suggests we should act' under three headings: *students' invest in their own learning, teachers and institutions are vital enablers of engagement*, and *engagement is assisted by enabling external environments*. Each proposition is intended as a reference for both students and teachers.

Students' Invest in Their Own Learning

Students are at the heart of engagement. They invest cognitively, emotionally and actively in learning in order to succeed (Fredricks et al. 2004). As the survey of engagement frameworks suggests, investment opportunities are many, varied and complex. While students invest in their own learning, teachers, institutions and significant outsiders help facilitate and grow the investment. Emerging from the engagement frameworks are indications of how students need to invest in their learning but also what supports are needed to grow that investment.

Student Self-belief Is Vital for Success

Emerging from the frameworks is an assumption that all students can engage; that they have strengths. To engage successfully they must believe that they have enough strengths to succeed. But self-belief is not given. It is built and maintained in various relationships between learners and teachers, learners and learners, learners and institutions and learners and their communities. Within both the 'inner' and 'outer' teaching learning environments discussed by Entwistle et al. (2002), a strengths-based approach to engagement assumes that while students have weaknesses they can learn to overcome them by enhancing their self-belief, by building their strengths. Strengths-based learning is rooted in Appreciative Inquiry (AI) developed by Cooperrider and Srivastva (1987) to overcome and solve problems in organizational behaviour. AI provides an important insight into higher education as it attempts to replace deficiency discourses that perceive disengagement as caused by problem students with poor achievement, negative behaviours and attitudes (Bushe 2013). For example, AI attempts to convince students that they bring cultural, age-related, educational and personality-related strengths to their learning. Take cultural strengths. Some students belong to cultures that value individualism and autonomy; others belong to collectivist cultures that value connection with others. Both strengths are useful in learning as long as learners and teachers believe that collaborative as well as autonomous learning leads to success. Some students are practical problem solvers; others think deeply by reflecting on their experiences; yet others theorize from reading and some do all three. Students need to believe that all strengths they bring into the classroom are appreciated.

Bushe (2013) suggests that five principles underpin AI. Together they have the capacity to help students build self-belief to engage. A constructionist principle proposes that what we believe to be true determines what we do. When applied to learning in higher education students co-construct new ideas, stories and images with significant others such as teachers, peers and outside influences to generate new possibilities for self-belief and success. A simultaneity principle proposes that as soon as we inquire into our own learning we change our understanding of how we learn and this plants seeds for change in our confidence and willingness to engage. A poetic principle proposes that self-belief and engagement is expressed in the stories people tell each other every day, and the story of our learning is constantly co-authored by significant others such as teachers, friends and colleagues. The stories we tell about ourselves and others have an impact far beyond just the words themselves. An anticipatory principle suggests that what we do today is guided by our image of the future. We project ahead of ourselves a horizon of expectation that brings the future powerfully into the present as a mobilizing agent. AI uses positive imagery on a collective basis to anticipate changes in self-belief. A positive principle emphasizes that change in self-esteem requires positive affect and feelings of belonging with others in our teaching-learning environment. These principles suggest the following actions by students, teachers and significant others: recognize and demonstrate, in word and deed that we appreciate our own and others strengths; engage with a variety of learning experiences that enable us to use and develop our particular strengths; and provide and accept feedback that enables us to build our and others' strengths.

Students' Motivation Grows from Self-belief

Motivation and self-belief go hand in hand in the engagement research literature. A number of researchers found that learners' self-belief to be a key motivator. Yorke and Knight (2004) for example found that the self-theories learners bring to their learning impact motivation, agency and engagement. Those with fixed self-theories tend to have fixed views about their own abilities. They adopt performance goals for their learning and lose motivation when these are not achieved. Those with malleable self-theories tend to adopt learning goals, seeing challenges as opportunities for learning. Such learners tend to stay engaged independently of their performance. They suggest that somewhere between 25 and 30% of learners have fixed self-theories that could impact negatively on their engagement. Related to this work is what Llorens et al. (2007) label a personal resources–efficacy–engagement spiral. They found that where learners believe they have the personal resources to complete a task, their self-efficacy grows and consequently so does their engagement. Fazey and Fazey (2001) reported that self-perceived competence is a key motivator for engagement. Students' confidence in their own competence within their context was a strong motivator for ongoing active learning. Such learners stayed motivated and engaged even in the face of short-term failure.

The work of Ryan and Deci (2000) on self-determination theory (SDT) has been influential in the way motivation and self-belief has been constructed in the engagement literature. From SDT, a synthesis emerges about how motivation and learner agency lead to engagement. SDT focuses on agentic individuals who have set themselves clear performance and learning goals, have positive self-theories and actively interact with their social environments. To be motivated means to be moved to do something. Ryan and Deci (2000) identify a trinity of intrinsic motivational factors that are vital for student engagement. They found that engaged students work autonomously, enjoy learning relationships with others and feel they are competent to achieve their own objectives. Of the three, feeling competent is the most important for motivation (Ryan and Deci 2000). This enhances students' self-belief, and Appreciative Inquiry offers examples of this. Set tasks that are challenging when within students' capabilities and offer feedback, help them to build feelings of competence. Autonomy does not just mean working independently; it can mean working interdependently. Belonging to and working within a group does not detract from autonomy or self-belief. A sense of belonging, or being in learning relationships with the teacher and other students, also enhances engagement. While perhaps less important than competence and autonomy, belonging is still important to student engagement and is enhanced through working in groups (Ryan and Deci 2000).

Social and Cultural Capital Enhance Engagement

Although engagement research, including that reported in this book, often looks at engagement in a generic way, it also acknowledges diversity. Whether due to social class, culture, ethnicity, age, gender, geographic location or sexual orientation diversity is likely to influence whether and how students engage. Two sociological theories alert us to this. The first is the notion of social capital. According to Putnam (2000) the shared values and understandings that enable us and others to trust each other and to work together create social capital. Having social capital enables us to connect to people with a common identity such as family and a shared ethnicity and culture; to relate to peers, colleagues and associates who do not share the same identity but nevertheless have similar characteristics; and under certain circumstances forge links to people who 'are not like us'. Cultural capital, according to Bourdieu, refers to symbolic elements such as skills, tastes, posture, clothing, mannerisms, material belongings, credentials that we acquires as members of a particular social class. Sharing similar forms of cultural capital with others—understanding and using academic language, for example—creates a sense of collective identity and group position. Not having cultural capital is a major source of social inequality (Bourdieu and Passeron 1990). Certain forms of cultural capital are valued over others, and can help or hinder a person's acceptance and respect just as much as income or wealth. In higher education holding social and cultural capital recognized and valued by the dominant majority in education, provides acceptance and respect that people from diverse minority groups may not have.

Students from minority groups, often labelled 'non-traditional', must still develop the social and cultural capital needed to succeed in mainstream education. They do not command the group memberships, relationships, networks of influence and support, the forms of knowledge, skills and education that will give them the capital to engage and succeed in higher education. They must learn the language of the subject they study, the attitudes and practices that are valued within the academy, gain a sense of belonging and understand how things work around here (Case 2007; Gavala and Flett 2005). To engage, all students including non-traditional ones need to feel that they can negotiate ways to succeed. Such negotiation means they need to engage with subject, institution and pedagogical cultures. Most importantly they must believe that such engagement is meaningful, reciprocated by peers, teachers and institution. Social and cultural capital grows when students feel they can negotiate, be accepted, enjoy constructive relationships with others, feel they have strengths they can contribute to the mainstream; in short when they feel like a 'fish in water' Thomas (2002). Johnson et al. (2007) found that, rather than merely placing the burden on students to adapt to an unalterable context, institutions wanting to engage learners respect the importance of students' perceptions of their educational environments and experiences and include such perspectives in developing institutional climates and curricula. Laird et al. (2007) did not find uniformly that 'minority' students feel alienated from their institutions; they did note that a greater effort was needed by teachers and institutions for them to ask deep questions about their cultures.

Engaged Learners Are Deep Learners

That engaged learners are deep learners has been widely accepted by researchers. For example, Coates et al. (2008) found that while students' attitudes to learning varied greatly, those who engaged in higher forms of learning such as analysing, synthesizing and evaluating tended to be most engaged. This finding was supported by Hockings et al. (2008) who suggested that students who reflect, question, conjecture, evaluate and make connections between ideas whilst drawing on the ideas, experiences and knowledge of others are most deeply engaged. The Higher Education Academy in the United Kingdom (n.d.) brought together a number of characteristics of deep learning gleaned from the research literature. These include: examining new facts and ideas critically, and tying them into existing cognitive structures; making numerous links between ideas; looking for meaning; focussing on the central argument or concepts needed to solve a problem; distinguishing between argument and evidence; having an intrinsic curiosity in the subject; and showing personal interest in the subject. These findings substantiate and refine the work of the originators of the 'approaches to learning' perspective like Marton and Säljö (1976) and Entwistle (2005) among others. The latter identified five aspects of deep learning: seeking meaning and understanding from learning; connecting ideas to enable independent thinking; weighing evidence by drawing conclusions, questioning author intent and finding reasons for it; and forward goal setting planning and evaluation. Underpinning and stimulating these aspects is intrinsic motivation that is driven by an interest in ideas originating inside and outside the classroom.

An important feature of deep learning is to confront an enduring myth about learners and learning in higher education. This is that students do not engage if they are challenged, if learning becomes difficult. On the contrary, the evidence is compelling that enriching experiences and academic challenge are engaging. Students respond to rigour, to experiences that take them out of their comfort zones, and to tasks that make them feel that they have grown intellectually and as people (Kuh et al. 2005). However, helping learners to meet such challenges requires support from teachers, institutions and the 'outer' environment. Among engaging support practices are convincing students that they are expected to meet high standards. Problem solving will only work when students are supported by suitable learning resources. Group work is not of itself disengaging but requires the opportunity for participants to get to know each other. Challenging academic tasks have to be clearly set out, and must allow students sufficient time to complete them. Challenging assessment activities are not disengaging if they are accompanied by timely and strengthening feedback. Indeed, challenge and extension work best in an environment in which students feel comfortable and safe in a strengths-based atmosphere (Báez 2011). The following ideas for challenging, enriching and extending students are offered in the research literature: convincing students that significant others have high expectations; expecting students to put sufficient time into tasks to complete them satisfactorily; supporting students when they get into academic trouble or when they want help to extend themselves; and encouraging students to share the results of their learning (Bryson and Hand 2007).

Teachers and Institutions Are Vital Enablers of Engagement

A number of the frameworks put the teacher and/or the institution at the centre of student engagement (Kuh et al. 2005; Nelson et al. 2012; Tinto 2010). According to Trowler (2010) this view dominates student engagement research. It is chiefly concerned with the 'how' of teaching and learning for engagement. While a generic view of teaching for engagement is necessary for learning and is unpacked in this section, it is not sufficient as will become clearer in Chaps. 7–11. This section canvasses some popular practical ideas that emerge from the frameworks about teaching but also proposes three teaching and institutional roles not so often surfaced in engagement discourses.

Quality Teaching and Institutional Support Enhance Engagement

Quality teaching is critical for quality learning. This is a key finding in much engagement research. Numerous meta-analyses attempt to quantify this finding. In their meta-analysis of how College affects student learning, Pascarella and Terenzini (2005) claim that literally hundreds of such studies show that teacher behaviour and student learning are positively correlated. They suggest that meta-analyses and narrative syntheses show that student perceptions of teacher behaviours and attributes are multi-dimensional, have reasonable reliability and have moderate positive correlations with successful learning. They found that under appropriate conditions more than 45% of the variation in student learning can be explained by student perceptions of teacher effectiveness. Feldman (1997) synthesis of meta-analyses showed moderately positive correlations for teacher behaviours such as clarity and understandability of explanations, avoidance of vague terms and use of concrete examples; teacher availability and helpfulness to discuss matters of concern; quality and frequency of feedback by teacher to student; and teacher effort to establish rapport with students. Experimental studies have shown that teacher expressiveness such as enthusiasm, humour, making eye contact and physical movement signifi-cantly enhance student content learning. Such studies have also shown that some teacher behaviours improve critical thinking. Edison et al. (1998), for example, reported that their experimental study revealed that how teachers organized teaching sessions could have a positive effect on critical thinking.

Teachers' work is vital to engagement but is most effective when backed by a strong philosophy and by institutional support. While a unitary philosophy for student engagement is hard to find, there are clear philosophical assumptions about quality teaching. One is that teaching for engagement is learner-centred, the other is that education is about students constructing their own knowledge (Krause and Coates 2008). This meets the requirements of Barr and Tagg (1995) notion of a learning paradigm where teaching is not about instruction but about producing learning with every student by whatever means work. This learner-centred view is made even clearer by the UK's Trowler (2010): student engagement encompasses ways in which students become active partners in shaping their learning experience. A particular feature of this learner-focused conception is learner participation in learning communities which Pike et al. (2011) claim is positively and significantly related to student engagement. Institutional support for learning is another impor-tant foundation for engaging teaching. Kuh et al. (2005) provide valuable research information about the nature and quality of institutional support for learning. An overview of what engaging institutions do is provided by this team of researchers. In researching the practices of 20 successful higher education institutions in the USA, they found cultures that focused on student success, fore-grounded learning, established high expectations, aimed for continuous improvement, invested money in support services, asserted the importance of diversity and difference and prepared students for learning in higher education.

Disciplinary Knowledge Engages Students

Solomonides et al. (2012) developed a relational model of engagement in which discipline knowledge plays a major role. They suggest that the inclusion of disci-pline knowledge as a key component of student engagement is evident in only a few frameworks. Yet, students enrol in higher education to gain subject or discipline knowledge and skills to achieve life goals. To help them achieve these requires "a teaching approach which begins to satisfy simultaneously a tacit demand for content, for understanding of content, for relevance and applicability of that content…" (Walker cited in Entwistle 2010). It is important then to include an explicit con-sideration of content in an engagement pedagogy that enhances quality learning. Entwistle (2003) does so when reporting on the *Enhancing teaching-learning environments in undergraduate courses project* (ETL) in the United Kingdom. This investigated quality learning in teaching-learning environments. He reports that stimulating interest in students about ways of thinking and practising in a subject is one of five factors leading to interest and engagement in learning. Engagement is developed on the back of growing conceptual understandings in a subject. Such understandings involve key terms, concepts and principles of a subject; higher order understandings such as possibilities for application in the 'real world'; fundamental skills such as designing programmes and communication skills; and higher order skills like evaluating and interpreting knowledge. But quality learning and teaching also requires a suitable pedagogy, ways to facilitate the understanding of content. He suggests that engagement in quality learning is achieved when teachers and learners together deal with content in pedagogically suitable ways.

Teaching disciplinary knowledge in a pedagogically engaging way, then, seems to be a vital element for quality learning and success. The ETL project investigated the potential of threshold concepts to explore the close link between content and learning-teaching. They are "akin to a portal, opening up a new and previously inaccessible way of thinking about something" (Meyer and Land 2003, p. 1). This seems to be a suitable construct to help develop disciplinary knowledge while stimulating student engagement. A threshold concept is discipline specific, focuses on understanding of the subject and, indeed, has the ability to transform learners' views of the content by providing a conceptual gateway to gain such understanding. Once through the gateway, a new way of understanding, interpreting or viewing a subject may emerge. Walker (2013) suggests that threshold concepts can be viewed as a product of learning, something developed in the minds of learners, or as a learning process, a transformative journey with distinct stages. As a product threshold concepts have a cognitive, deep learning focus that seeks understanding and seeing things in new ways. As a process it is transformative, integrative, bounded, troublesome and eventually tacit. Whether seen as product or process threshold concepts require students' cognitive investment in, active participation in and emotional commitment to their learning (Fredricks et al. 2004) and therefore require engagement in disciplinary learning.

Adapt to Changing Student Expectations

Engaging institutions and teachers, no matter how successful, are never satisfied with their performance. They change practices in response to evidence. There is evidence that political and social conditions are changing and that institutions and teachers must adapt to. McInnis (2003) observed a new reality in higher education with students increasingly studying part-time. In Australia, for example, James et al. (2010) found that more than half the students surveyed thought that paid work interfered with their academic performance. Such students expected study to fit their lives; not fit their lives around study. McInnis (2003) suggests that engagement can no longer be assumed; it must be negotiated with students. James et al. (2010) found that half of the students in part-time employment offered family reasons for seeking employment. Some wanted to gain greater financial independence from their family; others, and this was particularly so for aboriginal students, were supporting their families. Together, these studies suggest that factors created by changing conditions in wider society are important influences on engagement. Teachers and institutions must keep abreast of, adapt to and negotiate around ever-changing student expectations. While we will dance a fine line between maintaining standards and accommodating expectations, there are methods we can use that would not lower standards. Some flexibility is often permissible around content, assessment deadlines, and attendance requirements. In negotiating such items we must be very clear about our expectations.

Ever-changing student expectations are also apparent around the use of technology. In research of university students' attitude and use of media in the United States, Mihailidis (2014) found that students have different attitudes to media in their private and educational lives. In private life, they engaged avidly with social media such as Facebook, MySpace Twitter, WordPress, YouTube and Flickr. Most participants integrated all facets of daily communication into such social networks. They felt that they won strong relationships and a sense of belonging from that engagement. Mihailidis' research also revealed an ambivalent view of technology. Many students saw the use of technology in a negative light, feeling that their engagement with media tethered and controlled them. This ambivalence can extend into the classroom leading to reluctance to participate in formal online classroom activities while at the same time wanting to use social media for their own purposes in that setting. Deuze (2006) explains this ambivalence as a tension between technologies learners choose to use in their daily lives and technologies they are told to use in class. He suggests that bricolage, a third mode of engagement with technology, leads to constantly rethinking and questioning the use of teaching media in the classroom. Bricolage attempts to address learner ambivalence about using classroom-learning technologies by introducing diverse, perhaps less educationally orthodox technologies. For example, Cull et al. (2010) suggest including both social media and more formal technology teaching platforms into planning for engagement. They suggest that teachers who stay in touch, respond quickly, deliver material and engage in conversations in both social and formal media have a good chance to engage their students.

Engagement Requires Enabling External Environments

In general, engagement researchers focus on what teachers and institutions can do to enhance learning inside the classroom. While occasionally mentioned, influences that happen or originate outside the walls of the academy are neglected in some frameworks. The framework offered by Yorke and Longden (2008) is an exception. They found that seven factors explained disengagement and early departure. While five of these factors related mainly to institutional issues such as poor-quality teaching, and to personal considerations such as choosing the wrong course, two factors originated outside the institution: problems with finance and employment; and problems with social integration into aspects of institutional life due to their background. This suggests that influences on engagement from outside the institution can be important. Here I consider three motivations for engagement that occur outside the institution.

Engagement Occurs Across the Life-Span

Lawson and Lawson (2013) view of student engagement as a sociocultural ecological construct suggests that it involves more than behavioural, psychological, social and cultural understandings. They recognize that engagement involves the whole being and is nourished by experiences in classroom, the home, the community and their own virtual worlds. Engagement in this holistic view transcends formal education and can occur in several contexts sequentially, simultaneously or iteratively. This view draws on sociocultural theory (Vygotsky 1978), the ecological systems framework developed by Bronfenbrenner (1979) and experiential learning (Dewey 1938/1997). It also mirrors the idea of lifewide education and learning that sees learning and engagement as happening in several places simultaneously (Barnett 2010). This notion of lifewide learning adds an extra dimension to our understanding of student engagement. It suggests that we inhabit simultaneously multiple learning spaces and can draw inspiration for engagement in the classroom from all or some. Barnett highlights a number of potentially engaging spaces to make this point. He suggests that our engagement with classroom learning can be traced to multiple sites; formal learning in credit bearing courses may only be one of numerous spaces that engage us; and the most engaging stimulation for learning may be unaccredited, personally stretching, highly demanding yet transfer to the classroom. Of course, experiences in the sociocultural ecological spaces can have disengaging consequences in the classroom as well. Engagement and disengagement are not attributable only to the classroom.

A key strength of the lifewide view of student engagement is that it explains how emotions contribute to engagement in multiple spaces. As Kahu et al. (2014) observe, different emotions contribute to engagement and influence all stages of the learning process. But they are not contained in one site like a classroom. Rather, emotions in one space affect engagement and learning in other spaces in the lifeworld and so engagement can transfer between lifewide spaces. This is not to say that classroom experiences cannot stimulate engagement on their own, merely that it is not possible to say that emotional engagement is always contained within the classroom. Emotions that act on engagement for learning can be positive and negative. Positive learning emotions can be traced to students' private lives at home, at work and at leisure as well as to the classroom. Positive effects of emotion on engagement are enabled by background, skills, self-efficacy and success (Kahu et al. 2014) and stimulated by warm relationships, respect and success in what students want to achieve (Bryson and Hand 2007) whether inside or outside the classroom. The absence of such positive emotions experienced anywhere in the lifeworld can lead to disengagement or as Case (2007) puts it to alienation from learning. She attributes reasons for alienation to an undesirable separation from the self, disturbances in relationships with self, others and society.

Engagement Is Linked to Subjective Well-being

Subjective well-being is an area of research that has increasingly been connected with student engagement. This connection is two sided. On one side, well-being research sees engagement as an important indicator of subjective well-being. The New Economics Foundation (NEF) (2009) has created an international well-being accounting process using the European Social Survey to measure people's subjective well-being. The account is based on personal and social well-being as two headline measures. Personal well-being measures people's experiences of their positive and negative emotions, satisfaction, vitality, resilience self-esteem and sense of positive engagement in the world. Social well-being measures people's experiences of supportive relationships and sense of trust and engagement with others. The NEF developed a well-being manifesto based on these results. One of their manifesto findings claimed that "being actively engaged with communities has been shown … to give us a personal sense of well-being but also to have a positive knock-on effect for others" (Shah and Marks 2004, p. 3). Alternative approaches to this European set of indicators have been developed elsewhere. Indeed, in the United States, Forgeard, Jayawickreme, Kern and Seligman et al. (2011) suggested a new science of well-being containing five domains: positive emotion, engagement, relationship, meaning and accomplishment. Also in the United States, Ryan et al. (2008) identified four motivational well-being indicators based on Self-Determination Theory. They argued that by feeling competent, autonomous and belonging, people engaged with their community to the benefit of their community. On the back of such studies, I suggest that personal well-being requires autonomy, competence, engagement and self-esteem; social well-being involves social engagement, sound interpersonal relationships and social competence.

The other side of the connection between engagement and subjective well-being research considers well-being from an engagement perspective. In general, engagement research addresses well-being as a consequence of engagement (Bryson and Hardy 2012) and of how personal attributes like connection, autonomy and intrapersonal competence facilitate feelings of well-being and engagement (Wimpenny and Savin-Baden 2013). Bryson and Hardy's student learning pathways offer rich examples of how disengagement, particularly in the absence of social connection, can lead to alienation and ill health. Wimpenny and Savin Baden's literature synthesis identified four critical factors in engagement: inter-relational factors due to connection with others; personal shifts from self-consciousness to self-sufficiency in learning; intra-personal factors enabling resilience and persistence; and emotional factors leading either to connection with or disjunction from study. Indirectly both these studies support general insights about both engagement and subjective well-being—self-esteem, resilience and positive emotions; autonomy, competence and engagement; and positive relationships with students, teachers and significant others. These findings from engagement studies are supported by Field (2009), an education researcher who examined the relationship between learning and well-being. He argued that successful learning requires learners to be and feel well physically, socially and emotionally. He observed that successful learning impacts positively on feelings of well-being. "(T)here is, then, a growing body of evidence on the relationship between learning and well-being, as well as on the impact of learning on factors that help promote well-being" Field (2009 p.11).

Active Citizenship Is Important for Student Engagement

Powerful in helping students engage is for them to believe they are active citizens with a say in learning processes. Students want to feel they have a voice in what and how they learn and 'student voice' has become a powerful metaphor for active citizenship and engagement, particularly in Europe. But according to Toshalis and Nakkula (2012) research in the United States too has shown that where educators give students choice and opportunities for collaboration, their engagement will rise. Klemenčič (2011) suggests that student voice, and collaboration enhances active citizenship and serves as an indicator of democracy and a culture of dialogue. She argues that student voice is "of particular relevance for students' civic learning, as one of the purposes or social roles of higher education" (p. 76). But there is not just one form of student voice or participation for engagement. According to Toshalis and Nakkula (2012), participation lies on a continuum ranging from minimal participation to taking a full part in a learning democracy. Their examples range from students expressing opinions; to being consulted in feedback; to participating in decision-making meetings; to being involved in framing issues and planning actions; to acting in partnership with others on standard operations; to identifying problems and generating solutions in and outside the institutional context; and at the other end of the continuum to taking on a leadership role in co-planning, and accepting significant responsibility in group processes and conducting activities.

There are many examples of student voice leading to active citizenship in engagement research. Trowler (2010) offers a classification for student voice for engagement. Students as active citizens are co-producers of learning in the classroom, active co-workers in various institutional structures and identity builders in the wider community. A good example of this model is in a book co-edited by Nygaard et al. (2013) which reports on a collaboration between 18 academic staff and 15 students in writing a book of 16 chapters. This offers examples of student voice in an applied, evidence based approach to engagement. A number of chapters offer insights into students as partners. These show how students' identity has changed from being receptacles for knowledge transfer to participants in active learning relationships. A second selection of chapters presents ways collaborative authorship can contribute to engagement in the structures of an institution. A third group of chapters presents ways in which collaboration creates learning communities, the value of which has also been emphasized by American writers such as Tinto (2010) and Pike et al. (2011) who stress that learning community participation is positively and significantly related to student engagement. Collaborative research is also a feature of this approach to active citizenship. Taylor et al. (2012), for example, offer a case study of collaborative research in which the notion of student as consumer is critiqued and changed to student as producer.

Emergence: A Conceptual Organizer for Mainstream Student Engagement

These 10 propositions offer a coherent conceptual organizer for engagement synthesized from research. Solomonides et al. (2012) observed that engagement can be arranged in a number of such organizers (they refer to frameworks). While their frameworks differ from those discussed in Chap. 2 of this book and will not be discussed further, one of their frameworks seems suitable for summarizing the conceptual organizer developed in this chapter. They suggest that there is a multidimensional type of framework that can incorporate all the others. Given the complexity of engagement and its ability to assist the emergence of new ideas at the margins of a system, a multidimensional conceptual organizer seems appropriate and Table 3.1 presents one.

This organizer focuses on how students engage, how teachers and institutions promote student engagement and how enabling environments for students and teachers support it. The 10 propositions for practice synthesize engagement research from the multiple frameworks discussed in Chap. 2. The 'key concepts' column identifies concepts drawn from other research on student learning that illuminates particular propositions. They offer detail needed to make the general propositions generated by engagement research more meaningful.

The organizer is presented as a table. This gives clarity to the organizer but also hides some important considerations. The different contributions to the organizer are recognized by the discrete boxes within which each contribution is placed. The three organizing ideas focus on the roles of learners, teachers, institutions and ecological factors in engagement. Each organizing idea consists of three or four propositions drawn from the conceptual frameworks in Chap. 2. In the 'key concepts' column, I have connected each proposition to other educational research that further illuminates and supports the proposition. The placement of the different aspects of the organizer next to each other and the frame around the whole diagram suggests that the perspectives are both connected and distinct.

But the organizer also hides important information. It pictures student engagement as a bounded entity that is made up of separate parts that exist in an uncertain relationship with each other. While what differentiates the different aspects of the organizer is clear, how they are connected in a complex meta-construct is less so.

Table 3.1 Emergence: a conceptual organizer of propositions and key concepts of engagement

Organizing Idea	Proposition for practice	Key concepts
Students' investment in learning	1. Student self-belief is vital for success 2. Student motivation grows self-confidence 3. Social and cultural capital enhance engagement 4. Engaged learners are deep learners	Appreciative inquiry Self determination theory Social/cultural capital Deep learning
Teacher and institutional support	5. Quality teaching and institutional support enhance engagement 6. Disciplinary knowledge engages students 7. Quality teaching adapts to changing student expectations	Learner centred teaching Threshold concepts Social change
Enabling environments	8. Engagement occurs across the life-span 9. Engagement is supported by subjective well-being 10. Active citizenship is important for engagement	Lifewide education Subjective well-being Student voice

Neither is whether the boundaries between perspectives are permeable and, if they are, in what way. The organizer as presented in Table 3.1 does not show the dynamic processes and relationships that are distinguishing features of student engagement and are not seen in Table 3.1.

A synthesis of literature is a construction from what has been read and what the author thinks is important. Hence, it is limited as it cannot include all research on student engagement. While not overcoming this weakness, empirical evidence can help to validate such research. Appendix A offers some evidence that higher education student in New Zealand, in any case, do find the 10 propositions acceptable.

References

Báez, C. (2011). *Crafting programs to stimulate student engagement and persistence in higher education*. Paper presented at the 15th Biennial of the International Study Association on Teachers and Teaching (ISATT), University of Minho, Braga, Portugal.

Barnett, R. (2010). Life-wide education: A new and transformative concept for higher education? *Enabling a More Complete Education e-Proceedings On-line*. Retrieved from http://lifewidelearningconference.pbworks.com/w/page/24285296/E%20proceedings

Barr, R., & Tagg, J. (1995). From teaching to learning: A new paradigm for undergraduate education. *Change, 26*(6), 13–25.

Bourdieu, P., & Passeron, J.-C. (1990). *Reproduction in education, society and culture* (2nd ed.). London, UK: Sage.

Bronfenbrenner, U. (1979). *The ecology of human development: Experiments by nature and design*. Cambridge, MA: Harvard University Press.

Bryson, C., & Hand, L. (2007). The role of engagement in inspiring teaching and learning. *Innovations in Education and Teaching International, 44*(4), 349–362.

Bryson, C., & Hardy, C. (2012). The nature of academic engagement: What the students tell us. In I. Solomonides, A. Reid & P. Petocz (Eds.), *Engaging with learning in higher education.* Faringdon, UK: Libri Publishing.

Bushe, G. (2013). The appreciative inquiry model. In E. Kessler (Ed.), *The encyclopedia of management theory.* Thousand Oaks, CA: Sage Publications.

Case, J. (2007). Alienation and engagement: Exploring students' experiences of studying engineering. *Teaching in Higher Education, 12*(1), 119–133. doi:10.1080/1356251060110235

Coates, H., Hillman, K., Jackson, D., Tan, L., Daws, A., Rainsford, D., & Murphy, M. (2008). *Attracting, engaging and retaining: New conversations about learning. Australasian student engagement (AUSSE) report* Retrieved from Camberwell, Australia: https://minerva-access. unimelb.edu.au/bitstream/handle/11343/28878/264257_2008_coates_attracting_report.pdf? sequence=1

Cooperrider, D., & Srivastva, S. (1987). Appreciative inquiry in organizational life. In R. Woodman & W. Pasmore (Eds.), *Research in organizational change and development. Volume 1* (pp. 129–169). Stamford, CT: JAI Press.

Cull, S., Reed, D., & Kirk, K. (2010). *Student motivation and engagement in online courses.* Retrieved from http://serc.carleton.edu/NAGTWorkshops/online/motivation.html

Davis, B., & Sumara, D. (2008). *Complexity and education: Inquiries into learning, teaching and research.* London, UK: Routledge.

Deuze, M. (2006). Participation, remediation, bricolage: Considering principal components of a digital culture. *The Information Society, 22*(2), 63–75.

Dewey, J. (1938/1997). *Experience and education.* New York NY: Macmillan.

Edison, M., Doyle, S., & Pascarella, E. (1998). *Dimensions of teaching effectiveness and their impact on student cognitive development.* Paper presented at the Association of the Study of Higher Education, Miami, FL.

Entwistle, N. (2003). *Concepts and conceptual frameworks underpinning the ETL project. Occasional Report 3.* Retrieved from Edinburgh, UK: http://www.etl.tla.ed.ac.uk/docs/ ETLreport3.pdf

Entwistle, N. (2005). Contrasting perspectives on learning. In F. Marton, D. Hounsell & N. Entwistle (Eds.), *The experience of learning: Implications for teaching and studying in higher education* (3rd (Internet) ed., pp. 3–22). Edinburgh, UK: Centre for Teaching, Learning and Assessment, University of Edinburgh.

Entwistle, N. (2010). Taking stock: An overview of key research findings. In J. Hughes & J. Mighty (Eds.), *Taking stock: Research on teaching and learning in higher education.* Montreal, Canada: McGill-Queen's University Press.

Entwistle, N., McCune, V., & Hounsell, J. (2002). *Approaches to studying and perceptions of university teaching-learning environments: Concepts, measures and preliminary findings. Occasional Report 1.* Enhancing Teaching-Learning Environments (ETL) Project.

Fazey, D., & Fazey, J. (2001). The potential for autonomy in learning: Perceptions of competence, motivation and locus of control in first-year undergraduate students. *Studies in Higher Education, 26*(3), 345–361.

Feldman, K. (1997). Identifying exemplary teachers and teaching: Evidence from student ratings. In R. Perry & J. Smart (Eds.), *Effective teaching in higher education: Research and practice.* New York, NY: Agathon.

Field, J. (2009). *Well-being and happiness: Inquiry into the future for lifelong learning. Thematic Article 4.* Retrieved from Leicester, UK.

Fredricks, J., Blumenfeld, P., & Paris, A. (2004). School engagement: Potential of the concept, state of the evidence. *Review of Educational Research, 74*(1), 59–109.

Gavala, J., & Flett, R. (2005). Influential factors moderating academic enjoyment/motivation and psychological well-being for Maori university students at Massey University. *New Zealand Journal of Psychology, 34*(1), 52–57.

Heylighen, F. (1999). *The evolution of complexity.* Dordrecht, Netherlands: Kluwer.

Higher Education Academy. (n.d.). *Deep learning*. Retrieved from https://www.heacademy.ac.uk/enhancement/definitions/deep-learning

Hockings, C., Cooke, S., Yamashita, H., McGinty, S., & Bowl, M. (2008). Switched off? A study of disengagement among computing students at two universities. *Research Papers in Education, 23*(2), 191–201.

James, R., Krause, K.-L., & Jennings, C. (2010). *The first year experience in Australian universities: Findings from 1994 to 2009*. Centre for the Study of Higher Education, University of Melbourne, Australia.

Johnson, D., Soldner, M., Leonard, J., Brown, J., Alvarez, P., Inkelas, K., & Longerbeam, S. (2007). Examining sense of belonging among first-year undergraduates from different racial/ethnic groups. *Journal of College Student Development, 48*(5), 525–542.

Kahu, E., Stephens, C., Leach, L., & Zepke, N. (2014). Linking academic emotions and student engagement: Mature-aged distance students' transition to university. *Journal of Further and Higher Education, 39*(4), 481–497. doi:10.1080/0309877X.2014.895305

Klemenčič, M. (2011). The public role of higher education and student participation in higher education governance. In J. Brennan & T. Shah (Eds.), *Higher education and society in changing times: Looking back and looking forward* (pp. 74–83). London, UK: Centre for Higher Education Research and Information (CHERI).

Krause, K.-L., & Coates, H. (2008). Students' engagement in first-year university. *Assessment and Evaluation in Higher Education, 33*(5), 493–505. doi:10.1080/02602930701698892

Kuh, G., Kinzie, J., Schuh, J., Whitt, E., & Associates. (2005). *Student success in college: Creating conditions that matter*. San Francisco, CA: Jossey Bass.

Laird, T., Bridges, B., Morelon-Quainoo, C., Williams, J., & Salinas Homes, M. (2007). African American and Hispanic student engagement at minority serving and predominantly white institutions. *Journal of College Student Development, 48*(1), 39–56.

Lawson, M., & Lawson, H. (2013). New conceptual frameworks for student engagement research, policy and practice. *Review of Educational Research, 83*(3), 432–479.

Llorens, S., Schaufell, W., Bakker, A., & Salanova, M. (2007). Does a positive gain spiral of resources, efficacy beliefs and engagement exist? *Computers in Human Behavior, 23*(1), 825–841.

Marton, F., & Säljö, R. (1976). On qualitative differences in learning: Outcome and process. *British Journal of Educational Psychology, 46*(1), 4–11.

McInnis, C. (2003). *New realities of the student experience: How should universities respond?* Paper presented at the European Association for Institutional Research, Limerick, Ireland.

Meyer, J., & Land, R. (2003). *Threshold concepts and troublesome knowledge: Linkages to ways of thinking and practising within disciplines. Occasional Report 4*. Retrieved from http://www.etl.tla.ed.ac.uk/docs/ETLreport4.pdf

Mihailidis, P. (2014). The civic-social media disconnect: Exploring perceptions of social media for engagement in the daily life of college students. *Information, Communication & Society, 17*(9), 1059–1071. doi:10.1080/1369118X.2013.877054

Nelson, K., Kift, S., & Clarke, J. (2012). A transition pedagogy for student engagement and first-year learning, success and retention. In I. Solomonides, A. Reid, & P. Petocz (Eds.), *Engaging with learning in higher education* (pp. 117–144). Faringdon, UK: Libri Publishing.

New Economics Foundation. (2009). *National accounts of well-being: Bringing real wealth onto the balance sheet*. Retrieved from http://cdn.media70.com/national-accounts-of-well-being-report.pdf

Nygaard, N., Brand, S., Bartholomew, P., & Millard, L. (2013). *Student engagement: Identity, motivation and community*. Faringdon, UK: Libri Publishing.

Pascarella, E., & Terenzini, P. (2005). *How college affects students: A third decade of research*. San Francisco, CA: Jossey Bass.

Pike, G., Kuh, G., & McCormick, A. (2011). An investigation of the contingent relationships between learning community participation and student engagement. *Research in Higher Education, 52*(3), 300–322.

Putnam, R. (2000). *Bowling alone: The collapse and revivial of American Community*. New York, NY: Simon & Schuster.

Richardson, K., & Cilliers, P. (2001). Special editors' introduction: What is complexity science? A view from different directions. *Emergence, 3*(1), 5–23.

Ryan, R., & Deci, E. (2000). Self-determination theory and the facilitation of intrinsic motivation, social development and well being. American Psychologist, 55(1), 68–78.

Ryan, R., Huta, V., & Deci, E. (2008). Living well: A self-determination theory perspective on eudaimonia. *Journal of Happiness Studies, 9*(2), 139–170.

Seligman, M. (2011). *Flourish*. New York, NY: Simon & Schuster.

Shah, H., & Marks, N. (2004). *A well-being manifesto for a flourishing society*. Retrieved from London, UK: http://www.neweconomics.org/publications/entry/a-well-being-manifesto-for-a-flourishing-society

Solomonides, I., Reid, A., & Petocz, P. (2012). A relational model of student engagement. In I. Solomonides, A. Reid & P. Petocz (Eds.), *Engaging with learning in higher education* (pp. 11–24). Faringdon, UK: Libri Publishing.

Taylor, P., Wilding, D., Mockridge, A., & Lambert, C. (2012). Reinventing engagement. In I. Solomonides, A. Reid & P. Petocz (Eds.), *Engaging with learning in higher education* (pp. 259–278). Faringdon, UK: Libri Publishing.

Thomas, L. (2002). Student retention in higher education: The role of institutional habitus. *Journal of Education Policy, 17*(4), 423–442.

Tinto, V. (2010). From theory to action: Exploring the institutional conditions for student retention. In J. Smart (Ed.), *Higher education: Handbook of theory and research* (pp. 51–89). New York, NY: Springer.

Toshalis, E., & Nakkula, M. (2012). Motivation, engagement and student voice. Retrieved from http://www.studentsatthecenter.org/topics/motivation-engagement-and-student-voice

Trowler, V. (2010). Student engagement literature review. Retrieved from http://www.heacademy.ac.uk/assets/documents/studentengagement/StudentEngagementLiteratureReview.pdf

Vygotsky, L. (1978). *Mind and society: The development of higher mental processes*. Cambridge, MA: Harvard University Press.

Walker, G. (2013). A cognitive approach to threshold concepts. *Higher Education, 65*(2), 247–263.

Wimpenny, K., & Savin-Baden, M. (2013). Alienation, agency and authenticity: A synthesis of the literature on student engagement. *Teaching in Higher Education, 18*(3), 311–326. doi:10.1080/13562517.2012.725223

Yorke, M., & Knight, P. (2004). Self-theories: Some implications for teaching and learning in higher education. *Studies in Higher Education, 29*(1), 25–37.

Yorke, M., & Longden, B. (2008). *The first year experience of higher education in the UK: Final report*. Retrieved from https://www.heacademy.ac.uk/sites/default/files/fyefinalreport_1.pdf

Part II
Questioning the Mainstream View

Chapter 4
Higher Education in Neoliberal Times

Abstract The first three chapters examine current thinking about and practice of student engagement in higher education. They have shown that it is an extremely popular approach to learning and teaching, featuring in conversations about higher education policy, teaching and learning, educational research and in the media. The question addressed in this and the next chapter is "why is student engagement so popular"? The answer is that it suits the intellectual and political climate of our time which is dominated by neoliberalism. This chapter explores the influence of neoliberalism in setting higher education aims, policies and the culture of teaching and learning these create. The chapter examines the drivers that enable neoliberal ideas to dominate in higher education, uses a case study to show how these drivers operate in higher education in one country and outlines the key educational neoliberal ideas that shape student engagement.

So far I have introduced a number of research frameworks for student engagement, their theoretical underpinnings and practical applications in a learning centred and constructionist pedagogy I call *mainstream student engagement*. We have seen that engagement has become ever present in conversations about higher education policy, teaching and learning, educational research and even in the media (Kuh 2009). It has been called a popular buzz phrase and a hot topic; a universal label for any appealing form of teaching that encourages learning (Ramsden and Callender 2014). This popularity has led to a wide array of claims about its contributions to engaging learning and teaching. It is said to measure reflective accountability of institutions (McCormick 2009), to promote student success (Thomas 2012), to assure quality teaching (McCormick et al. 2013), to support individual and social wellbeing (Field 2009), to transform students from consumers to co-producers of knowledge (Nygaard et al. 2013), and to achieve active student citizenship and participation (McMahon and Portelli 2004, 2012). With such an array of uses, definitions become plentiful. I added to this profusion by calling engagement complex; a metaphor for effective learning and teaching consisting of entwining continuities and discontinuities across multiple frameworks and methodologies. The question that this discussion raises is *why is student engagement so popular*?

© Springer Nature Singapore Pte Ltd. 2017
N. Zepke, *Student Engagement in Neoliberal Times*,
DOI 10.1007/978-981-10-3200-4_4

The complex, far-reaching promise of and widespread research, practice and publicity about student engagement undoubtedly contributes to its own popularity. But its long list of generic and practical suggestions for improving learning and teaching cannot be sheeted home solely to an increased interest in improving classroom practice. In the next two chapters I argue that the main reason for its prominence is that it suits the political climate of the times we live in, neoliberal times. The purpose of these chapters is to explore the relationship between student engagement and politics and to argue that neoliberal times enhance the appeal of student engagement theory and practice in higher education. In this chapter I will outline key features of neoliberalism and how they help shape the conduct of higher education generally, discuss important ideas that contribute to the relationship between neoliberalism and higher education and investigate effects neoliberalism has on the conduct of learning and teaching there.

The choice of neoliberalism as the major reason for student engagement's attractiveness to higher education is not arbitrary. Student engagement flourishes in a supportive intellectual and political environment. For the last 30 or so years this has been provided by neoliberalism which Finger and Asún (2001) labelled 'turbo capitalism'. Saunders (2010) argues that neoliberal ideas have come to dominate cultural, social and political life almost everywhere. It is based on the belief that individuals are primarily self-interested and that self-interest benefits the whole society. The best way to support self-interested individuals is to allocate resources through free market economics and governance. It is the role of government to ensure that the free market operates efficiently. However, like student engagement, neoliberalism functions in diverse ways in different contexts both at the geopolitical level through globalization and at a local level of the individual who is expected to be work ready for the market place (Davies and Bansel 2007).

So neoliberalism is just as complex as student engagement. To establish a relationship between them we have to explain neoliberalism as more than a combination of economic theories and policies that impact higher education by way of government legislation and regulation. We have to follow Saunders (2010) into understanding how neoliberalism dominates political, cultural, intellectual and social life in most parts of the world; the way it establishes and shapes a new moral order of subjects by which the conduct of individuals or of groups can be conducted (Foucault 1991). According to Foucault (2008) neoliberalism is about the relations of power and how it is exercised. Power is not just used to impose the will of the institution called government through legal instruments. It functions in a domain of relationships between subjects who regard themselves as free but who are tightly governed by self-imposed political, cultural, intellectual and economic norms. Consequently government is everywhere. It involves not only the administration and management of the state, but expects self-control by subjects about every aspect of life such as the conduct in families, of children, management of the household and investment in education, training and learning. Government affects subjects in ways ranging from legislating and regulating to self-regulation by subjects creating technologies of the self (Lemke 2001). Foucault (2008) referred to this continuum of activity as *governmentality,* the conduct of conduct, a term he employed as an analytical grid to explore the workings of neoliberalism.

In this chapter I explore how *governmentality* illuminates the relationship between higher education and neoliberalism. While neoliberal ideas have struck root in political and cultural frameworks around the world, their application can vary. On the local and individual level neoliberalism has also become a dominant presence. It turns out to be an umbrella term supported by a number of contributing theories. Together these theories construct what Foucault (1991) called *governmentality,* the systems, technologies, processes and practices the state uses to govern individual citizens and citizens use to govern themselves. But how has neoliberalism spread so widely across the world? Its expansion is partially explained because it seemed to address problems, particularly in the western world, that caused economic difficulties. Neoliberalism was portrayed as being the only economic approach that could fix those problems. It's seemingly reasonable ideas offered an economic and technical rationality that promises ready solutions to these economic and political challenges. At the geopolitical level neoliberalism has spread around the world on the back of a process Edwards and Usher (2000) call 'policy migration'. Policy migration of neoliberal solutions is assisted by the use of new communication technologies that speed their adoption.

Neoliberalism, Globalization and Governmentality in Higher Education

Globalization

In trying to describe globalization, Perry (1998, p. 167) decided that it is only ever "glimpsed, but not grasped". So it may be safer to think of multiple globalizing processes rather than a singular process. For example, Apple (2010) identifies three interlinked discourses as helping to drive globalization. Neoliberalism is one such discourse. Others are neo-conservative and managerial impulses that also have a global impact. Through television, movies, social and other media in the Internet and popular music, people become aware of information, ideas and symbols that move around the world at great speed. These communication streams feature telecommunication, finance and electronic technologies, products and services. They have penetrated and overwhelmed national and cultural borders. Huge multinational concerns, sometimes bigger than nation states, shift capital around the world to suit the availability of cheap labour and their own bottom line. Ever more sophisticated goods and services result. These require applied research and a highly skilled labour force to develop and maintain. Economic globalization is further advanced by free trade. The General Agreement on Trade of Services (GATS), for example, has the potential to remove all limitations of market access or commercial presence to any corporations wanting to do business in signatory states (Kelsey 2002). Yet, as Jameson (1998, p. xi) observes, while globalisation is the "universalizing of the particular" it is also "a particularisation of the universal". Neoliberalism fosters both uniformity of economic systems and variability.

Much has been written about the impact of globalization on higher education. More and more emphasis is placed on education as of service to economic development. Both modernizing and western countries have used higher education as a keystone to make their way in the modern global economy (Martin 2003). Knowledge and skills become key sources of competitive advantage in the global market place. Education becomes both the provider of the knowledge and skills required and a marketable service (Codd 2002). Indeed, neoliberalism recognizes knowledge as capital (Burton-Jones 1999). He suggests that knowledge has been the most undervalued of all economic resources but that with the revolution in communication and other technologies it is becoming the most important capital in business, work arrangements, education, learning and work—the market. The way neoliberalism and globalization affects higher education is debated. It is possible to argue that globalization, the internet, and the scientific community will level the economic playing field in a new age of knowledge interdependence. But it is also feasible to claim that globalization leads to worldwide inequality and the McDonaldization of higher education. What is reasonably safe to suggest is that the contemporary shape of higher education stems from the pursuit of a knowledge economy/society initiated by neoliberalism and globalization.

Governmentality

If globalization explains the international approval and spread of neoliberal ideas, governmentality refers to the way conduct is normalized within societies. It is dubbed 'Foucault's hypothesis' by Lemke (2002, p. 51) and "is characterized by inquiring into the conditions of a consensus or the prerequisites of acceptance" of relationships of power. Mutual acceptance explains the relationship between neoliberalism and higher education, and by extension student engagement. Foucault (2008, p. 186) sees governmentality as "a proposed analytical grid" for enabling relations of power to be examined. The term is used to analyse "the way in which one conducts the conduct of men (sic)". The grid can be applied to government at the level of the individual right through to "the management of a whole social body" (Foucault 2008, p. 186). According to Bye (2015) governmentality is valuable for analysing both the management of society and the management of the actual practice of individuals: what they do and what they think. It offers a view of how the state, which according to Foucault (2008, p. 98) is "nothing more than the mobile effect of a regime of multiple governmentalities [that] conducts conduct in neoliberal times, not in a single all powerful entity called government, but as a dynamic collection of relations that has multiple effects on power in society".

Governmentality is "at once internal and external to the state, since it is the tactics of government which make possible the continual definition and redefinition of what is within the competence of the state and what is not ..." (Foucault 1991, p. 103). Hence conduct is not shaped by single all-powerful entities such as governments or educational institutions, but in relationships that occur in more or less open fields of possibility: within and between individuals, groups and their members, and institutions and their associates. With this concept Foucault tries to show how the state collaborates through its multiple relationships with individuals, groups and communities in determining the conduct of conduct.

Dean (1999, p. 18) offers a very broad understanding of how governmentality works through multiple reflexive relationships.

> On the one hand, we govern others and ourselves according to what we take to be true about who we are, what aspects of our existence should be worked upon, how, with what means, and to what ends. On the other hand, the ways in which we govern and conduct ourselves give rise to different ways of producing truth.

In the relationship between neoliberalism and higher education and subsequently student engagement, the state has initially shaped the conduct of conduct of all actors in the educational process by using "the mechanisms that try to shape, sculpt, mobilise and work through the choices, desires, aspirations, needs, wants and lifestyles of individuals and groups" (Dean 1999, p. 12). But the conduct of conduct is not just decreed by a government. Dean divides governmentality into 'govern' and 'mentality' that is into the mentalities of governing or a mental disposition to govern. Governments have such mental dispositions and use these to introduce neoliberal theories into the conduct of conduct in education. By living neoliberal values and practices in their homes and communities, most citizens find them practical and reasonable; a desirable way of meeting universally attractive economic and political aspirations. As Duggan (2003, p. 10) observed "who could be against greater wealth and more democracy"? With neoliberalism present in all aspects of their lives, citizens also acquire the mental disposition to govern themselves using neoliberal ideas of proper conduct (Usher et al. 1997).

Laclau and Mouffe (2001) suggest that the mental disposition in favour of neoliberalism is so great that Antonio Gramsci's concept of cultural hegemony comes into play. Hegemony exists when a dominant idea establishes its authority as common sense and gains popular acceptance to the extent that the population at large believes that there can be no other way of thinking or operating. As a result neoliberal ideas and practices have come to redefine the purposes and roles of economic, social, cultural and political practices and institutions. But as Mouffe (2005) also notes, society is always hegemonically constituted through structures of power relations and so the neoliberal hegemony will not necessarily be permanent or remain the same. Indeed, Collier (2005) observed that neoliberalism as an ideology undergoes constant change and renewal. He shows that it began a third incarnation in 2005. Its bedrock beliefs in "weak government and powerful markets" had changed to belief in strong government to maintain powerful markets.

As incarnations change so do the multiple relations of governmentality and the conduct of conduct.

Governmentality is valuable for understanding the rise of and changes in neoliberalism and its current role in higher education. While not a new idea when it became influential in the 1970s, neoliberalism's rise can be attributed to economically troubled times (Saunders 2010). Governments could not get stagflation under control using Keynesian demand-side economics and policy makers turned to new accounts of liberalism to address economic difficulties. According to Saunders governments around the world introduced policies based on neoliberal accounts of the economy and society out of necessity. Neoliberalism is an umbrella term sheltering a number of related but distinct theories on markets, the role of the state, human capital, accountability and knowledge (Olssen and Peters 2005). These theories were manufactured into economic, social and ecological policies for which 'there is no alternative' (TINA). TINA became the catch cry for transforming societies. But as Saunders (2010) observed, catch cries do not make people accept blindly that there is no alternative. The claim has to seem to be true to be acceptable to the majority of people. The claims of neoliberalism had to be accepted as part of people's lived experiences. As economies improved, people were ready to reject old policies on the back of their experience of the new, change their own conduct of conduct and that of others by embracing new ways of thinking and doing so to solve large scale economic problems and personal financial issues.

Neoliberal ideas came to define the conduct of conduct in the public service sectors of many societies, including in higher education. But neoliberalism is not a single theory of action. Originally an economic rationality, it comprises multiple economic theories to define the conduct of conduct in societies and subsequently higher education. Table 4.1, following Olssen (2002), Peters and Hume (2003) and Olssen and Peters (2005), summarizes key theories (Table 4.1).

Table 4.1 Selected theories informing higher education policy in the twenty-first century

Theory	Examples of theorists	Key ideas
Spontaneous order	Hayek	Unregulated markets are superior to central regulation in developing creativity and progress
Public choice	Buchanan, Tullock	Theories of institutional redesign to increase economic efficiency in public institutions
Agency	Williamson	Efficient personal and institutional performance is achieved via principal-agent contracts
Human capital	Becker, Denison, Schulz	Education is an investment in people. It improves capacities, increases productivity and earning power
Knowledge capitalism	Stiglitz, Burton-Jones	Knowledge is the most important form of capital in the 21st century to assist development

Neoliberalism and Higher Education

Together these theories sought to establish competition between institutions in higher education by creating market place conditions. But competition is controlled by an active state that continues to finance higher education according to strategic plans approved by the government in negotiations with providers. Investment is made on the assumption it will produce graduates who will, through their study, enhance their value in the market place and help develop the economy. Learners are required to fulfil a contract with their institutions to achieve desired outcomes, with both students and institutions being accountable for its achievement. Students are expected to gain knowledge and skills suitable in the market place. While there are many critics of the application of neoliberal ideology to higher education, administrators, teachers, students and members of communities have in the main accepted its ideas and practices as common sense. The chapter now discusses these theories before illustrating their effects in higher education using New Zealand as a case study.

Spontaneous Order Theory

According to Olssen and Peters (2005) the 'spontaneous order' theory originated with Hayek. It alludes to the role of the market in the economy and society. The market, he suggested, facilitates the spontaneous growth of orderly social structures, of law and morals, of language and also the growth of technological knowledge. In his view the market provides the most efficient means of allocating resources. Central planning is undesirable as it distorts the working of the market, is less efficient and is also a morally inferior mechanism to the market. Because of its ability to facilitate spontaneous order, the market should also be self-regulating as self-regulation is more efficient than regulations imposed by the state or any other outside force. People in the spontaneous order state are economically self- interested subjects, rational optimisers and the best judge of their own interests. While many of these beliefs are shared with liberalism, neoliberalism moves away from the idea that value of resources, goods and services should be judged objectively. Hayek argued that value is conferred on resources by the subjective preferences of agents (Olssen and Peters 2005). Initially neoliberals showed a distinct distrust of government power. They sought to limit state power to the protection of the rights of individuals. In this view of the world higher education is a market where commodities, primarily knowledge, are traded. To be effective and efficient in the marketplace requires higher education institutions to be autonomous actors.

Public Choice Theory

Neoliberal theorists like Hayek were challenged by others who had a more positive view of state power than the spontaneous order market liberals. Buchanan and the Public Choice theorists wanted to create markets in the public sector including higher education using the deliberate actions of the state (Olssen and Peters 2005). They had little trust that markets could on their own spontaneously order economic or social evolutionary processes. These theorists thought markets if not helped by state steerage would produce social chaos and dysfunction as well as harmony and equilibrium. Public choice theorists did not believe that social evolution supported by markets alone will ensure the arrival of efficient institutions. Whereas Hayek's version of neoliberalism viewed the influence of the state negatively, public choice theory saw the state as the mechanism to create and maintain the appropriate market conditions to ensure smooth economic and social development. So the state was not dismissed from the operation of the public sector or higher education. It was assigned two roles: safeguarding independence in the market place and ensuring that that independence is accountable to state agencies. In the marketplace, autonomy stands for freedom to compete; accountability gives the state power to both ensure and define the freedom. However, like Hayek and his spontaneous market liberals, public choice theorists rejected the view that the state was there to protect individuals. But they did see a role for the state as policeman and active participant (Reisman 1990).

Agency Theory

Agency theory is one of a cluster of economic and management theories intended to re-design institutions into agents of the neoliberal state (Olssen and Peters 2005). It expands on public choice theories that an active state should be involved in creating and ordering public sector markets. In particular, agency theories seek to ensure that management controls the design and operation of institutions. Agency theorists think of working relationships in public sector institutions as dualistic and hierar-chical, with different kinds of contracts used to enable managers or principals to motivate, supervise, control and monitor the work of agents. Underpinning agency theory and its managerialist allies is accountability, the notion that government through management needs to be able to measure performance in objective and transparent ways. Biesta (2004) suggests that an 'accountability culture' has emerged in the neoliberal world. He argues that this is used as a system of governance that results in an audit society. This has re-conceptualized the relationship between government and citizens from the political to the economic. It is a relationship between consumers and providers, with government as principal and institutions as agents at one level; institutions as principals and their employees and students as agents at another. The role of government is to create and manage this complex, layered market by providing the conditions, laws and contractual regulations necessary to create and maintain it (Olssen 2002). One central assumption of this arrangement is that statistics provide transparent, fair and objective information about outcomes. Another is that scientific evidence will also provide the information from which improvements can be made. A third assumption is that evidence must be practical, informing both policy-making and practice. This focus on practicality has given rise to the mantra "what matters is what works" (Sanderson 2003).

Human Capital Theory and Knowledge Capitalism

Many theories connect education to economic development and growth. One such theory at the heart of neoliberalism is human capital theory (Becker 1994). He argues that human capital is similar to the physical capital that generates outputs in factories and on farms. To achieve growth in factory outputs, capital investment is needed to obtain returns on investment. Human capital does the same job as its physical cousin. But instead of returns being produced in factories they are produced in educational institutions and from there in the market place. So investment in education is also an investment in economic development and growth. For Simkovic (2013) human capital aggregates all the competencies, *knowledge*, skills, habits, personal attributes used by people, including *creativity* and cognitive abilities, to perform *labour* and produce *economic value* and returns on investment. It attempts to capture the social, biological, cultural and psychological complexity of market economics in education. Human capital theory is an economic view of people and their functions in the neoliberal state. They are expected to produce value for the economy through their knowledge, skills and work. Former British Prime Minister Blair boiled this thinking into the memorable "education is the best economic policy we have" (cited in Martin 2003, p. 567). The dominant policy discourse that emerged is one that focuses "on learning for earning" in support of economic growth and global competitiveness (Biesta 2005 p. 688).

The Effects of Neoliberalism on Higher Education: A Case Study

To be meaningful, theories generated by neoliberalism become clearer when placed into a context that shows how they are applied. Without such application, theories run the danger of remaining abstractions. I have suggested throughout this chapter that neoliberalism manifests in many countries of the world. Examples of its application are available from Australia and New Zealand, the Americas, Western Europe including the United Kingdom, and Asia (Saunders 2010). This global spread provides the opportunity to study the application of neoliberalism in multiple contexts. But an extensive let alone exhaustive survey of application is impractical given the purpose of the book and chapter and I have chosen New Zealand as a single case study to illustrate how neoliberalism has been applied in a specific context. New Zealand is a credible example both for showing the integration of neoliberal thinking into a policy framework for higher education and the operation of governmentality as government, institutions, teachers and learners collaborate to conduct the conduct of higher education. But there is also a caution attached to such a case study approach. A case study does not explain how neoliberalism has been applied universally. Saunders (2010) reminds us that while the application of neoliberal theories in different countries is similar, it is not the same. New Zealand case study then is, but one, although credible example of neoliberal theories in practice.

As I mentioned earlier, Collier (2005) observed that neoliberalism is not static. It is a collection of ideas that undergoes constant change and renewal. He identified three distinct phases and these apply to New Zealand. The first he calls *proto neoliberalism*. Largely an intellectual movement, proto neoliberalism views the world through economic lenses and supports the establishment of a free market. It reminds of spontaneous order theory and often precedes the actual introduction of neoliberal policies. Collier designates a second phase as *roll-back neoliberalism*. In this phase neoliberalism is implemented by the state with the express purpose of mobilizing state power to steer markets and society. This stage reminds of public choice, agency and human capital theories and the effects of managerialism. A third stage, he called *rollout neoliberalism*, which involves a deliberate attempt by the state to sort out anomalies and contradictions incurred in the second phase. Higher education, as part of a post-school policy framework in New Zealand seems to have gone through these phases, although perhaps not in a strictly sequential way as overlaps and revisions are observable. As Openshaw (2012) suggested, the strands of neoliberalism in higher education were evident years before government documents began to build a neoliberal policy framework. After 1987 policy papers rained on the higher education landscape to establish government control and steerage of market policies. This stage was superseded after 1999 with the introduction of a third way neoliberalism in public policy.

Colliers first phase, *proto neoliberalism* was well signalled internationally before it hit New Zealand in the early 1980s. It had been well discussed in economic circles since the 1930s and its ideas were circulated by the Mont Pelerine Society from the 1950s. In West Germany Ludwig Erhard implemented economic policies drawing on neoliberal ideas in the 1950s and 1960s. The Thatcher and Reagan eras in the United Kingdom and the United States brought neoliberal ideas to the attention of the world in the 1980s. In New Zealand there was an awakening of interest in neoliberal ideas throughout the 1980s. Fargher (1985), for example, an influential Trade Union secretary and not a neoliberal, nevertheless argued strongly that work and post-school education were two sides of the same coin and students had to learn to be competent in the workforce. While education had a responsibility to respond to economic conditions, in his view it remained a public good.

New Zealand's Treasury department dismissed this idea. In its 'Government Management Vol II' (1987) it made its bid to apply neoliberal economic analysis to education. 'Government Management' argued that despite its complexity, education must be exposed to rigorous economic analysis. This will show that education is a commodity in the market place and a private good. Once government recognises that education is just another commodity, consumer sovereignty and the market will rule and government's role decline. A government commissioned report (Hawke 1988) softened the uncompromising market economic views of Treasury, but agreed that post school education was a private good for which students should pay.

The next phase, *roll-back neoliberalism* arguably began with another policy document. 'Learning for Life II' (New Zealand Government 1989) stipulated that all post-school education institutions including higher education "are of equal value in their personal, social and economic worth" (p. 12). It mapped out its proposed post-school education landscape in considerable detail. In doing so it reaffirmed market based spontaneous order theory but also referred to public choice and agency theories

> Institutions will be given as much independence and freedom to make operational and management decisions as is consistent with the nature of their service, the efficient use of national resources and the demands of accountability... Post-school education and training institutions (and other non-institutional providers) will now make their own operational decisions - and this will enable them to respond to local conditions and the needs of their clients with a speed and sensitivity that has not been possible in the past (New Zealand Government 1989, p. 8).

But it was the next, a centre-right government after 1990 that pushed the economic purposes of education in a competitive market. Its first Minister of Education, energetically spread the idea of enterprise as a keystone of educational policy. It was the government's purpose to

> ... enhance educational achievement and skill development to meet the needs of the highly competitive, modern international economy.... The government is committed to an education system that prepares New Zealanders for the modern competitive world (Smith 1991, pp. 1–2).

These themes repeatedly appeared throughout the 1990s in government policies. Indeed, elements of *roll back neoliberalism* remained after the demise of the centre-right government in 1999. Roberts (2008), for example, suggested that economic concerns, competition and the commodification of knowledge remained priorities under subsequent governments as well.

Human capital theory became increasingly prominent in the 1990s. A discussion document on 'Education for the 21st Century' (New Zealand Ministry of Education 1993) emphasised New Zealand's place in the global market place. In order for New Zealand to compete "we must invest in people, our greatest economic resource" (p. 7). The government's succession of green and white papers between 1997 and 1999 reinforced the economic purposes of post-school including higher education. For example, 'A Qualifications Policy for New Zealand' (1997, p. 3) stated that employers want high skill employees in order to gain advantage over competitors: "(n)ationally, the capability of our people drives New Zealand's overall competitiveness and our economic and social success".

Collier's third phase of *roll out neoliberalism* was introduced by the next, a centre-left government after 1999. Four reports by a 'Tertiary Advisory Commission' (TEAC) (TEAC 2000, 2001a, b, c) defined a third way for neoliberalism to steer post-school (higher education) between market economics and social inclusion. The third way is a pragmatic response to needs: "what counts is what works" (Giddens 2001, p. 5); what works also changes and so did post-school education policy. TEAC's reports used public choice, agency, and human capital theories to give the government a greater ability to shape and steer post-school education. They also introduced the idea of a knowledge society as a key priority for the government. In the foreword to the third report, 'Shaping the Strategy' (2001b), the Associate Minister of Education (Tertiary Education) conceded that post school education, as one of the major public investments in developing skills and capabilities needed in the future, required a paradigm shift. The system could no longer be driven by consumer choice or market demand.

> Rather, the focus of the tertiary education system will now be to produce the skills, knowledge and innovation that New Zealand needs to transform our economy, promote social and cultural development, and meet the rapidly changing requirements of national and international labour markets (TEAC 2001b, p. 1).

This was a significant step away from the spontaneous order theory of the market so prevalent during the *proto neo liberal* phase.

Competition was now frowned on as institutions were encouraged to shift their attention from attracting customers to meeting government priorities. Programme mixes for different kinds of institutions and agencies were determined centrally through institutional profiling. The whole sector was to be planned, directed and monitored by a Tertiary Education Commission (TEC) that "steers the system in the direction specified by the government, but in a manner consistent with the principles of provider autonomy, academic freedom and responsiveness...." (TEAC 2001a, p. viii). The Education Amendment (No. 2) Bill proposed strengthening the government's power over post-school education institutions. Any institution seen as at risk financially and operationally could result in the appointment of a Crown observer to protect the Crown's investment. While this provision was carefully hedged, it could result in compromising any education provider's autonomy.

Carried over from times prior to TEAC, agency theory governed the relationships that developed between the state, institutions and students. These were contractual with one party (the principal) purchasing 'outputs' from another party (the agent). The post-school education system turned into a network of principal-agent relationships. The State invested in programmes for specified educational outputs and students paid institutions to gain qualifications. But the interests of agents and principals were expected to conflict. As a result post-school education was governed by a series of formal contracts. The institution provided a statement of what it expected to achieve from a set of government priorities. The Tertiary Education Commission (TEC) purchased outputs on the basis of this document. TEC monitored and judged to what extent plans were achieved. These achievements are reported publically in annual reports.

The TEAC strengthened accountability regimes imposed on post-school education. The governing process now seemed more one of central control than accountability for autonomy in the market. In its second report, 'Shaping the System' (TEAC 2001a) TEAC extended the use of charters to all publicly funded providers, introduced a new profiling system, established the TEC, and foreshadowed a centralising quality assurance mechanism extending to all publicly funded providers. While institutional differences were recognized in charter prescriptions, "there must be more active use of the Minister's current powers to specify mandatory requirements for charters" (p. 53). The profiling system used functional classifications by which the government could determine the programmes taught in institutions and sectors and hold institutions accountable through the public funding mechanism. The Tertiary Education Commission ensured a whole host of matters including accountabilities of providers and "sustainable wealth creation" (p. 39). While centralized quality assurance processes were just hinted at then, a centralizing audit agency has been established since TEAC to monitor the quality of university provision.

A component of agency theory, what Boston (1991, p. 9) dubbed the new managerialism, was introduced during the 1990s. "Its slogans include the now familiar 'let the managers manage' and 'managing for results'". Under these slogans, managers were encouraged to manage the institution to achieve mandated objectives. As a result they accrued considerable powers of decision-making. Chief Executives, not the state or councils, employed and deployed all staff. They achieved sole control over implementing council policies while in academic matters they reigned supreme with the help of academic boards. In the framework created by TEAC after 1999, Chief Executives and senior managers maintained their powerful positions as long as the institutions they led met contracted performance criteria. Chief Executives seem convinced by neoliberal theories. For example, a sampling of reports and press releases coming out of 'Universities New Zealand—Te Pokai Tara' (2011)—the organization representing universities and their CEOs —exhibits a strong economic mission. It is focused on proving the value of universities to the economy. It lauds the role of universities in increasing wealth, productivity, and value for money and emphasises that universities' research outputs assist business.

Athough Roberts (2008) suggestion that overall policies since TEAC have shown continuities from the market led priorities of the 1990s is credible, there have also been significant departures from these. Regardless of whether governments have been left or right of centre politically the influence of third way ideas and the framework create by TEAC continues to dominate at the time of writing in 2015. Governments have been obliged to publish strategic documents including setting and monitoring priorities for the system since the time of TEAC. Institutional investment plans have been based on such priorities. These have remained quite stable since the first 'Tertiary Education Strategy' was published in 2002 (New Zealand Government 2002). Priorities have been focused on strengthening general system capabilities, contributing to the development of Māori (New Zealand's indigenous people) and Pasifika (people oiginating in Pacific Island nations), raising foundation skills for a knowledge society, strengthening research and knowledge creation and having a presence in the world. Such priorities are visible in the latest strategy for 2014–2019 (New Zealand Ministry of Education 2014). This focuses on delivering skills for industry, getting at risk young people into careers, boosting achievement of Māori and Pasifika, improving adult literacy and numeracy, strengthening research based institutions and growing international linkages. System progress towards achieving these undergoes rigorous monitoring using largely quantitative indicators. Stringent monitoring reveals that accountability is an unstated priority. Indicators show achievements on priority outcomes, research outputs, completions and retention and financial performance. These are published in numerous books and on public web sites. They create what de Santos (2009) calls fact totems, cultural items used to steer, maintain and support the system.

Theory to Practice

I have argued in this chapter that neoliberal ideas and theories have achieved a geopolitical dominance right around the world via globalization and that these theories have been adopted internally by states and the people living in them by regulating the conduct of conduct through governmentality. Many states have turned neoliberal ideas and theories into policies. New Zealand has been used as a case study to show effects such policies have had on higher education. What is missing is an examination of what impact such policies have had on the practices of learning and teaching. To round out this chapter 1 sketch how three particular aspects of neoliberalism have impacted on practice in higher education and student engagement.

The first is that what is learnt is practical and economically useful in the market place. Higher education is a particular market where commodities, primarily knowledge, are traded. The emphasis on what is marketable has impacted on the meaning of knowledge. Høstaker and Vabø (2005) argue that, prior to the establishment of the neoliberal hegemony, knowledge was generated within academic disciplines and research traditions associated with a search for truth based on reason. Neoliberalism has transformed this to a knowledge that is judged more on how it performs in a context of application—in this case, the marketplace. This transforms knowledge to what Giddens (1990) calls Type 2 knowledge—transdisciplinary, transient, useful and applied. It connects well to the precepts of neoliberalism. Not only can knowledge be presented as a commodity sold in the marketplace, it is also seen as the only source of comparative economic advantage, particularly for small countries (Gilbert 2005). Type 2 knowledge lies at the heart of the 'information society'. Funding and subject matter are determined by how useful knowledge is to the information economy (Dyer-Witheford 2005). The pursuit of knowledge becomes a search for information that is practical and useful, able to be turned into profit (Roberts 2005).

The second particular application of neoliberalism to practice is how local higher education performs in the global education market. Olssen (2002, p. 55) suggests that neoliberalism functions as a performance idea that establishes a new relationship between the state and its subjects. Lyotard used the term 'performativity' to describe governance in higher education (Barnett 2000) in which academic leaders are executives managing the performance of institutions, teachers, researchers and students according to set criteria. According to Codd (2012) universities operate in the market employing policies and practices that commodify not only knowledge, but teaching, learning and research into sets of performance standards. These judge the performance of teachers and students as countable qualities. Macfarlane (2015) argues that this results in a lack of trust extending to both teachers and students. Higher education becomes a carefully controlled input–output system with an economic production function. It manages inputs using behavioural objectives and learning outcomes, recruiting academics, administrators and students, determining course offerings and content—all in line with market demands. For institutions and teachers outputs are quantified by means of verifiable criteria counting such things as successful pass rates, financial performance and research impacts. Students' performativity is demonstrated through attendance registers and assessment-related proxies for attendance such as in-class tests and presentations. According to Yates (2009) this emphasis on countable qualities has the effect of fashioning learners in certain generic ways.

Accounting for how well higher education performs in the market is the third particular application of neoliberalism to higher education. El-Khawas (2007) suggested that accountability refers to a general trend to publically measure performance. As a result of this, an 'accountability culture' emerges (Biesta 2004) that works within a complex web of accountability relationships including students, teachers, institutions, sponsors, as well as local communities. Accountability takes many forms: legal requirements, such as licensing, extensive planning documentation to obtain funding, financial and academic audits; quality assurance procedures, such as accreditation and review of programmes; comparisons across universities published as league tables; budget allocations that reward performance; and new oversight structures, such as governing boards with external participants and performance league tables (Salmi 2007). A regime of audited self-reviews is mandated with results published in public media. This leads to both self-disciplining by institutions and external surveillance of them (Olssen 2002). Similarly, individual and institutional research outputs are audited with results published as league tables in national and international media. While research audits do not overtly curtail academic freedom, they do tend to channel researchers' intellectual attention and political engagement, "influencing what they study, how they do it, and how they report and write" (Middleton 2009, p. 193). These multiple requirements and practices ensure that the products of higher education are suitable for the market.

These three applications of neoliberal thinking to higher education will be examined again in Chaps. 5 and 6. Chapter 5 will examine the relationship between neoliberalism and student engagement research and practice. Chapter 6 will critique the relationship between student engagement and neoliberalism. This chapter has set the stage for them. It argued that neoliberalism is nothing out of the ordinary. Its special features and influences on policy and practice are marked by an acceptance that their application to higher education are normal. People working in and for higher education increasingly accept neoliberal disciplines and discipline themselves in its service. This normalization is shown by multiple questions asked of a speaker at a recent international conference that puzzled "what is neoliberalism?"

References

Apple, M. (2010). Global crises, social justice, and education. In M. Apple (Ed.), *Global crises, social justice, and education* (pp. 1–22). New York: Routledge.

Barnett, R. (2000). University knowledge in an age of supercomplexity. *Higher Education, 40*(4), 409–422.

Becker, G. (1994). *Human capital: A theoretical and empirical analysis with special reference to education*. Chicago, IL: The University of Chicago Press.

Biesta, G. (2004). Education, accountability, and the ethical demand: Can the democratic potential of accountability be regained? *Educational Theory, 54*(3), 233–250.

Biesta, G. (2005). The learning democracy? Adult learning and the condition of democratic citizenship. *British Journal of Sociology of Education, 26*(5), 687–703.

Boston, J. (1991). The theoretical underpinnings of public sector restructuring in New Zealand. In J. Boston, J. Martin, J. Pallot, & Walsh (Eds.), *Reshaping the state: New Zealand's bureaucratic revolution* (pp. 1–26). Auckland, New Zealand: Oxford University Press.

Burton-Jones, A. (1999). *Knowledge capitalism: Business, work and learning in the new economy*. Oxford, UK: Oxford University Press.

Bye, J. (2015). Foucault and the use of critique: Breaching the self-evidence of educational practices. *International Journal of Qualitative Studies in Education, 28*(4), 394–414.

Codd, J. (2002). The third way for tertiary education policy: TEAC and beyond. *New Zealand Annual Review of Education, 11*, 31–57.

Codd, J. (2012). Selected article: Educational reform, accountability and the culture of distrust. In R. Openshaw & J. Clark (Eds.), *Critic and conscience: Essays on education in memory of John Codd and Roy Nash* (pp. 29–46). Wellington, New Zealand: NZCER Press.

Collier, S. (2005). *The spatial forms and social norms of 'actually existing neoliberalism': Toward a substantive analytics. New School University International Affairs Working Paper 2005-04*. Retrieved from New York, NY: https://stephenjcollier.files.wordpress.com/2012/07/spatial-forms.pdf

Davies, B., & Bansel, P. (2007). Neoliberalism and education. *International Journal of Qualitative Studies in Education, 20*(3), 247–259. doi:10.1080/09518390701281751

Dean, M. (1999). *Governmentality: Power and rule in modern society*. London: UK: Sage.

de Santos, M. (2009). Fact-totems and the statistical imagination: The public life of a statistic in Argentina 2001. *Sociological Theory, 27*(4), 466–489.

Duggan, L. (2003). *The twilight of democracy: Neoliberalism, cultural politics and the attack on democracy*. Boston, MA: Beacon Press.

Dyer-Witheford, N. (2005). Cognitive capitalism and the contested campus. In G. Cox & J. Krysa (Eds.), *Engineering culture: On 'the author as (digital) producer'* (pp. 71–93). New York, NY: Automedia.

Edwards, R., & Usher, R. (2000). *Globalisation and pedagogy: Space, place and identity*. London, UK: Routledge Falmer.

El-Khawas, E. (2007). Accountability and quality assurance: New issues for academic inquiry. In J. Forest & P. Altbach (Eds.), *International handbook of higher education* (pp. 23–37). Heidelberg, Germany: Springer.

Fargher, R. (1985). Continuing education and New Zealand society. In N. Zepke & L. Webber (Eds.), *Continuing education in New Zealand*. Wellington, New Zealand: Association of Teachers in Technical Institutes (ATTI).

Field, J. (2009). *Well-being and happiness: Inquiry into the future for lifelong learning. Thematic Article 4*. Retrieved from Leicester, UK:

Finger, M., & Asún, J. (2001). *Adult education at the crossroads: Learning our way out*. London, UK: Zed Books.

Foucault, M. (1991). Governmentality. In C. Gordon & P. Miller (Eds.), *The Foucault effect: Studies in governmentality* (pp. 87–104). Chicago, IL: University of Chicago Press.

Foucault, M. (2008). *The birth of biopolitics: Lectures at the College de France 1978–1979*. New York, NY: Picador.

Giddens, A. (1990). *The consequences of modernity*. Cambridge, UK: Polity Press.

Giddens, A. (2001). *The global third way debate*. Cambridge, UK: Polity Press.

Gilbert, J. (2005). Catching the knowledge wave? 'Knowledge society' and the future of public education. In J. Codd & K. Sullivan (Eds.), *Education policy directions in Aotearoa New Zealand* (pp. 53–70). Southbank, Australia: Thomson Dunmore Press.

Hawke, G. (1988). *Report of the working group on post-compulsory education and training*. Retrieved from Wellington, New Zealand:

Høstaker, R., & Vabø, A. (2005). Higher education and the transformation to cognitive capitalism. In I. Bleiklie & M. Henkel (Eds.), *Governing knowledge* (pp. 227–243). Heidelberg, Germany: Springer.

Jameson, F. (1998). Notes on globalization as a philosophical issue. In F. Jameson & M. Miyoshi (Eds.), *The cultures of globalization* (pp. 54–77). Durham, NC: Duke University Press.

Kelsey, J. (2002). *At the crossroads: Three essays*. Wellington, New Zealand: Bridget Williams Books.

Kuh, G. (2009). The national survey of student engagement: Conceptual and empirical foundations. *New Directions for Institutional Research, 141*, 5–20. doi:10.1002/ir.v2009: 141/issuetoc

Laclau, E., & Mouffe, C. (2001). *Hegemony and socialist strategy: Towards a radical democratic politics* (2nd ed.). London: UK: Verso.

Lemke, T. (2001). 'The birth of bio-politics': Michel Foucault's lecture at the Collège de France on neo-liberal governmentality. *Economy and Society, 30*(2), 190–207.

Lemke, T. (2002). Foucault, governmentality, and critique. *Rethinking Marxism, 14*(3), 49–64.

Macfarlane, B. (2015). Student performativity in higher education: Converting learning as a private space into a public performance. *Higher Education Research & Development, 34*(2), 338–350. doi:10.1080/07294360.2014.956697

Martin, I. (2003). Adult education, lifelong learning and citizenship: Some ifs and buts. *International Journal of Lifelong Education, 22*(6), 566–579.

McCormick, A. (2009). Toward reflective accountability: Using NSSE for accountability and transparency. *New Directions for Institutional Research, 141*, 97–106. doi:10.1002/ir.v2009: 141/issuetoc

McCormick, A., Gonyea, R., & Kinzie, J. (2013). Refreshing engagement: NSSE at 13. *Change: The Magazine of Higher Learning, 45*(3), 6–15. doi:10.1080/00091383.2013.786985

McMahon, B., & Portelli, J. (2004). Engagement for what? Beyond popular discourses of student engagement. *Leadership and Policy in Schools, 3*(1), 59–76.

McMahon, B., & Portelli, J. (2012). The challenges of neoliberalism in education: Implications for student engagement. In B. McMahon & J. Portelli (Eds.), *Student engagement in urban school: Beyond neoliberal discourses* (pp. 1–10). Charlotte, NC: Information Age Publishing.

Middleton, S. (2009). Becoming PBRF-able: Research assessment and education in New Zealand. In T. Besley (Ed.), *Assessing the quality of educational research in higher education* (pp. 193–208). Rotterdam, Netherlands: Sense Publishers.

Mouffe, C. (2005). *On the political*. Abingdon, UK: Routledge.

New Zealand Government. (1997). *A qualifications policy for New Zealand*. Wellington, New Zealand: New Zealand Government.

New Zealand Government. (1989). *Learning for life two*. Wellington, New Zealand: Government Printer.

New Zealand Government. (2002). *Tertiary Education Strategy 2002–2007*. Wellington, New Zealand: New Zealand Government.

New Zealand Ministry of Education. (1993). *Education for the 21st century*. Wellington, New Zealand: Ministry of Education.

New Zealand Ministry of Education. (2014). Tertiary education strategy 2014–2019. Retrieved from   http://www.education.govt.nz/further-education/policies-and-strategies/tertiary-education-strategy/

New Zealand Treasury. (1987). *Government management: Brief to the incoming Government 1987*. Wellington: New Zealand Treasury.

Nygaard, N., Brand, S., Bartholomew, P., & Millard, L. (2013). *Student engagement: Identity, motivation and community*. Faringdon, UK: Libri Publishing.

Olssen, M. (2002). *The neoliberal appropriation of tertiary education policy in New Zealand: Accountability, research and academic freedom. State-of-the-Art monograph No. 8*. Wellington, New Zealand: New Zealand Association for Research in Education.

Olssen, M., & Peters, M. (2005). Neoliberalism, higher education and the knowledge economy: From the free market to knowledge capitalism. *Journal of Education Policy, 20*(3), 313–345. doi:10.1080/02680930500108718

Openshaw, R. (2012). Researching New Zealand's education reforms: Problems and prospects 1988–2011. In R. Openshaw & J. Clark (Eds.), *Critic and conscience: Essays on education in memory of John Codd and Roy Nash* (pp. 63-86). Wellington, New Zealand: NZCER Press.

Perry, N. (1998). *Hyperreality and global culture*. London, UK: Routledge.

Peters, M., & Hume, W. (2003). Education in the knowledge economy. *Policy Futures in Education, 1*(1), 1–19.

Ramsden, P., & Callender, C. (2014). *Review of the national student survey: Appendix A: Literature review*. Retrieved from London, UK: http://www.hefce.ac.uk/pubs/rereports/year/2014/nssreview/#alldownloads

Reisman, D. (1990). *The polticial economy of James Buchanan*. College Station, TX: A&M University Press.

Roberts, P. (2005). Tertiary education, knowledge and neoliberalism? In J. Codd & K. Sullivan (Eds.), *Education policy directions in Aotearoa New Zealand* (pp. 39–52). Southbank, Australia: Thomson Dunmore Press.

Roberts, P. (2008). Beyond the rhetoric of 'quality' and 'relevance': Evaluating the tertiary education strategy 2007–2012. *New Zealand Annual Review of Education, 17*, 41–57.

Salmi, J. (2007). Autonomy from the state vs responsiveness to markets. *Higher Education Policy, 20*(3), 223–242.

Sanderson, I. (2003). Is it 'what works' that matters? Evaluation and evidence-based policy-making. *Research Papers in Education, 18*(4), 331–345. doi:10.1080/0267152032000176846

Saunders, D. (2010). Neoliberal ideology and public higher education in the United States. *Journal for Critical Education Policy Studies, 8*(1), 42–77.

Simkovic, M. (2013). Risk-based student loans. *Washington and Lee Law Review, 70*(1), 527–648.

Smith, L. (1991). *Education policy: Investing in people, our greatest asset*. Wellington, New Zealand: Ministry of Education.

Tertiary Education Advisory Commission. (2000). *Shaping a shared vision*. Wellington, New Zealand: Tertiary Education Advisory Commission.

Tertiary Education Advisory Commission. (2001a). *Shaping the system.* Wellington, New Zealand: Tertiary Education Advisory Commission.

Tertiary Education Advisory Commission. (2001b). *Shaping the strategy.* Wellington, New Zealand: Tertiary Education Advisory Commission.

Tertiary Education Advisory Commission. (2001c). *Shaping the funding framework.* Wellington, New Zealand: Tertiary Education Advisory Commission.

Thomas, L. (2012). *Building student engagement and belonging in higher education at a time of change: Final report from the what works? student retention and success project.* Retrieved from

Universities New Zealand—Te Pokai Tara. (2011). *Academic quality assurance of New Zealand universities.* Retrieved from http://www.nzvcc.ac.nz/publications

Usher, R., Bryant, I., & Johnston, R. (1997). *Adult education and the postmodern challenge: Learning beyond the limits.* London, UK: Routledge.

Yates, L. (2009). From curriculum to pedagogy and back again: Knowledge, the person and the changing world. *Pedagogy, Culture and Society, 17*(1), 17–28.

Chapter 5
Student Engagement and Neoliberalism: An Elective Affinity?

Abstract In the previous chapter, I showed that higher education is governed and operates in the shadow of neoliberalism. In this chapter, I argue that this connection is also evident when we examine student engagement research and practice. To support the argument, the chapter investigates a number of underlying issues. It first examines on a very general level, whether and how educational research can be connected to an overarching political rationality such as neoliberalism. Second, focusing specifically on student engagement, it asks whether research into this pedagogy has been suborned by neoliberalism. A response to these two issues generates a third investigation: how the relationship between neoliberalism and student engagement can be conceptualized. The answer to this inquiry offers the metaphor of *elective affinity*. The fourth issue investigated in this chapter focuses on how this elective affinity impacts the practice of student engagement as seen from neoliberal and research points of view.

Chapter 4 investigated the spread and impact of neoliberalism on higher education. It established that neoliberalism has achieved dominance in economic and social policy discourses in many countries through processes of globalization and governmentality. In this chapter, I turn the spotlight more squarely on student engagement and its relationship with neoliberalism. I ask whether student engagement is so embedded in neoliberalism that it shapes how teaching and learning are practiced. To be able to conduct such an inquiry, I investigate a number of underlying questions: first, whether and how educational research in general can be connected to an overarching political rationality, such as neoliberalism; second, and more specifically, whether student engagement research has been suborned by neoliberalism; third, arising from the answers to the first two questions, how can the relationship between neoliberalism and student engagement be conceptualized; and fourth, if there is a relationship between student engagement and neoliberalism, how does it impact student engagement practices in higher education. I will argue that the answer to the first question is 'yes', the second 'no'. This means that the relationship cannot be a totalizing one. I suggest that Weber's use of a metaphor,

© Springer Nature Singapore Pte Ltd. 2017
N. Zepke, *Student Engagement in Neoliberal Times*,
DOI 10.1007/978-981-10-3200-4_5

elective affinity, is more appropriate for describing the relationship. This means that theory, research and practice of student engagement are by choice influenced by and allied to neoliberalism but not entirely subsumed by it.

Research Culture and Neoliberalism

I have suggested that governmentality is vital to an understanding of how neoliberalism works in higher education and how it affects student engagement. It is the conduct of conduct, the process by which behaviour is shaped via a series of commonly accepted norms. These provide a general frame for ideas, strategies and technologies, shaping behaviours that are not exclusively economic but fashion people across a whole range of issues in complex relationships involving individuals, the community and the state. Neoliberal norms have transformed actors in higher education, such as policy makers, academics and students into market participants and competitors who contribute to the development of knowledge capitalism. This results in educational research that displays a deep neoliberal turn (Gonzales et al. 2014) giving educational research two directions: research *for* and *of* policy development (Lingard 2013) for higher education. Lingard suggests that educational research both assists policy-making and helps determine the questions asked, topics examined and methods used by researchers. Research *for* refers to research that assists the development and support of actual policy. Such research might ask how certain practices, like student engagement, help improve student outcomes. Research *of* identifies policy problems that require solutions. Such problems are often identified to provide evidence in support of ideological assumptions, for example, the best way to measure accountability. Such research is framed by the interests and intentions of policy makers and is taken up willingly by researchers (Lingard 2013). He suggests that this type of research is ammunition for or legitimation of a particular policy direction taken politically. The combined impact of research *for* and research *of* policy creates a research culture that suits neoliberal ideas and practices.

Three norms mark the neoliberal research culture. The first emerges from human capital theory and seeks the development of a knowledge economy and knowledge society. These require research that is closely connected to neoliberal ideas. They privilege the pursuit of practical, market relevant Type 2 knowledge that offers useable answers to immediate problems. Researchers become knowledge capitalists that produce marketable knowledge (Gonzales et al. 2014). The second norm focuses on research performance. Performativity becomes a key component of the neoliberal research culture. According to Leathwood and Read (2013), performativity is about obtaining grants from government agencies and commercial firms, productivity by publishing in prestige journals, being cited and addressing practical problems. Meeting such performance requirements produces considerable pressures. Gonzales et al. (2014, p. 1107) cite the example of one academic:

> I have learned to more efficiently perform my teaching responsibilities so that I can focus more on research including grant writing and publishing. I had difficulty finding the time to write manuscripts with all of my other duties but have been able to slowly change that. I have tried to spend more time on research activities, but … if I want to do more research I must work harder and faster.

The third norm is about institutions, academics, administrators and students being accountable for their performance and the funding showered on them. Accountability in a neoliberal research culture measures performance against narrow standards such as planned outcomes. According to Leathwood and Read (2013) accountability measures result in active surveillance by measurement of others and the self.

These norms are important when identifying research questions, topics and methods. Bernasconi (2014) suggests that in a relatively stable policy environment, there is a general consensus about what questions are asked and what topics researched. The general consensus in neoliberal times is that educational research should focus on addressing practical problems using evidence of what works. According to Bernasconi evidence for what works enables a tacit agreement between policy makers and academics about what and how to research. Evidence-based policy research of what works has enjoyed a very high profile throughout the western world since the late 1990s. For example, evidence-based policy was adopted in the UK in 1999. Since then, it has remained a vital part of public management strategies and policy practice (Strassheim and Kettunen 2014). They cite a paper produced by the Cabinet Office in 2013 announcing creation of a network of evidence centres to build 'what works' into policy. The attraction between educational research of what works and neoliberalism is illustrated in a paper summarizing a large research project on what works for student retention and success in the UK (Thomas 2012). Evidence from this project showed that what works to improve student retention and success is "helping all students to become more engaged and more effective learners in higher education, thus improving their academic outcomes and their progression opportunities after graduation…" (Thomas 2012, p. 10). This focus on outcomes and success in employment suggests a strong connection with neoliberal norms.

Evidence connecting research topics and neoliberal policy agendas further emerges when considering the kind of research published. A content analysis by Zepke and Leach (2012) of projects funded by the Teaching and Learning Research Programme (TLRP) in the United Kingdom between 1999 and 2009, for example, suggests that neoliberal priorities were heavily represented. During its 10 years of operations it funded 21 projects in the post-school education space. Project proposals were expected to be practical, to demonstrate what works and were intended to address political and social issues of the day. Of the 21 projects included in the analysis nine addressed topics associated with a widening participation agenda. The remaining 12 TLRP funded projects can be associated with three other areas important to neoliberal policy making: practices to improve student success (eight projects); transitions from further to higher education (two projects); and impacts of policy on teaching practice (two projects). The student success agenda is further evident in the content analysis when examining the publications in four international journals specializing in teaching and learning: *Active Learning in Higher Education* (UK), *Higher Education Research and Development* (Australasia), *Journal of College Student Development* (USA) and *Teaching in Higher Education* (UK). Of 1074 articles published in these journals between 2003 and 2011, 312 (29%) report research that investigated student success in various guises.

It is of course common sense that evidence should underpin every report and journal article assisting policy-making and practice in higher education. The question is what counts as evidence. Strassheim and Pekunen (2014) suggest that in neoliberal times an 'ideology of scientism' has developed based on quantitative methods. As a result the research–policy relationship tends to expect quantitative evidence based on the positivist and absolutist assumptions offering factual solutions to problems (Jankowski and Provezis 2014). Consequently in the US, for example, acceptable evidence is based on quantitative scientific research, preferably randomised control experiments (Feuer et al. 2002). Such research is also valued in many other jurisdictions similarly influenced by neoliberal ideas. With slight variations the arguments supporting quantitative evidence contend that when the stakes associated with the development of a knowledge economy/society, performance standards and accountability are high, research that can identify causal, empirically valid relationships between actions and outcomes, must be considered as the gold standard (Feuer 2006). The question 'what works?' is a causal question and can only be addressed validly and safely using statistical methods. Feuer further argues that research often raises diverse and competing claims of what works. Policy-makers require rigorous ways to distinguish between such claims. He argues that because quantitative scientific research enables even small effects on variables to be detected, such research is well placed to disentangle competing claims. Moreover, a key assumption of quantitative scientific research is that its results can often be generalized and thus form a firm foundation for policy-making.

The use of numbers to demonstrate performance does not just account for the performance of institutions, staff and students. In neoliberal times educational research should also be accountable to the public. For example, student choice is expected to be a determining factor for enrolment in particular institutions and even disciplines. Choice must be informed by information about institutional performance on a large variety of variables. This includes pricing information and the quality of the student experience. Students are made aware publically of retention, completion rates and employment outcomes. Institutional ratings across a number of indicators like research outputs and financial performance are captured in a variety of media. This information is usually conveyed via statistics available for public view in digestible form, usually in the form of league tables. For example, in the United Kingdom the Higher Education Statistics Agency publishes such information annually for each institution (Thomas 2012). Statistics of how well-participating institutions in the National Survey of Student Engagement in the USA engage students are publicly available from extensive reports analyzing and summarizing results. In addition to informing student choice, such statistics are also published more widely to inform the interested public about performances of institutions. de Santos (2009, p. 467) calls such statistics fact-totems, cultural objects that have deep seated meanings for their audiences.

> Fact-totems are powerful symbols that condense social attention and evoke passionate responses from broad audiences. This concentrated attention gives rise to statistical dramas that have diffuse but powerful effects on actors' perceptions of social and economic reality, included policy interventions.

They are very useful in aligning research findings to knowledge capitalism, performativity, accountability and the interests of neoliberal rationality.

Student Engagement and Neoliberalism

I have suggested that neoliberalism has a significant influence on research culture in higher education. I now argue that this influence is extended to the way student engagement is conceived and practiced. I use the word *influence* deliberately because I do not want to imply that student engagement research is a creature of neoliberalism. While its emergence as a powerful player in higher education research and practice is connected to neoliberalism, student engagement is neither caused by nor embedded in it. The neoliberalism—student engagement relationship will be unpacked at greater length in the third section of this chapter. In this section, I just want to suggest that student engagement is a subset of the general education research culture. As such it is aligned with neoliberalism which influences the conduct of student engagement research. However, as Dean (1999) pointed out, the way research in higher education and therefore student engagement is conducted in neoliberal times is complex. It involves the state setting research agendas in its own image. This assumes that research provides countable evidence of what works in education and so meets the norms set by knowledge capitalism, performativity and accountability. But the research agenda is not just set, controlled and managed by government. Researchers and institutions themselves govern each other to meet the terms of the neoliberal agenda and also govern themselves to conduct their research according to accepted norms.

Krause (2012) suggested that scanning the higher education landscape in both developed and undeveloped countries reveals a strong focus on quality. She agrees that quality is not easy to define, but uses the Australian experience to summarize how quality issues are handled by the use of centrally set performance-based funding indicators, mission-based institutional contracts and the monitoring of quality standards. Quality reviews and audits at institutional and classroom levels use student feedback, institutional self-review and external audit procedures according to quality criteria established both centrally and locally. The quality discourse used here is strongly influenced by the neoliberal norms of performativity and accountability. They bind higher education generally and student engagement into neoliberal quality discourses. This is as it should be argued Coates (2005) as student engagement offers a perspective on quality student learning that is often neglected by institutional reviews about such things as reputation, financial performance, resourcing and pathways into employment. With its focus on learning, engagement is a key indicator of the quality of the student experience (Krause 2012) and of teaching and institutional performance (McCormick 2009). Kuh (2009) argued that student engagement is an important predictor of retention and success in higher education. It is apparently positively correlated with a range of student outcomes such as critical thinking, cognitive development, self-esteem, student satisfaction and improved grades and persistence (Pascarella et al. 2010). Engagement researchers not associated with variable-centred quantitative research (Lawson and Lawson 2013) also recognize the close association of engagement with quality. In their case, it is often that engagement is developed through positive relationships and emotion (Bryson and Hand 2007; Wimpenny and Savin-Baden 2013).

In neoliberal times the focus on quality and student engagement is associated with student success: retention, completion and employment after graduation. These indicators of success suit the needs of the neoliberal state to justify government spending in higher education. They ensure accountability and enable funding to be directed to institutions and programmes that provide quantitative evidence not only of student but also of institutional success. These success indicators also put individual students at the centre of the educational process as they support student choice and responsibility at the same time. In this context student engagement becomes a useful proxy for researchers searching for what works in helping students and institutions achieve successful outcomes. Outcomes such as retention, completion and productive employment often feature as indicators of success embedded in engagement. Kuh et al. (2006) suggested that engagement matched the requirement of a knowledge-based economy. According to McMahon and Portelli (2004, 2012) this has led to a technical and operational rationality about engagement that reflects neoliberal assumptions. Hence, the prolific research programmes of quantitative and qualitative data accumulations about engaging student behaviours, thinking and institutional practices. In the United States, McCormick (2009) and Kuh (2009) found some evidence that a high level of engagement predicts student success. In the United Kingdom Bryson and Hardy (2012) suggested that by engaging in a variety of educationally productive activities students can develop the foundation of skills and dispositions people need to live a productive, satisfying life after graduation.

Success indicators such as engagement suit a one size fits all perspective appropriate for neoliberal times. They produce generic evidence that can be applied in any situation and context, nationally and internationally. They enable benchmarking of institutional and national performances. According to Kuh (2009), a key benefit of engagement research is offered through the insights gained from surveys such as the NSSE and its many international offspring. Student experience questionnaires that do not actually employ the term 'engagement' but nevertheless assess student participation in the student experience (Krause 2012) and 'approaches to learning' inventories that assess cognitive dimensions such as deep learning (Entwistle 2005) also identify generic qualities of student engagement.

Such research monitors engagement as measurable, objective and generic. The roles of specific cultural, power and other contextual differences seem imperfectly recognized even though Kuh et al. (2006) suggest that quality in engagement requires institutional cultures that cater for diversity. Engagement research seems blind to cultural and other differences. For example, in an edited book on engaging culturally diverse learners (Harper and Quaye 2009), chapter authors acknowledge differences in conceptions of learning by different cultural groups but suggest techniques and practices from NSSE engagement surveys to address them, and so do not recognize that engagement might reveal itself differently in diverse cultural contexts. The very construct of engagement is presented generically. For example, Kinzie (2010) consolidates engagement research into four generic propositions that do not distinguish different contexts, learners and teachers. Similarly, wellness, a contributor to engagement research, is often described by universal indicators sited in national and international repositories (Forgeard et al. 2011).

According to Yates (2009) this uniform view of quality is a feature of pedagogy which seeks to fashion learners in certain generic ways. And pedagogy—the method and practice of teaching—is at the heart of student engagement research. But pedagogy is just one of three interdependent message systems—the others being curriculum and evaluation (Bernstein 1996). Yates (2009) unpicks the interdependence of the three message systems by assigning them particular functions. She suggests that pedagogy serves teaching and learning processes by focusing on the individual and their subjectivities, on evidence about interpersonal instructional or facilitative behaviours and the conscious application of particular assumptions about instructional methods. Her characterisation of pedagogy fits engagement which shares similar understandings about learning and teaching. To her, pedagogy is but a subset of curriculum and therefore offers only a partial understanding of students' learning. Student engagement research, with its focus on providing countable evidence of what works takes a lead role in how pedagogy is constructed and so meets the requirements of research in neoliberal times. Whether visualizing student engagement as reflective accountability, as a collection of teaching methods to facilitate student success, or as an indicator of well-being, student engagement describes a learner fashioned to actively commit to a task, to problem solve and to feel a strong sense of belonging (Thomas 2012). Phelan (2011) concurs that pedagogy in neoliberal times is mainly interested either in 'the doing' of teaching (and learning) or in improving 'the doing'.

Elective Affinity: A Metaphor for the Relationship

I have argued that student engagement and neoliberalism are powerful influences in early twenty-first century higher education and that they are linked. But they could be linked in various ways. Student engagement could be seen as a "hard wired" and necessary consequence of a neoliberal hegemony. Support for this view is credible. In many neoliberal jurisdictions, New Zealand is one example, educational research generally and engagement research specifically is funded almost exclusively by governments or related state agencies. As suggested by Lingard (2013) such funded research is expected to assist policy-making. Funders expect researchers to ask preferred questions, examine favoured topics and use accepted methods. Such research might ask how certain practices, like student engagement, help improve student outcomes. Researchers not funded pick up on the favoured agenda and conduct unfunded research addressing similar questions, related topics and using approved methods. Research on student choice and success, quality, belonging and even well-being and active citizenship is prized as it finds strong echoes in neoliberal thought and government policies. The use of a predetermined and generic pedagogical framework to provide quantitative survey data as 'fact-totems' (de Santos 2009) helps gain public acceptance for the technical rationality embedded in such research. The often mentioned generic "one size fits all" and "what counts is what works" mantras of neoliberalism (Giddens 2001) also apply to engagement research which tends to cloak differences, such as ethnicity, class and other privilege.

Yet an assumption that student engagement is totally embedded in and controlled by neoliberal necessities is not convincing as there are research programmes and practices that do not fit comfortably into a neoliberal hegemony. Chronologically student engagement research and neoliberal times do not correspond exactly. For example, early research on student engagement in the United States started well before the high tide of neoliberalism (Kuh et al. 2006). Neither have I found evidence that early research into 'approaches to learning' was influenced by, let alone is a creature of neoliberalism. Then the critique of the technical, economic and operational nature of engagement research by, for example McMahon and Portelli (2012), critiques the neoliberal web. So does the work of Neary (2013) and Bryson (2014) in the United Kingdom. They counter normative views of engagement by involving their undergraduate students in research as producers of knowledge. Neary (2013), for example explicitly opposes neoliberal ideas in his engagement research. He bases his research on Marxist thought as voiced particularly by Walter Benjamin and the Soviet psychologist Lev Vygotsky. Neary's vision of engagement is *Student as Producer* which connects intellectual and manual labour so learners feel part of the production of knowledge and meaning. In *Student as Producer* the learner is a creative subject within the academic project. This reshapes the relationship between teaching and research from neoliberal concepts of the learner as a consumer of teaching and knowledge to a producer of potentially revolutionary ideas.

So an alternative and less causal connection between student engagement and neoliberalism is needed to explain the links. The concept of *elective affinity* offers such an explanation. This considers the strong connection between student engagement and neoliberalism as one of mutual attraction. Jost et al. (2009) suggested that *elective affinities* can develop between political ideologies and seemingly unrelated ideas of social groups such as educators in higher education. Such affinities can increase the influence of both the ideologies and the apparently unrelated social groups. I argue that student engagement has an elective affinity with neoliberalism. This has helped it to prominence in educational research and practice. Similarly, it has led to neoliberal ideas being generally accepted, but not unquestioned, by theorists and researchers working in learning and teaching. Three key understandings of neoliberalism in particular share this elective affinity with engagement: that what is to be learnt is practical and economically useful in the market place; that learning is about performing in certain ways in order to achieve specified outcomes; and that quality is assured by measurable accountability processes. While these ideas support the argument for an elective affinity between engagement and neoliberalism, they deliberately do not suggest that the spirit or form of student engagement is connected causally to neoliberalism.

The suggested elective affinity between student engagement and neoliberalism is both more complex and more subtle than this. The idea of elective affinity owes much to Max Weber who used it to link the Protestant ethic and the "spirit" of capitalism (McKinnon 2010). Weber did not define elective affinity and indeed, seems to have been ambiguous in the way he used it. According to Thomas (1985) and McKinnon (2010) this ambiguity has led to materialist and nonmaterialist interpretations of elective affinity. They largely agree in their analysis of the two interpretations. The materialist interpretation provides an analysis of emergence in the chemistry of social relations. It holds that the term elective affinity was Weber's means of connecting materialist interests and ideas. Materialists see this as a decisive concept as it connects the material world (interests) with the spiritual (ideas). Nonmaterialist interpretations typically stress "quite rightly, that Weber sometimes uses the term to describe the relation between two beliefs" (McKinnon 2010, p. 110). They stress that mutual attraction of ideas and beliefs can naturally connect because they share an internal logic. Thomas (1985) observes that 'elective affinity' is shorthand for identifying a relationship between the ideas and beliefs connected by the term. He agrees that it is a nondeterministic and ambiguous concept, more a metaphor for connection and affinity than a chemistry of social relations.

Despite this ambiguity Thomas (1985) and McKinnon (2010) affirm that the concept played a major part in Weber's thinking and writing. According to Thomas (1985) it is an attempt by Weber to construct a new analytic for comprehending the social world. He suggested that elective affinity is Weber's way of showing that there is a close relationship between two ideas. The relationship is elective in that it emphasises the mutual accommodation of ideas between social groups because they are on the lookout for ideas, and ideas are on the lookout for sympathetic groups. Consequently elective affinities cannot be understood in terms of cause and effect. The two forces interact in ways that make it difficult to say who led and who followed. Elective affinity is a complex relationship that gives rise not to new ideas but to the emergence of an accommodation, a mutual acceptance. McKinnon (2010) argues that this mutual accommodation is an indispensable dimension of Weber's concept of elective affinity. It allows for independent carriers of ideas to bring them together and to mutually reinforce them.

Student Engagement Practice in Neoliberal Times

It is one thing to theorize elective affinity between neoliberalism and student engagement; to demonstrate how it might work in practice is quite another. In this section, I use two different views of the elective affinity between neoliberalism and student engagement to investigate how this works in practice. I first examine engagement from the neoliberal point of view by exploring how three key neoliberal policy expectations first discussed in Chap. 4—knowledge acquisition, performativity and accountability—relate to student engagement. I then discuss the elective affinity from the student engagement perspective. I adapt the conceptual organizer of 10 propositions for engagement introduced in Chap. 3 to discuss student learning, pedagogy and external influences.

A Neoliberal Perspective of an Elective Affinity with Engagement

A neoliberal expectation for higher education is that what is taught involves practical knowledge and skills; develops abilities and attributes that enable learners to successfully transition from higher education to being effective contributors to the economy. Knowledge is valued, but as a tool that is useful in the market and not as something that is pursued for the sake of truth based on reason. Such knowledge is used to construct behaviours and competencies that are generic, instrumental and useful in the job market (Clarke 2012). This view of knowledge and learning finds echoes in student engagement (Lawson and Lawson 2013). Engaged students are more successful than disengaged learners in meeting learning outcomes and completing courses, expectations of the neoliberal state (McCormick et al. 2013). It becomes very important to know how well students engage and what educational practices nurture such engagement. An industry has developed around measuring generic indicators of engaging practices and behaviours (Trowler 2010). The leading example is the National Survey of Student Engagement (NSSE) in the USA. This measures 10 indicators and six high impact practices for engagement (McCormick et al. 2013). Such behavioural engagement indicators connect to a neoliberal view that higher education contributes to the development of human capital.

Ball (2004) observed that neoliberal thinking defines success as performance outcomes in the market place. Such performativity provides a system of governance that focuses on what can be produced, observed, measured, recorded and reported (Barnett 2000). To a large extent this view of success is shared in student engagement research and practice. It is another elective affinity between neoliberalism and student engagement. Kuh (2008), for example, bracketed student engagement and success. He suggested that NSSE research showed that success in the form of retention and completion are more likely where students participate in at least two high impact learning activities as measured in the NSSE survey. The NSSE and its various cousins, as well as other research measuring engagement, for example approaches to learning inventories, produce calculable success indicators. The widespread use in governance of measuring, recording and reporting is labelled by de Santos (2009) as creating 'fact totems' to influence public choice about which institutions perform well/or not in engaging students according to, for example, the NSSE indictors. In this way, a public picture of institutional success is projected. When used to measure success 'fact-totems' spotlight another dimension of an elective affinity between neoliberalism and student engagement.

Being able to account for the quantity and quality of performance is a key neoliberal expectation of institutions, organizations, businesses, individuals and communities. This lays the basis for another elective affinity with student engagement. Internationally, public accountability demands on higher education institutions range from finance to teaching and learning; and are increasing and widening. Entities have to be able to supply evidence in concrete, observable and measurable ways of the quality of learning and teaching (Strydom et al. 2012) According to Hagel et al. (2011) student engagement occupies an important place on the accountability agenda of higher education as a proxy for educational quality and success. Institutions that engage students successfully are thought to contribute to student success more generally, such as achieving high levels of successful course completions and attaining a passport to employment with a positive attitude to lifelong learning (Yorke 2006). McCormick (2009) separates accountability into accountability that is externally required and is summative, and accountability that is reflective or formative. He suggests that institutional data on student engagement provides a suitable mechanism for reflective accountability and so help to improve the quality of the student experience and student outcomes (Kuh 2009). But results from, for example, the NSSE survey, when used as 'fact-totems' to publicly benchmark institutions against one another can lead to an effective form of summative accountability. Consequently, how students engage and what they, institutions and educators do to improve student engagement, and hence student success can be monitored through such survey research (Horstmanshof and Zimitat 2007).

Elective Affinity from a Student Engagement Perspective

Student engagement then is aligned with neoliberalism's expectation for higher education to be practical, efficient, accountable and to lead to student success. It goes further though, as mainstream engagement research proposes a generic pedagogy of what works. This researched generic pedagogy matches the expectations of neoliberalism. As I pointed out in Chap. 3, students are at the heart of engagement research and if there is a connection between student engagement and neoliberalism, it must be made visible here. Students invest cognitively, emotionally and actively in learning in order to succeed (Fredricks et al. 2004). Investment opportunities are many, varied and complex. While students invest in their own learning, teachers, institutions and significant outsiders help facilitate and grow the investment. I used the 'investment' metaphor deliberately to indicate that engagement research has adopted neoliberal ideas and values. Chapter 3 discussed the emergence of a synthesis of mainstream engagement research made up of 10 propositions and key concepts as a conceptual engagement organizer. Table 5.1 largely repeats the table presented in Chap. 3 but with a major change in the third column. The educational theories underpinning the propositions in Chap. 3 give way to affinities between student engagement and neoliberalism. Neoliberal influences on student investment in learning can be traced to identity, choice and success; those on teacher and institutional support on quality, knowledge capitalism and what works; those on enabling external influences on lifelong learning and student voice.

The first organizing idea in Table 5.1 focuses on the effort of individuals to engage with learning for success. The four propositions expand on this organizing idea. They promote self-belief, self-motivation and the investment of social and cultural capital in learning. In neoliberal times all are won by individual energy and determination. Engagement research and practice emphasise the value of such individual effort. While students have weaknesses, they can learn to overcome them by enhancing their self-belief in their strengths. Motivation and self-belief go hand in hand. A number of engagement researchers found that learners' self-belief is a key motivator. Yorke and Knight (2004), for example found that the self-theories learners bring to their learning impact motivation, identity, agency and engagement. Self-belief is influenced by self-identity which in turn is affected by the cultural capital students can invest in the learning process. Not having sufficient appropriate cultural capital is a major source of social inequality (Bourdieu and Passeron 1990)

Table 5.1 A conceptual organizer of propositions of engagement and their relationship with neoliberalism

Organizing idea	Propositions	Affinities to neoliberalism
Students' investment in learning	1. Student self-belief is vital for success 2. Student motivation grows self-confidence 3. Social and cultural capital enhance engagement 4. Engaged learners are deep learners	Identity Choice Success
Teacher and institutional support	5. Quality teaching and institutional support enhance engagement 6. Disciplinary knowledge engages students 7. Quality teaching adapts to changing student expectations	Quality Knowledge capitalism What works
Enabling external environments	8. Engagement occurs across the life-span 9. Engagement is supported by subjective wellbeing 10. Active citizenship is important for engagement	Lifelong learning Positive emotions Student voice

and hence a potential barrier to engagement and success. The focus on rational individual effort in pursuit of personal achievement is a feature of neoliberalism (Peters 2001). Individuals can only succeed on the back of their personal effort. While teachers, peers and institutions can support such endeavour, students can overcome obstacles only if they work hard enough. In their pursuit of personal success, students need more opportunities to exercise choice in order to engage for success. As a result they have more control, gain more responsibility over their learning and grow into their identity as agentic learners (Klemenčič 2013).

The second organizing idea in Table 5.1 focuses on the work of teachers and institutions in supporting engagement. The three propositions here pinpoint the importance of quality teaching and institutional support for student engagement, particularly in their discipline of choice. Engagement research has constructed numerous frameworks that position teachers and/or institutions as chief facilitators of what works in engagement (Lawson and Lawson 2013). Moreover, engaging practice is never static. It changes in response to new expectations. The effects of such developments as students' need for part-time employment and the impact of ever changing technologies changes not only the way students engage with learning, but the way teachers and institutions facilitate it. McInnis (2003) is right, engagement can no longer be assumed; but must be constantly negotiated. Most students enrol in higher education to gain practical knowledge and skills in their subject of choice to achieve life goals, particularly employment. To help them achieve these goals requires a teaching approach that meets student expectations of relevant and applicable content (Entwistle 2010). It is important then to include an explicit consideration of content in an engagement pedagogy that enhances quality learning. This organizing idea for engagement fits well with neoliberalism's idea of learning and teaching in higher education. It offers evidence of what works in teachers and institutions supporting quality learning in a pedagogy that shapes learners to perform in certain ways.

The third organizing idea in Table 5.1 focuses on the contribution external environments make to student engagement. Its three propositions draw on Lawson and Lawson's (2013) socio-cultural ecological framework that involves the whole being across the lifespan. It is nourished by experiences of striving for personal success in classrooms, the home, the community and their own virtual worlds. For successful engagement positive emotions are vital (Kahu et al. 2014). Positive emotions are enabled by background, skills, self-efficacy and success and stimulated by affirming relationships, respect and success in what students want to achieve (Bryson and Hand 2007). Engaged students also want to feel they have a voice in what and how they learn and 'student voice' has become a powerful metaphor for active citizenship and engagement (Toshalis and Nakkula 2012). All three propositions have an affinity with neoliberalism. They feature lifelong and life-wide learning, subjective wellbeing and active citizenship. Tony Blair's observation that education is the best economic policy available (Martin 2003) highlights the importance of learning across the lifespan. This, Bagnall (2010) observed has acquired a distinctive human capital turn since the 1990s in which engaged individuals operate successfully in the marketplace. Positive emotional feelings are associated with engagement, personal success in life, autonomy, competence and the wherewithal to exercise lifestyle choices (Field 2009). While 'student voice' seems to promise a culture of democratic dialogue (Klemenčič 2013), student voice in neoliberal times is limited. It has no guaranteed influence for change on policy settings and is only occasionally seen as a partner in the classroom (Fielding 2001).

Looking Back, Looking Forward

This chapter shows that the relationship between student engagement and neoliberalism is complex. It is just not amenable to a simple definition. Clear is that the two are connected strongly but I have argued that the connection is not so strong that we can claim that engagement is subsumed or caused by neoliberalism. Rather, I suggest that the relationship is more akin to Weber's metaphor of an *elective affinity* where key ideas in engagement are attracted by key ideas in neoliberalism and vice versa.

I have argued that this elective affinity with neoliberalism has helped student engagement to a powerful position in discourses about learning and teaching in higher education. It is central in mainstream thinking about learning and teaching. This positioning of student engagement seems to have uplifted it to an "uncritically accepted academic orthodoxy" (Brookfield 1986, p. 96). In the next chapter, I place mainstream engagement thinking under a more critical microscope.

References

Bagnall, R. (2010). Citizenship and belonging as a moral imperative for lifelong learning. *International Journal of Lifelong Education, 29*(1), 449–460.

Ball, S. (2004). Performativities and fabrications in the educational economy: Towards the perfect society. In S. Ball (Ed.), *The Routledge Falmer reader in sociology of education* (pp. 143–155). London, UK: Routledge Falmer.

Barnett, R. (2000). University knowledge in an age of supercomplexity. *Higher Education, 40*(4), 409–422.

Bernasconi, A. (2014). Policy path dependence of a research agenda: The case of Chile in the aftermath of the student revolt of 2011. *Studies in Higher Education, 39*(8), 1405–1416. doi:10.1080/03075079.2014.950448.

Bernstein, B. (1996). *Pedagogy, symbolic control and identity: Theory, research, critique.* London, UK: Taylor and Francis.

Bourdieu, P., & Passeron, J.-C. (1990). *Reproduction in education, society and culture* (2nd ed.). London, UK: Sage.

Brookfield, S. (1986). *Understanding and facilitating adult learning.* Milton Keynes, UK: Open University Press.

Bryson, C. (2014). Clarifying the concept of student engagement. In C. Bryson (Ed.), *Understanding and developing student engagement* (pp. 1–22). London: Routledge.

Bryson, C., & Hand, L. (2007). The role of engagement in inspiring teaching and learning. *Innovations in Education and Teaching International, 44*(4), 349–362.

Bryson, C., & Hardy, C. (2012). The nature of academic engagement: what the students tell us. In I. Solomonides, A. Reid, & P. Petocz (Eds.), *Engaging with learning in higher education.* Faringdon, UK: Libri Publishing.

Clarke, M. (2012). The (absent) politics of neo-liberal education policy. *Critical Studies in Education, 53,* 297–310. doi:10.1080/17508487.2012.703139.

Coates, H. (2005). The value of student engagement for higher education quality assurance. *Quality in Higher Education, 11*(1), 25–36.

de Santos, M. (2009). Fact-totems and the statistical imagination: The public life of a statistic in Argentina 2001. *Sociological Theory, 27*(4), 466–489.

Dean, M. (1999). *Governmentality: Power and rule in modern society.* London: UK: Sage.

Entwistle, N. (2005). Contrasting perspectives on learning. In F. Marton, D. Hounsell, & N. Entwistle (Eds.), *The experience of learning: Implications for teaching and studying in higher education* (3rd (Internet) ed., pp. 3–22). Edinburgh, UK: Centre for Teaching, Learning and Assessment, University of Edinburgh.

Entwistle, N. (2010). Taking stock: An overview of key research findings. In J. Hughes & J. Mighty (Eds.), *Taking stock: Research on teaching and learning in higher education.* Montreal, Canada: McGill-Queen's University Press.

Feuer, M. (2006). Response to Bettie St. Pierre's "Scientifically based research in education: Epistemology and ethics". *Adult Education Quarterly, 56*(4), 267–272.

Feuer, M., Towne, L., & Shavelson, R. (2002). Scientific culture and educational research. *Educational Researcher, 31*(8), 4–14.

Field, J. (2009). *Well-being and happiness: Inquiry into the future for lifelong learning. Thematic Article 4.* Retrieved from Leicester, UK.

Fielding, M. (2001). Students as radical agents of change. *Journal of Educational Change, 2,* 123–141.

Forgeard, M., Jayawickreme, E., Kern, M., & Seligman, M. (2011). doing the right thing: Measuring wellbeing for public policy. *International Journal of Wellbeing, 1*(1), 79–106.

Fredricks, J., Blumenfeld, P., & Paris, A. (2004). School engagement: Potential of the concept, state of the evidence. *Review of Educational Research, 74*(1), 59–109.

Giddens, A. (2001). *The global third way debate.* Cambridge, UK: Polity Press.

Gonzales, L., Martinez, E., & Ordu, C. (2014). Exploring faculty experiences in a striving university through the lens of academic capitalism. *Studies in Higher Education, 39*(7), 1097–1115. doi:10.1080/03075079.2013.777401.

Hagel, P., Carr, R., & Devlin, M. (2011). Conceptualizing and measuring student engagement through the Australasian Survey of Student Engagement (AUSSE): A critique. *Assessment and Evaluation in Higher Education, 37*(4), 475–486.

Harper, S., & Quaye, J. (2009). *Student engagement in higher education: Theoretical perspectives and practical approaches for diverse populations.* New York, NY: Routledge.

Horstmanshof, L., & Zimitat, C. (2007). Future time orientation predicts academic engagement among first year university students. *British Journal of Educational Psychology, 77*(3), 703–718. doi:10.1348/000709906X160778.

Jankowski, N., & Provezis, S. (2014). Neoliberal ideologies, governmentality and the academy: An examination of accountability through assessment and transparency. *Educational Philosophy and Theory, 46*(5), 475–487. doi:10.1080/00131857.2012.721736.

Jost, J., Federico, C., & Napier, J. (2009). Political ideology: Its structure, functions and elective affinity. *Annual Review of Psychology, 60,* 307–337.

Kahu, E., Stephens, C., Leach, L., & Zepke, N. (2014). Linking academic emotions and student engagement: Mature-aged distance students' transition to university. *Journal of Further and Higher Education, 39*(4), 481–497. doi:10.1080/0309877X.2014.895305.

Kinzie, J. (2010). Student engagement and learning experiences that matter. In J. Christensen Hughes & J. Mighty (Eds.), *Taking stock: Research on teaching and learning in higher education* (pp. 139–153). Montreal, Canada: McGill-Queens University Press.

Klemenčič, M. (2013, 13 December). Student engagement: Between policy-making and scholarship. *University World News Global Edition.* Retrieved from http://www.universityworldnews.com/article.php?story=20131210124920672

Krause, K.-L. (2012). Addressing the wicked problem of quality in higher education. Higher Education Research & Development, 31(3), 285-297. doi: 10.1080/07294360.2011.634381

Kuh, G. (2008). *High-impact practices: What they are, who has access to them, and why they matter.* Retrieved from Washington, DC.

Kuh, G. (2009). The national survey of student engagement: Conceptual and empirical foundations. *New Directions for Institutional Research, 141,* 5–20. doi:10.1002/ir.v2009: 141/issuetoc.

Kuh, G., Kinzie, J., Buckley, J., Bridges, B., & Hayek, J. (2006). *What matters to student success: A review of the literature.* Retrieved from http://nces.ed.gov/IPEDS/research/pdf/Kuh_Team_Report.pdf

Lawson, M., & Lawson, H. (2013). New conceptual frameworks for student engagement research, policy and practice. *Review of Educational Research, 83*(3), 432–479.

Leathwood, C., & Read, B. (2013). Research policy and academic performativity: Compliance, contestation and complicity. *Studies in Higher Education, 38*(8), 1162–1174. doi:10.1080/03075079.2013.833025.

Lingard, B. (2013). The impact of research on education policy in an era of evidence-based policy. *Critical Studies in Education, 54*(2), 113–131. doi:10.1080/17508487.2013.781515.

Martin, I. (2003). Adult education, lifelong learning and citizenship: Some ifs and buts. *International Journal of Lifelong Education, 22*(6), 566–579.

McCormick, A. (2009). Toward reflective accountability: Using NSSE for accountability and transparency. *New Directions for Institutional Research, 141,* 97–106. doi:10.1002/ir.v2009: 141/issuetoc.

McCormick, A., Gonyea, R., & Kinzie, J. (2013). Refreshing engagement: NSSE at 13. *Change: The Magazine of Higher Learning, 45*(3), 6–15. doi:10.1080/00091383.2013.786985.

McInnis, C. (2003). *New realities of the student experience: How should universities respond?.* Limerick, Ireland: Paper presented at the European Association for Institutional Research.

McKinnon, A. (2010). Elective affinities of the protestant ethic: Weber and the chemistry of capitalism. *Sociological Theory, 28*(1), 109–125.

McMahon, B., & Portelli, J. (2004). Engagement for what? Beyond popular discourses of student engagement. *Leadership and Policy in Schools, 3*(1), 59–76.

McMahon, B., & Portelli, J. (2012). The challenges of neoliberalism in education: Implications for student engagement. In B. McMahon & J. Portelli (Eds.), *Student engagement in urban school: Beyond neoliberal discourses* (pp. 1–10). Charlotte, NC: Information Age Publishing.

Neary, M. (2013). Student as producer: A pedagogy for the avant-garde; or, how do revolutionary teachers teach? Retrieved from http://josswinn.org/wp-content/uploads/2013/12/15-72-1-pb-1.pdf

Pascarella, E., Seifert, T., & Blaich, C. (2010). How effective are the NSSE benchmarks in predicting important educational outcomes? *Change: The Magazine of Higher Learning, 42*(1), 16–22.

Peters, M. (2001). *Poststructualism, Marxism and neoliberalism: Between theory and politics.* New York, NY: Rowman and Littlefield.

Phelan, A. (2011). Towards a complicated conversation: Teacher education and the curriculum turn. *Pedagogy, Culture and Society, 19*(2), 207–220.

Strassheim, H., & Kettunen, P. (2014). When does evidence-based policy turn into policy-based evidence? Configurations, contexts and mechanisms. *Evidence & Policy: A Journal of Research, Debate and Practice, 10*(2), 259–277. doi:10.1332/174426514X13990433991320.

Strydom, J., Basson, N., & Mentz, M. (2012). *Enhancing the quality of teaching and learning: Using student engagement data to establish a culture of evidence.* Retrieved from Pretoria, South Africa: http://www.che.ac.za/media_and_publications/research/enhancing-quality-teaching-and-learning-using-student-engagement

Thomas, J. (1985). Ideology and elective affinity. *Sociology, 19*, 39–54. doi:10.1177/0038038585019001005.

Thomas, L. (2012). *Building student engagement and belonging in higher education at a time of change: Final report from the what works? student retention and success project.* Paul Hamlyn Foundation, Higher Education Funding Council for England, The Higher Education Academy and Action on Access.

Toshalis, E., & Nakkula, M. (2012). Motivation, engagement and student voice. Retrieved from http://www.studentsatthecenter.org/topics/motivation-engagement-and-student-voice

Trowler, V. (2010). Student engagement literature review. Retrieved from http://www.heacademy.ac.uk/assets/documents/studentengagement/StudentEngagementLiteratureReview.pdf

Wimpenny, K., & Savin-Baden, M. (2013). Alienation, agency and authenticity: A synthesis of the literature on student engagement. *Teaching in Higher Education, 18*(3), 311–326. doi:10.1080/13562517.2012.725223.

Yates, L. (2009). From curriculum to pedagogy and back again: Knowledge, the person and the changing world. *Pedagogy, Culture and Society, 17*(1), 17–28.

Yorke, M. (2006). *Student engagement: Deep, surface or strategic?* Paper presented at the Pacific Rim First Year in Higher Education Conference, Griffith University, Gold Coast Campus, Australia.

Yorke, M., & Knight, P. (2004). Self-theories: Some implications for teaching and learning in higher education. *Studies in Higher Education, 29*(1), 25–37.

Zepke, N., & Leach, L. (2012). *The contribution of the Teaching and Learning Research Initiative to building knowledge about teaching and learning: A review of tertiary sector projects 2003–2011.* Wellington, New Zealand. Retrieved from: http://www.tlri.org.nz/sites/default/files/pages/A%20review%20of%20tertiary%20sector%20projects%202003%E2%80%932011.pdf

Chapter 6
A Critique of Mainstream Student Engagement

Abstract Mainstream student engagement, with its affinity with neoliberalism, can arguably be called an academic orthodoxy. It focuses on what works in the classroom, relies heavily on psychology research, largely ignores ethical and political considerations, assists in the development of a knowledge economy, is used to measure the performance of institutions, managers, teachers and students, and uses accountability systems to do the measuring. These critiques are discussed in this chapter both to add to a paucity of critique of engagement in the literature, and to set the stage for subsequent chapters which seek to find ideas and practices that go beyond the hegemony of the mainstream.

McMahon and Portelli (2012, p. 3) are right to suggest that "it is self-evident that no one wants to argue against student engagement…." Intuitively, active physical, mental and emotional involvement in the world and learning has so much more potential for achieving a satisfying life than alienation, disengagement and apathy. In this light, out and out critique of the importance of students engaging in learning seems untenable. The many research findings offering learners, teachers and institutions ideas about what works in practice also make engagement attractive for all. On the political stage, engagement's elective affinity with neoliberalism about the purposes of, performativity and accountability in higher education gives engagement power and legitimacy. Such a profile places student engagement research and practice into the vanguard of mainstream educational thinking. It may have become what Brookfield (1986) called an uncritically accepted academic orthodoxy. While the metaphor for successful learning offered by student engagement may be beyond critique, its application in higher education is not. The elective affinity with neoliberal ideas narrows the potential of engagement. It confines its horizon to what works in practice and is welcome to neoliberal sensibilities. Not all researchers are happy with this narrowing and have critiqued it both on technical and theoretical grounds.

In this chapter I first summarize some of these operational and theoretical critiques in the literature before developing my own. However, critique, particularly of a theoretical nature, creates the temptation of throwing the mainstream baby out with the bathwater. This is not intended. Mainstream engagement research has an important place in higher education. My critique prepares to widen, not eliminate the focus on what works in classrooms. It seeks to engage students in widening their intellectual and emotional horizons, not just to prepare them for jobs in a neoliberal economy. It wants to encourage the development of critical faculties, not just an acceptance and promotion of dominant norms as highlighted in governmentality.

Selected Critiques in the Student Engagement Research Literature

Even though mainstream student engagement research, practice and thinking are widely accepted by politicians, the general public, students and teachers, such acceptance also gives rise to some critique. While not extensive, critique often focuses on technical issues about validity of instruments used to measure engagement as well as more theoretical issues. This section canvasses both kinds of critiques.

Technical Critiques

Questions about the instruments used to conceptualize and measure student engagement such as NSSE, its derivatives and the 'approaches to learning' inventories and surveys introduced in Chap. 2 are increasing. Various critiques have emerged about the way engagement is conceptualized and presented in these frameworks. McMahon and Portelli (2004), for example, raised concerns about the operational, technical and instrumental nature of engagement research. The two most popular conceptual frameworks examined in Chap. 2 rely heavily on students' self-report on the effects of their learning efforts. For example, the behavioural framework represented by Kuh and colleagues in this book and the cognitive 'approaches to learning' framework use a variety of questionnaires and inventories such as NSSE, Bigg's Learning/Study Process Questionnaire and some versions of the Approaches to Studying Inventory to identify deep learning and thinking. According to Axelson and Flick (2010) such frameworks unduly simplify and generalize the messy reality of student engagement. Generic instruments are incapable of picking up the complexities of learning, teaching and their relationships with life outside the academy. Porter (2009) even considers self-report questionnaires invalid and unreliable. He cites research evidence that suggests that students cannot report their behaviours, cognitive processes and attitudes accurately and that they have problems even answering simple factual questions correctly. Moreover, the label 'scientific rigour' that underpins this kind of research seems mainly to involve collecting data in order to confirm existing ideas (Howie and Bagnall 2013).

Porter (2009) applied his analysis of the general lack of validity of self-report questionnaires to the NSSE. He suggested that research on behaviour as a proxy for learning and learning success should be abandoned. A number of recent studies support aspects of this general critique. According to Kahn (2014) only a relatively small proportion of the variation in learning success can be attributed to measures of student engagement used in the NSSE instrument. Campbell and Cabrera (2011) conducted a case study to assess the validity of NSSE. They found the construct validity of certain benchmarks was either marginal or poor; they were highly inter-correlated as they did not appear to measure distinct domains of student engagement; and, they did not appear to be strongly associated with important student outcomes, like GPA. Indeed, as a predictor of cumulative GPA, the NSSE benchmark model was not valid, at least regarding predictive validity according to Campbell and Cabrera. One of the NSSE derivatives, the Australasian University Survey of Student Engagement (AUSSE), was also questioned on technical grounds. Hagel et al. (2011) and Krause (2012), for example, found the reflective accountability purposes of the AUSSE wanting. The former questioned the predictive validity of such instruments in connecting engagement with student success; the latter argued that assumptions about engagement as defined in such instruments are challengeable as they cannot account for cultural and linguistic diversity.

The 'approaches to learning' framework also comes in for criticism. One is that as a generic view of learning it is initially attractive but as with all general models, it does not support teachers and learners in specific contexts (Haggis 2003; Howie and Bagnall 2013). It assumes that deep learning is good, surface learning bad; strategic learning is a mixture of both (Howie and Bagnall 2013). Haggis (2003) suggests that this framework can be seen to have been constructed in the image of academics themselves, rather than as a likeness of a wide range of student learners. Students who are not deep learners are seen as lacking the correct approach to learning. She argues (p. 95).

> ...the model is arguably acting as a normative paradigm, within which further research studies can only ever further articulate the paradigm's underlying assumptions (Kuhn 1970). In this situation, ideas that fall outside or challenge the foundations of the paradigm become invisible.

Howie and Bagnall (2013) suggest that the strength of the 'approaches to learning' paradigm was that it provided the 'big answer' to questions about students' learning in higher education in Europe and elsewhere, particularly Australasia. The ready uptake of its ideas about learning and teaching meant it was not theorized extensively. Consequently not sufficient account is taken of epistemological and cultural matters. It is overly psychological in focus without taking sufficient interest in sociocultural aspects of learning.

In the third and fourth conceptual frameworks distilled in Chap. 2 engagement in the classroom has antecedents and consequences outside of the classroom (Kahu 2013; Barnett and Coate 2005). These frameworks, although different in many ways, share the view that engagement is lifewide, a holistic process that includes psychological, sociological, cultural and ecological processes that originate and play out beyond classrooms in the wider community. Axelson and Flick (2010) critique such holistic frameworks as creating definitional, research and planning difficulties. Such an expansive definition of engagement includes multiple variables that create a single measure or index of engagement. Variables that apply only to classroom practice cannot be readily identified. A holistic framework obscures some of the very phenomena and relationships classroom researchers want to study. Such a framework makes it difficult to measure specific instances of engagement and prevents study of the factors that enable and prevent it. Axelson and Flick argue that in order to improve student engagement, a narrower definition of the term is needed, one that is restricted to students' level of involvement in a learning process. To gain information about classroom engagement specific questions need to be asked. According to Axelson and Flick (2010, p. 41) "we might ask, how do we engage (cognitively, behaviorally, and/or emotionally) type X students most effectively in type Y learning processes/contexts so that they will attain knowledge, skill, or disposition Z?"

Critiques Originating in Philosophical/Theoretical Concerns

Other critiques argue that it is not enough to focus on engagement's technical shortcomings. More effort is needed to develop an overarching theoretical framework for the construct. McMahon and Portelli (2004) offer a democratic-critical conception of engagement that goes beyond strategies, techniques or behaviours— beyond pedagogy; a conception in which engagement is participatory and dialogic, leading not only to academic achievement but success as active citizens. Such an overarching theoretical conception weakens conservative and student-centred views that tend to focus on technical concerns. Conservative and student-centred views interpret engagement as psychological dispositions and academic achievement often leading to learning lacking social context. Such views, they argue, are too narrowly focused on operational matters. Barnett and Coate (2005) support and expand this critique. They advocate for operational engagement to be supplemented by a more ontological approach. The former encompasses conservative and student-centred engagement; the latter reflects a level of commitment to learning that extends beyond narrow interpretations of competence and success. This requires the extension of the current boundaries of an operational 'what works' curriculum. They suggest three curriculum projects in ontological engagement for active citizenship. Here engagement requires students to (i) engage by learning to make justifiable claims in a changeable world and to answer objections to such claims; (ii) learn to act positively and assertively in addressing issues of common concern; and (iii) become self-aware and confident in where they stand on contentious issues and realize their potential to create change in an uncertain world.

Despite the efforts of McMahon and Portelli and Barnett and Coate, Kahn (2014) argues that the very concept 'student engagement' is relatively weakly theorized. But he attributes this more to a surfeit of theories for engagement than a shortage. He cites Harper and Quaye's (2009) edited book about student engagement in diverse settings to observe that engagement is theorized in many different ways (but see Chap. 5 for an observation that chapter authors expect it to be measured by the NSSE). Kahn identifies self-perception theory, transition theory, critical race theory and attribution theory among others apparently connected to the NSSE version of engagement. Numerous other theories have also been advanced. For example, constructionism, the idea that when engaged learners construct knowledge from experience, is widely accepted as an underpinning theory. So is learner centredness, the notion that students are co-producers of knowledge who share responsibility for their learning with teachers and institutions (Krause and Coates 2008). But learner centredness can be theorized in different ways. Neary (2013) uses Marxist thinking to connect intellectual and manual labour to develop the notion of co-production, while Thomas (2012) uses the imperative of what works to support co-production. Further, a theoretical construct originating in the American school sector is now widely accepted in higher education. This theorizes that engagement is rooted in psychology as a meta-construct involving right behaviours, cognitive investment and emotional commitment to learning (Fredricks et al. 2004). Kahn (2014) himself offers critical realism as an underpinning theory for student engagement. He uses the work of Margaret Archer to help theorize engagement as the interplay between student agency and structure in educational settings. Classroom engagement in this view is a reflexive process that actively progresses individual and collegial learning projects through reflexive deliberations in specific social settings.

I will leave a discussion of whether this profusion of engagement theories is boon or bane to later in this chapter. Kahn (2014) considers it a weakness and launches critical realism as a suitable theory to address his critique. But it is his related analysis of the role of agency and structure in engagement research and thinking that interests me here. There is clearly ambivalence about the place of engagement in the agency–structure continuum. On the surface most engagement theorizing is close to the agency end of the spectrum. It is supposed to focus on the agency of the student in constructing knowledge, in being actively engaged in their own learning. But as Kahn observes, student engagement research and practice pays more attention to the structural end of the agency–structure continuum. Thomas (2012) demonstrates this in her summary of the 'What Works' project in the United Kingdom. She argues that engagement is using structural factors such as teachers, curricula, institutional and government policies to further student success in academic outcomes, progression and jobs after graduation. This supports Kahn's critique that engagement thinking is closer to structure than agency. The work of Neary (2013) casts doubt on this view. He follows radical thinkers such as Benjamin and Vygotsky who theorize the student as producers not consumers of knowledge and ideas. His project, 'Student as Producer', centres on student agency as students are regarded as creative subjects within a learning context. Students collaborate with teachers in the production of knowledge and meaning.

Another criticism of mainstream engagement research and practice is gaining momentum. This focuses on the way student success is narrowly conceived as obedient academic behaviour leading to retention, increased achievement, graduation and employment (Taylor and Parsons 2011; McMahon and Portelli 2012; Taylor et al. 2012). While educators want students to be successful, definitions of success can vary greatly. Many such definitions are not restricted to academic success as conceived in the mainstream (Taylor and Parsons 2011). According to McMahon and Portelli (2012) such a limited view leads to a narrow view of engagement. The responsibility for such a view of success and engagement is often attributed to the dominating influence of neoliberalism. Alternative views of success seek to escape this. At least two alternative but related meanings of success and engagement have been developed using key phrases like 'student voice' and 'student as producer'. Both expand the mainstream meaning of success and engagement. Student voice involves active involvement of students in educational structures and processes (Trowler 2010). These range from giving feedback, to taking active roles on committees and in having roles in governance and decision-making about the curriculum. Student as producer visualizes learners as active producers of knowledge and meaning, often in collaboration with teachers. A number of studies by students as producers of knowledge have been published. These range from books of case studies (Nygaard et al. 2013) to projects based on radical theory as the one developed by Neary (2013) and applied by, for example, Taylor et al. (2012).

Questioning an Academic Orthodoxy

Despite these varied critiques in the literature, the student engagement construct continues to be ever-present in discussions about higher education policy and practice, in research literature, and even in the popular media (Kuh 2009). It is unquestioned as an invaluable model to inform higher education of what works in learning and teaching, and so few want to argue against student engagement (McMahon and Portelli 2012). Yet, the brief discussion of critiques voiced in the literature suggests that student engagement as a construct could benefit from even a closer investigation of possible shortcomings. This is the intention of the remainder of the chapter in which I question.

- the way the elective affinity between neoliberal ideas and student engagement has become normalized as part of the accepted fabric of higher education;
- the idea that engagement research provides a generic 'one size fits all' understanding of engagement;
- how engagement is cast as pedagogy, the study and practice of 'what works' in learning and teaching and the idea of curriculum is given a backseat;
- the way psychology has become the bedrock on which engagement thinking has been built.

Investigating such questions is not intended to diminish the value of mainstream engagement research and practice to higher education, but to offer openings for expanding and enriching this construct which is the purpose in subsequent chapters.

Elective Affinity, Normality and Governmentality

I discussed the elective affinity between neoliberalism and student engagement in Chap. 5. In this section I critique this mutual attraction. Although a number of researchers explicitly recognize the important influence of neoliberalism on student engagement in higher education (Kuh et al. 2006; Thomas 2012; Trowler 2010), they tend to note its influence but do not question it directly. Kuh et al. (2006) recognized that student engagement research and practice as represented by the NSSE benefits from the emergence of neoliberal economic realities such as the demands of a knowledge-based economy and subsequent policy definitions for student outcomes and success. It is the task of the NSSE to support these developments. Thomas (2012) records influences on engagement of neoliberal policy in the UK and led a research project that attempts to meet such policy expectations. Carey (2013), in examining the role of neoliberalism in engagement, takes a more critical view. He argues that the popularity of student engagement in higher education results from the extension of neoliberal ideology into government policies and higher education. Its reforms have replaced publically funded state education with a business model and a managerialist ideology such as public choice, agency and human capital theories. Carey (2013, p. 136) writes that as a consequence "universities are judged on student engagement..., so engagement becomes part of management orthodoxy".

A major issue arises when researchers and educators concentrate on implementing government policies. This traps higher education and engagement researchers into accepting or even supporting neoliberal policy discourses. It normalizes neoliberal thinking and so shapes the conduct of conduct of engagement research and practice. Neoliberal discourses and policies are not only accepted but are reinforced and supported as common sense by opinion leaders in society, higher education and student engagement. While some engagement researchers such as McMahon and Portelli (2012), Carey (2013) and Neary (2013) question this assumption, the general picture in the literature suggests that researchers, practitioners, managers and also students accept even welcome, often unconsciously, neoliberal ideas and practices. Such ideas and practices are accepted as part of people's lived experience. They are understood as normal and without alternative. By living neoliberal values and practices in their homes and communities, educators along with most citizens find them practical and reasonable; an acceptable way of meeting universally desirable educational, economic and political aspirations (Saunders 2010). With neoliberalism present in all aspects of their lives, citizens acquire the mental disposition to govern themselves using neoliberal ideas of what is proper conduct (Usher et al. 1997). Consequently researchers and teachers and other actors in higher education discipline themselves in the conduct of research, teaching practice, management and learning to meet neoliberal precepts. Because we accept neoliberalism, we ensure that engagement's affinity with neoliberalism is elective and mutual.

Yet critique is expected to be at the heart of academic life. I now turn to critique the affinity between neoliberalism and student engagement research and practice in three key areas: the commodification of knowledge, performativity and account-ability. As I observed in Chap. 4 and again in Chap. 5 neoliberalism regards knowledge as a commodity to be traded. Higher education is a market where desirable knowledge and skills are bought and sold. If the market chooses not to buy a certain kind of knowledge, it devalues and in some cases its presence in the academy diminishes, disappears entirely or is not admitted. Classics, history, phi-losophy, languages, not obviously useful in commerce, for example, are threatened with decline or extinction; type 2 knowledge, practical, applied and useful in trade becomes dominant (Olssen 2012). It is in this climate that student engagement's affinity with neoliberalism prospers. Knowledge valued in engagement suits the market place. It is what works, a practical element in achieving success in a market-orientated society. Quality learning is achieved when learners acquire useful knowledge in pedagogically suitable ways (Entwistle 2003). This offers a partial view of knowledge as it focuses narrowly on technical and instrumental human interests. According to Habermas' (1987) definition of human interests, such knowledge draws on just one of three knowledge domains. I agree with Stuckey et al. (2014) that this focus on the practical limits both education and student engagement. In focusing on knowledge of what works, the affinity between engagement and neoliberalism encourages surface and strategic learning. Habermas' interpretative and critical knowledge domains are neglected or even ignored.

Performativity, the measuring, recording, and reporting of success has become a dominant discourse, a technology of control that judges and compares performances (O'Neill 2005). High-performance individuals and organizations come to dominate the market place and so ensure emotional compliance to its views, which, according to Fielding (2006), can lead to totalitarian behaviours that put substantial pressures on people to perform in certain ways. Student engagement research shows affinity with performativity. The prevalence of quantitative indicators is one example of this affinity. The results of NSSE and AUSSE are used to compare the engagement of students in different institutions, different departments and subject areas. The engagement results of teachers are measured and compared. Institutions are benchmarked against others and the results from one country are compared to the results of another (Coates 2008). Moreover, the indicators contained in such questionnaires normalize and narrow the meaning of engagement. Satisfactory performance on such normative indicators is then required. Qualitative research also develops indicators for judging performance. Leach and I (2010), for example, produced ten indicators of engagement from a literature review; Bryson and Hand (2007) suggested five from interviews with students. These articles have been widely accessed and have the potential to further contribute to the normalization of engagement practices. Although Solomonides et al. (2012) show that engagement research offers diverse engagement frameworks, the pressure on facilitators to perform on indicators connected to neoliberal ideals is considerable, narrowing conceptions of engagement.

Performance is monitored and assessed using summative accountability processes often based on quantitative evidence. Suspitsyna (2010, p. 567) observed that such accountability constitutes a technology of control, "a sacred language' that supports and maintains neoliberal political rationality". Biesta (2004) finds that audit accountability supports a culture of teaching and learning that shapes what and how knowledge and skills are taught. As a proxy for student success and educational quality, engagement research and practice have emerged as important tools in this culture (Hagel et al. 2011). Engaging institutions and teachers and engaged learners contribute to success by achieving high levels of course completions, ready employment opportunities and a positive attitude to lifelong learning (Yorke 2006). But as Biesta (2004) argues, accountability carries two distinct meanings. One emphasizes the countable; another carries connotations of 'being answerable to'—students, colleagues and, yes, government for funding received. The first is a good fit for neoliberal rationality; the second requires working in relationships of mutual responsibility and trust (Codd 1999). The emphasis on mutual responsibility is important. Accountability theorized in this way results in negotiation of goals, standards and their evaluation; in discussions about means and processes; in greater democracy. Distance between the various actors on the educational stage is reduced. I agree with Sanderson (2003) who argued that accountability via performativity-driven evidential processes is narrow and limiting. In pursuing only 'what works' in engagement, researchers and practitioners are liable to leave to others such vital tasks as conceptualizing ideas and issues, opening up the range of policy options available and challenging taken-for-granted assumptions about appropriate methods.

The elective affinity between student engagement and neoliberalism drives mainstream research on student engagement. It provides a wealth of information about what works in enabling a generic student to achieve success. This information is useful, but it severely restricts the field of strategic possibilities for student engagement (Foucault cited in Lather 2004). It is this limited vision of engagement that forms the sharp end of my critique. Not only is the accent on marketable knowledge, expectations of performativity or countable measures of accountability questionable, but more important, as a consequence of the elective affinity the curriculum narrows to the extent that student engagement is reduced to a generic pedagogy which serves as a technology of control. This technology is created and maintained not just by an all-powerful state or management. It is supported and sustained by the compliant conduct of researchers and teachers, students and the public. It is governmentality in action: conduct is shaped in relationships that occur in more or less open fields of possibility within and between individuals, groups and their members, and institutions and their associates (Foucault 1991). The elective affinity and resulting narrow compass of student engagement research and practice are seen as common sense, as a natural part of life and learning by participants in higher education. As such it is almost impossible to disrupt. But perhaps, it is possible to upset it at the margins. This is what I attempt next in the chapter by questioning the notion of the generic learner and pedagogy that focuses on what works.

Quality and the Generic Learner

According to Kuh (2009) engagement leads to quality learning and positive outcomes. Yet Krause (2012) argues insightfully that the idea of quality poses a wicked problem. Quality is an ill-defined concept with many possible meanings subject to constant change. Quality is not amenable to a single generic understanding. But engagement research in both its NSSE and 'approaches to learning' guises envisage student engagement enhancing all quality learning. Quality is seen through a single lens as desirable behaviours or a deep approach to learning. Of three possible ideological perspectives on quality—a rational/technical, an interpretive and a critical transformative perspective—it is conceptualized as a technical construct focusing on behavioural or cognitive processes. Both suggest that the quality of engagement is measurable, objective and universal. I argue that quality is not singular; nor is engagement generic. Hagel et al. (2011) are right when they suggest that quality cannot be reduced to predetermined behaviours or learning approaches. Students must have control of and autonomy in their learning. They must also be encouraged to take a critical view of their learning and be able to disengage at times without being characterized as alienated. In short, engagement is a much deeper and more complex process than often pictured in the research. The generic nature of the NSSE and the 'approaches to learning' frameworks provide only a limited view of engagement. Hagel et al. (2011) suggest that what is seen as disengagement in the AUSSE framework is not in all disciplines and cultures. Howie and Bagnall (2013) argue that the 'approaches to learning' framework does not support teachers or learners in diverse cultural contexts as only deep learners achieve the gold standard of quality engagement.

Indeed, the effects of specific cultural, power and other contextual differences seem imperfectly recognized in engagement research. True, the more holistic frameworks proposed by, for example Kahu (2013), Lawson and Lawson (2013) recognize the importance of contextual influences on engagement. At the sharp end of the learning and teaching process in the classroom, however, engagement seems generic, the result of psychological factors separated from culture, power and politics. Although Kuh et al. (2006) recognize that quality in engagement requires institutional cultures that cater for diversity; engagement research tends to be blind to cultural and other differences. For example, in an edited book focusing on engaging diverse learners (Harper and Quaye 2009), chapter authors discuss diverse learners acknowledging their different needs and points of view but treat engagement as generic behaviours mostly captured in NSSE engagement surveys. According to Yates (2009) this uniform view of quality is a feature of pedagogy which seeks to fashion learners in certain generic ways. The very construct of engagement is generic. For example, Kuh (2009) prescribes universal tools such as NSSE for gauging engagement and Kinzie (2010) consolidates engagement research into four generic propositions that do not distinguish different contexts, learners and teachers. Wellness is often described by universal indicators sited in national and international repositories (Forgeard et al. 2011). Similarly generic are the purposes for engagement. Success is frequently mentioned (Thomas 2012). But the meaning of success tends to be connected to completion of programmes and winning paid jobs rather than to more personal and perhaps socially and politically less valued goals.

Engagement Pedagogy: Only a Partial Understanding of Student Learning

I argue here that mainstream student engagement offers a narrow and depleted view of higher education. I adopt Bernstein's (1996) view that schooling comprises curriculum, pedagogy and evaluation operating as three interdependent message systems. These message systems involve complex relationships between teachers, students and society that together construct the purposes, knowledge, values and practices that make up education, including higher education. As I noted in Chap. 5 , Yates (2009) acknowledged the interdependence of these message systems. Each has played equally important and distinct roles contributing to higher education. Traditionally pedagogy has described teaching and learning processes used in classrooms; curriculum has been concerned with wider issues such as purposes, knowledge and values; evaluation has judged the extent of student learning and the quality of educational provision. In neoliberal times the roles played by these message systems have changed. They are no longer distinct or equal with pedagogy rendering curriculum and evaluation as distinct message systems largely invisible. Curriculum is reduced to statements about expected outcomes, content and methods. Evaluation serves as a measure of performance and audit accountability. This reading of pedagogy diminishes education and mirrors how student engagement is portrayed in mainstream research and practice as a collection of practical 'how to' techniques leading to student success in employment, well-being in life and as active citizens.

There is support in educational research for this critique. Phelan (2011), for example, supports the view that pedagogy offers only a partial understanding of education. She argues that researchers into teacher education are mainly interested either in 'the doing' of teaching (and learning) or in improving 'the doing'. Priestley (2011) argues that this is because curriculum theory is impoverished as it has become dominated by pedagogy. Purposes, knowledge and values are stripped out of curriculum statements in pursuit of meeting the demands of a global market. He argues that consequently thinking about the curriculum is dominated by behavioural outcomes, generic skills, capacities and key competencies. While Priestley (2011) writes about the dominance of pedagogy in general, engagement research has similar operational and technical characteristics. Biesta (2007) argued that education and, therefore, engagement is a moral practice, not merely a technical project. In a 2011 article he examines *Erziehung*, a German word for pedagogy, to suggest that beyond pedagogy a curriculum should include purposes, knowledge and values about becoming human, interpersonal interactions, social justice, contemporary social life and perspectives for the future. Phelan (2011) adds that curriculum research that espouses such qualities is subjected to different views and arguments and is not marginalized by the technical focus so evident in the engagement approach to pedagogy.

Questioning an Affinity with Psychology

Whenever we discuss engagement research and practice we meet psychology. Its importance in student engagement research and practice cannot be overstated. In Chap. 3 I synthesized 10 propositions from the engagement literature, five are situated in psychology; another two are influenced by it. So it is unsurprising that engagement is typically theorized by reference to three psychological constructs: behavioural, cognitive and emotional (Lawson and Lawson 2013). As I described in Chap. 2, the NSSE and 'approaches to learning' frameworks discussed there draw on behavioural or/and cognitive constructs with some recognition of emotional aspects. While it is reassuring to think of these constructs as an overarching explanatory meta-construct (Fredricks et al. 2004), such thinking also leads to conceptual difficulties. Psychology is not a unitary discipline. It is braided into multiple perspectives and sometimes into oppositional schools of thought with different assumptions, visions, methods and even facts (Walsh et al. 2014). Teo (2011) identifies three perspectives as currently important, two are mainstream and dominant. A natural-scientific perspective assumes that psychology is a science using experimental methods to explain specified mental processes in whole populations. A human-scientific perspective seeks to understand holistically psychological phenomena in human contexts using a variety of research techniques. While these perspectives overlap, they use different approaches and often reach dissimilar conclusions. As engagement's meta-construct draws its energy mainly from the human-science perspective, it offers a partial view of mainstream psychology. The question arises whether an incomplete meta-construct is defensible. Haggis (2003) writing about 'approaches to learning' argues that this research is normative and forces new research to confirm but not deny its assumptions. I suggest that this critique applies to the research supporting engagement's meta-construct as well.

Teo (2011) recognizes a third, a critical perspective in psychology. This is informed by Marxist, feminist, postmodern and post-colonial discourses. It takes issue with the other perspectives, particularly in relation to a perceived lack of recognition of ethical and political questions. Teo uses the work of Habermas (1987) to explain the thinking behind this critical perspective. Habermas proposed a relationship between knowledge and human interest. Knowledge is related to technical, interpretive and critical interests. Applied to psychology these interests correspond to the natural-scientific, human-scientific and critical perspectives. Critical interests are emancipatory and call for a focus on self-reflection, ideological critique, social involvement and a concern for ethical and political issues. Neither the two mainstream perspectives nor the critical perspective are internally unified. They express varied ideas and voices of concern. However, mainstream and critical perspectives do stand opposed to each other in a number of ways. Teo suggests that neither of the mainstream perspectives is interested in critical human interests. This lack of interest in emancipatory concerns in psychology applies to the overarching engagement meta-construct as well. Research developed around this meta-construct values technical and interpretive interests but shows little engagement with critical interests (Howie and Bagnall 2013). McMahon and Portelli (2012) and others highlight the focus on technical interests in what works in teaching and learning in schools and I have done the same for higher education (Zepke 2013, 2015). Lawson and Lawson's (2013) and Kahu's (2013) holistic sociocultural frameworks are attuned to interpretative interests but scarcely to critical ones. I join others (e.g. Smyth 2012; Teo 2011) in finding this lack of involvement with critical interests in the mainstream psychological and engagement literature troubling.

Neither mainstream psychology nor mainstream engagement researchers who accept the overarching validity of the meta-construct take great interest in ethical–political issues, a key aspect of the critical perspective. Critical psychologists share an assumption that there is a relationship between politics, power and psychology. While they may differ on the strength and exact nature of the relationship, they agree that psychology has an obligation to consider moral, ethical and political influences in the lives of societies, communities and individuals. Ethical–political influences must therefore be researched and addressed (Walsh et al. 2014). While the ethical–political dimension forms part of the research agenda of critical psychology, it does not in natural-scientific and only minimally in human-scientific psychology (Teo 2011). I have argued that engagement research has an elective affinity with neoliberalism, an ethical–political ideology that infuses higher education. This suggests that ethical–political issues are alive but hidden in engagement research. Elective affinity is not usually acknowledged explicitly by those working within the meta-construct and mainstream engagement research largely excludes ethical–political issues. In producing generic statements of what works, mainstream engagement research ignores issues pertaining to human rights, social justice, ideological critique and political action. Only the ecological social–cultural frameworks (Kahu 2013; Lawson and Lawson 2013) give a hint that such ethical–political issues may have a part to play in engagement.

Mainstream Engagement Research: Anticipating a New Direction

The critique offered in this chapter does not invalidate the mainstream engagement enterprise. It does, however, offer an opportunity for critically reflecting on and rethinking some of its problem areas in order to strengthen it. The chapter concludes with preliminary thoughts on developing an expanded view of engagement.

- Engagement researchers could accept a more holistic view of engagement that moves the discourse beyond the classroom. Axelson and Flick's (2010) critique that such holistic frameworks create definitional, research and planning difficulties implies that the actual lived experiences of students and their families, cultures and communities do not count in learning and teaching, condemning them to a technical education that prepares them for the market place and little else.
- Engagement researchers could raise their consciousness about the political implications of their enterprise. This is a call to widen engagement enquiry beyond the marketization of knowledge, performativity, accountability, the search for generic indicators, meta-constructs and what works. For example, they could include well-being (Field 2009) and active citizenship (McMahon and Portelli 2004) in a broader research agenda: well-being as a precondition for and outcome of engagement; active citizenship as a process and an outcome of active learning and construction of knowledge beyond the instrumental. They might consider a more interpretative and critical theory in addition to the technical and operational concerns of classical American research.
- Engagement researchers could begin to accept that the current understanding of engagement offered by engagement research is partial. Yates' (2009) distinction between pedagogy and curriculum could alert the engagement research community that there is more to know about engagement than practices and techniques. Entwistle (2003) offers a start for thinking about a more inclusive view. His is a dualistic framework for thinking about learning and teaching. On one side is pedagogy—involving the design and use of the learning environment. On the other is content, necessary for quality in learning. While he focuses on content selection, organization and assessment, his framework could easily accommodate other attributes of curriculum: consideration of moral purposes, the nature of knowledge and values.
- Engagement researchers could recognize contextual and personal diversity when researching engagement pedagogy. Thomas (2002) suggested students who arrive in a tertiary institution with cultural capital or 'familial habitus' congruent with the existing institutional habitus, are likely to be 'fish in water' and succeed. Where learners think their cultural and personal practices are incongruent, they are likely to feel like 'fish out of water' and not engage. Engagement researchers need to keep in mind more the impact of ethnicity, age, gender, socioeconomic status, lifestyle and beliefs on engagement.

- Engagement researchers could recognize that engagement is more than a 'one size fits all' set of 'how to' suggestions. They could consider ideas mooted by curriculum researchers such as Phelan (2011) who suggest that educational research should offer critique as well as practical suggestions, entertain diverse ways of understanding and imagining engagement as well as ready generic solutions through generic questionnaires, recognize the significance and complexity of teachers' work as well as offering recipes for engaging students. Such research pursues deep understanding rather than quick improvements, tolerates difficult and continuous questions, and does not try to find a 'quick fix' for all the difficulties that its findings surface. It ceases to be an unquestioned academic orthodoxy.
- Researchers could move beyond a mainstream psychological meta-construct to consider other disciplines such as sociology (Haggis 2003).

References

Axelson, R., & Flick, A. (2010). Defining student engagement. *Change: The Magazine of Higher Learning, 43*(1), 38–43. doi:10.1080/00091383.2011.533096

Barnett, R., & Coate, K. (2005). *Engaging the curriculum in higher education*. Maidenhead, UK: Society for Research into Higher Education and Open University Press.

Bernstein, B. (1996). *Pedagogy, symbolic control and identity: Theory, research, critique.* London, UK: Taylor and Francis.

Biesta, G. (2004). Education, accountability, and the ethical demand: Can the democratic potential of accountability be regained? *Educational Theory, 54*(3), 233–250.

Biesta, G. (2007). Why 'what works' won't work: Evidence-based practice and the democratic deficit in educational research. *Educational Theory, 57*(1), 1–22.

Biesta, G. (2011). Disciplines and theory in the academic study of education: A comparative analysis of the Anglo-American and continental construction of the field. *Pedagogy, Culture and Society, 19*(2), 175–192.

Brookfield, S. (1986). *Understanding and facilitating adult learning*. Milton Keynes, UK: Open University Press.

Bryson, C., & Hand, L. (2007). The role of engagement in inspiring teaching and learning. *Innovations in Education and Teaching International, 44*(4), 349–362.

Campbell, C., & Cabrera, A. (2011). How sound is NSSE? Investigating the psychometric properties of NSSE at a public, research-extensive institution. *Review of Higher Education, 35*(1), 77–103.

Carey, P. (2013). *Student engagement in university decision-making: Policies, processes and the student voice.* (Doctoral), Lancaster University, Lancaster, UK.

Coates, H. (2008). *Attracting, engaging and retaining: New conversations about learning. Australasian Student Engagement Report.* Camberwell, Victoria: Australian Council for Educational Research.

Codd, J. (1999). Educational reform, accountability and the culture of distrust. *New Zealand Journal of Educational Studies, 34*(1), 45–53.

Entwistle, N. (2003). *Concepts and conceptual frameworks underpinning the ETL project. Occasional Report 3.* Retrieved from Edinburgh, UK: http://www.etl.tla.ed.ac.uk/docs/ETLreport3.pdf

Field, J. (2009). *Well-being and happiness: Inquiry into the future for lifelong learning. Thematic Article 4.* Retrieved from Leicester, UK.

Fielding, M. (2006). Leadership, radical student engagement and the necessity of person-centred education. *International Journal of Leadership in Education, 9*(4), 299–313.

Forgeard, M., Jayawickreme, E., Kern, M., & Seligman, M. (2011). Doing the right thing: Measuring wellbeing for public policy. *International Journal of Wellbeing, 1*(1), 79–106.

Foucault, M. (1991). Governmentality. In C. Gordon & P. Miller (Eds.), *The Foucault effect: Studies in governmentality* (pp. 87–104). Chicago, IL: University of Chicago Press.

Fredricks, J., Blumenfeld, P., & Paris, A. (2004). School engagement: Potential of the concept, state of the evidence. *Review of Educational Research, 74*(1), 59–109.

Habermas, J. (1987). *Knowledge and human interests* (J. Shapiro, Trans.). Oxford, UK: Polity Press.

Hagel, P., Carr, R., & Devlin, M. (2011). Conceptualizing and measuring student engagement through the Australasian Survey of Student Engagement (AUSSE): A critique. *Assessment and Evaluation in Higher Education, 37*(4), 475–486.

Haggis, T. (2003). Constructing images of ourselves? A critical investigation into 'Approaches to Learning' research in higher education. *British Educational Research Journal, 29*(1), 89–104.

Harper, S., & Quaye, J. (2009). *Student engagement in higher education: Theoretical perspectives and practical approaches for diverse populations.* New York, NY: Routledge.

Howie, P., & Bagnall, R. (2013). A critique of the deep and surface approaches to learning model. *Teaching in Higher Education, 18*(4), 389–400. doi:10.1080/13562517.2012.733689

Kahn, P. (2014). Theorising student engagement in higher education. *British Educational Research Journal, 40*(6), 1005–1018.

Kahu, E. (2013). Framing student engagement in higher education. *Studies in Higher Education, 38*(5), 758–773. doi:10.1080/03075079.2011.598505

Kinzie, J. (2010). Student engagement and learning experiences that matter. In J. Christensen Hughes & J. Mighty (Eds.), *Taking stock: Research on teaching and learning in higher education* (pp. 139–153). Montreal, Canada: McGill-Queens University Press.

Krause, K.-L. (2012). Addressing the wicked problem of quality in higher education. *Higher Education Research & Development, 31*(3), 285–297. doi:10.1080/07294360.2011.634381

Krause, K.-L., & Coates, H. (2008). Students' engagement in first-year university. *Assessment and Evaluation in Higher Education, 33*(5), 493–505. doi:10.1080/02602930701698892

Kuh, G. (2009). The national survey of student engagement: Conceptual and empirical foundations. *New Directions for Institutional Research, 141,* 5–20. doi:10.1002/ir.v2009:141/issuetoc

Kuh, G., Kinzie, J., Buckley, J., Bridges, B., & Hayek, J. (2006). *What matters to student success: A review of the literature.* Retrieved from http://nces.ed.gov/IPEDS/research/pdf/Kuh_Team_Report.pdf

Lather, P. (2004). Scientific research in education: A critical perspective. *British Educational Research Journal, 30*(6), 759–772.

Lawson, M., & Lawson, H. (2013). New conceptual frameworks for student engagement research, policy and practice. *Review of Educational Research, 83*(3), 432–479.

McMahon, B., & Portelli, J. (2004). Engagement for what? Beyond popular discourses of student engagement. *Leadership and Policy in Schools, 3*(1), 59–76.

McMahon, B., & Portelli, J. (2012). The challenges of neoliberalism in education: Implications for student engagement. In B. McMahon & J. Portelli (Eds.), *Student engagement in urban school: Beyond neoliberal discourses* (pp. 1–10). Charlotte, NC: Information Age Publishing.

Neary, M. (2013). Student as producer: A pedagogy for the avant-garde; or, how do revolutionary teachers teach? Retrieved from http://josswinn.org/wp-content/uploads/2013/12/15-72-1-pb-1.pdf

Nygaard, N., Brand, S., Bartholomew, P., & Millard, L. (2013). *Student engagement: Identity, motivation and community*. Faringdon, UK: Libri Publishing.

O'Neill, A.-M. (2005). Individualism, enterprise, culture and curriculum policy. In J. Codd & K. Sullivan (Eds.), *Education policy directions in Aotearoa New Zealand* (pp. 71–86). Southbank, Melbourne: Thomson Learning Australia.

Phelan, A. (2011). Towards a complicated conversation: Teacher education and the curriculum turn. *Pedagogy, Culture and Society, 19*(2), 207–220.

Porter, S. (2009). Do college student surveys have any validity? *Review of Higher Education, 35* (1), 45–76.

Priestly, M. (2011). Whatever happened to curriculum theory? Critical realism and curriculum change. *Pedagogy, Culture and Society, 19*(2), 221–237.

Sanderson, I. (2003). Is it 'what works' that matters? Evaluation and evidence-based policy-making. *Research Papers in Education, 18*(4), 331–345. doi:10.1080/0267152032000176846

Saunders, D. (2010). Neoliberal ideology and public higher education in the United States. *Journal for Critical Education Policy Studies, 8*(1), 42–77.

Smyth, J. (2012). When students 'speak back': Student engagement towards a socially just society. In B. McMahon & J. Portelli (Eds.), *Student engagement in urban school: Beyond neoliberal discourses* (pp. 73–90). Charlotte, NC: Information Age Publishing.

Solomonides, I., Reid, A., & Petocz, P. (2012). A relational model of student engagement. In I. Solomonides, A. Reid, & P. Petocz (Eds.), *Engaging with learning in higher education* (pp. 11–24). Faringdon, UK: Libri Publishing.

Stuckey, H., Taylor, E., & Cranton, P. (2014). Developing a survey of transformative learning outcomes and processes based on theoretical principles. *Journal of Transformative Education*, 1–18. doi:10.1177/1541344614540335

Suspitsyna, T. (2010). Accountability in American education as a rhetoric and a technology of governmentality. *Journal of Education Policy, 25*(5), 567–586.

Taylor, L., & Parsons, J. (2011). Improving student engagement. *Current Issues in Education*. Retrieved from http://cie.asu.edu/

Taylor, P., Wilding, D., Mockridge, A., & Lambert, C. (2012). Reinventing engagement. In I. Solomonides, A. Reid, & P. Petocz (Eds.), *Engaging with learning in higher education* (pp. 259–278). Faringdon, UK: Libri Publishing.

Teo, T. (2011). *The critique of psychology: From Kant to postcolonial theory*. New York, NY: Springer.

Thomas, L. (2002). Student retention in higher education: The role of institutional habitus. *Journal of Education Policy, 17*(4), 423–442.

Thomas, L. (2012). *Building student engagement and belonging in higher education at a time of change: Final report from the what works? student retention and success project*. Paul Hamlyn Foundation, Higher Education Funding Council for England, The Higher Education Academy and Action on Access.

Trowler, V. (2010). Student engagement literature review. Retrieved from http://www.heacademy. ac.uk/assets/documents/studentengagement/StudentEngagementLiteratureReview.pdf

Usher, R., Bryant, I., & Johnston, R. (1997). *Adult education and the postmodern challenge: Learning beyond the limits*. London, UK: Routledge.

Walsh, R., Teo, T., & Baydala, A. (2014). *A critical history and philosophy of psychology: Diversity of context, thought and practice*. Cambridge, UK: Cambridge University Press.

Yates, L. (2009). From curriculum to pedagogy and back again: Knowledge, the person and the changing world. *Pedagogy, Culture and Society, 17*(1), 17–28.

Yorke, M. (2006). *Student engagement: Deep, surface or strategic?* Paper presented at the Pacific Rim First Year in Higher Education Conference, Griffith University, Gold Coast Campus, Australia.

Zepke, N. (2013). Student engagement: A complex business supporting the first year experience in tertiary education. *International Journal of the First year in Higher Education, 4*(2), 1–14. doi:10.5204/intjfyhe.v4i1.183

Zepke, N. (2015). Student engagement research: Thinking beyond the mainstream. *Higher Education Research & Development, 34*(6), 1311–1323. doi:10.1080/07294360.2015.1024635

Zepke, N., & Leach, L. (2010). Improving student engagement: Ten proposals for action. *Active Learning in Higher Education, 11*(3), 167–179. doi:10.1177/1469787410379680

Part III
Student Engagement Beyond the Mainstream

Chapter 7
Student Engagement Beyond the Mainstream

Abstract This chapter looks to critical theory to provide a theoretical foundation for thinking beyond mainstream student engagement. But critical theory, like student engagement is a diverse field and in this chapter, five critical theorists have been chosen to represent it and to provide a foundation for thinking of student engagement beyond the mainstream. However, critical theory by definition is theoretical and busy teachers and researchers may want very practical ways to improve student engagement. On the assumption that nothing is as practical as a good theory, this chapter concludes by offering 10 *proposals for action* which are drawn from the theories and provide the opening for an innovative approach to student engagement to be developed in the following four chapters.

The way I have named this chapter raises an important question. Given the elective affinity between neoliberalism and what I label mainstream student engagement research and practice, what could '*beyond* the mainstream' refer to? Two possible answers suggest themselves. One imagines the affinity between neoliberalism and student engagement broken and a new theory and practice of student engagement invented. The other continues to accept but weakens the affinity. This means that new ideas about teaching and learning are introduced; ideas that look beyond the neoliberal concerns with practical knowledge, performativity and audit accountability. As I have noted in previous chapters, mainstream engagement research has generated many valid and valuable insights into teaching and learning. It seems wasteful to even think of abandoning the many years of research and practice that have afforded these insights. In any case, student engagement cannot just end its elective affinity with neoliberalism. The effects of power infusing all facets of governmentality cannot simply be turned off. Educational researchers, teachers and administrators, even if they had the will, cannot break the neoliberal mindset without some immediate economic and/or political crisis occurring in the economy at large. It seems unlikely therefore that neoliberalism's alignment with student engagement as a pedagogy comprising practical behavioural, emotional and cognitive indictors will end. A more feasible way to think *beyond* neoliberalism is to enrich mainstream student engagement with theories, research and practices that do

© Springer Nature Singapore Pte Ltd. 2017
N. Zepke, *Student Engagement in Neoliberal Times*,
DOI 10.1007/978-981-10-3200-4_7

not have an elective affinity with neoliberalism. To enable us to think about student engagement beyond the mainstream is the purpose of the remainder of the book.

This chapter looks to critical theory to provide a theoretical foundation for thinking *beyond* mainstream student engagement. Critical theory offers a broader, a more socially and culturally aware view of student engagement. In contrast to neoliberalism, which centres its analysis on the individual striving to succeed in a capitalist economy, critical theory and critical pedagogy, its educational application, focus more on engagement for greater social justice and emancipation using ideological critique and a raised consciousness. With these emphases it aligns with the holistic engagement frameworks discussed in Chap. 2 but adds social agency inside and outside traditional classrooms. Shor (1992, p. 129) defines critical pedagogy, the educational practice of critical theory, as

> habits of thought, reading, writing, and speaking which go beneath surface meaning, first impressions, dominant myths, official pronouncements, traditional clichés, received wisdom, and mere opinions, to understand the deep meaning, root causes, social context, ideology, and personal consequences of any action, event, object, process, organization, experience, text, subject matter, policy, mass media, or discourse.

Critical pedagogy, as identified in Shor's definition, involves a conscious disengagement from tacit assumptions, beliefs and practices; a critical distancing from the status quo. Brookfield (2005) argues that this kind of distancing primarily involves teachers and students being able to engage in ideological critique. But there are other processes of theorizing critically. He discusses transformation theory, experiences that enable people to become critically aware of their personal assumptions to help determine who they are and how they relate to others. Critical theory also values reason to shape our thinking to enable us to detect fallacies in others' thinking. Brookfield finds another facet of critical theory in pragmatism which encourages us to continuously experiment in order to discover our own and others' fallibilities and so develop an agenda for change.

The educational project conceived in critical theory seems contrary to the disciplining rationality observed in governmentality. The conduct of conduct with its intertwining loops of discipline and self-disciplinary power appears as a closed system difficult to critique and change. The discipline of the market is reinforced by the discipline and self-discipline of performativity and accountability. My first challenge in this chapter is to suggest how neoliberalism as theorized in governmentality can share theoretical space with critical pedagogy as conceived in critical theory. Foucault (2000) himself offers the possibility of such a shared space. He acknowledged that critique of the status quo is possible and can lead to the invention of new things. Such invention occurs when a crisis point is reached and our "threshold of tolerance is breached" (p. 234). This suggests a clear link between critique and the possibility of change. But the change resulting from critique is not a recipe for wholesale change as there is "no question of trying to dictate 'what is to be done'" (Foucault 2000, p. 236). Policy makers such as politicians and educational administrators do not dictate change. Critique leading to change is affected by "those who have a stake in that reality" (p. 236). As Bye (2015) concludes, change is always contextualized to the problem space recognized by locals. When it comes, it will be local change in higher education and classrooms.

I do not want to replace mainstream engagement research, but I do want to critique and change it. As noted in Chap. 6 I find it lacks vision and a critical dimension to achieve greater social justice. This chapter identifies ideas from critical theory that offer a vision for engagement where students and teachers learn to work towards a more democratic classroom and society. This will fill vacant spaces in student engagement theories and practice and take them beyond the mainstream. I use the work of selected critical theorists who have influenced education to lay a foundation for a student engagement that is emancipatory as well as practical. I use Jürgen Habermas and his project to restore reason to public and private life through communicative action and a theory of knowledge that reaches beyond the technical; Paolo Freire and his call for critical consciousness, reflection, action and dialogue; bell hooks and her enrichment of Freire's work through an anti-racist feminism; Linda Tuhiwai Smith and others who focus on indigenous people who lack recognition of their diverse identities in mainstream education; and Theodore Brameld and his idealistic vision of the reconstruction of society. I use these theorists selectively to plug gaps in mainstream student engagement research; gaps I first noted in Chap. 6:

- Little recognition of the actual lived experiences—sociological and cultural as well as psychological—of students, their families, cultures and communities;
- a lack of a critical dimension that encourages learners, teachers and administrators' to think and act beyond the marketization of knowledge, performativity and accountability;
- an exclusive focus on pedagogy that neglects the political importance of curriculum, evaluation and leadership;
- an unquestioning assumption that engagement is "one size to fit them all" and a collection of generic 'how to' prescriptions.

The work of these selected theorists does not plug any of these specific gaps. Rather, their combined efforts sketch overlapping ideas for creating clear spaces for student engagement research beyond the mainstream.

Jürgen Habermas: Reason, Communicative Action and Emancipatory Knowledge

Habermas is one of the most influential critical theorists in adult and higher education (Brookfield 2005). This is not because he is an educational theorist. His main interests are to restore reason to democratic politics (Flyvbjerg 2000). Habermas sees three crises that have led to the decline of reason. The first is in the public arena where people discuss matters of common interest; the second is in voluntary organizations and associations which act as counterpoints to the power of the state;

and the third is in the lifeworld which shapes peoples' understanding of their world and communicates to others that understanding. Habermas has not examined in detail the practical implications and consequences of these crises for education. That task has been taken up by others such as Shor (1992), Welton (2001) and Brookfield (2005). In this chapter, the importance of Habermas' work is his understanding of how the three crises can be overcome in the public sphere and the lifeworld. Habermas (1984) argues that an instrumental rationality is responsible for the crisis in democratic politics and social life. This values success over critique, compliance over understanding, and technical considerations over what he calls discourse ethics. The result is an increase in central coordination through steering media such as state power and market forces in place of reasoned argument. To combat the crisis he offers communicative action leading to consensus (King 2009). This opens a theoretical space that enables higher education and student engagement to move beyond neoliberalism and governmentality.

According to Habermas (1984, p. 17) communicative action is "oriented to achieving, sustaining and reviewing consensus—and indeed a consensus that rests on the intersubjective recognition of criticisable validity claims". This is impeded by what he calls (1984, p. 25) "the colonization of the lifeworld" by instrumental rationality. Communicative action counters this as it "excludes … all motives except that of a cooperative search for the truth". This social theory advances the goals of human emancipation by outlining an inclusive universal moral framework which has the goal of mutual understanding and establishing that people are competent to communicate such understanding. This shifts the focus of decision-making from the individual to a collective and away from the economic individualism of success and choice that are vital ingredients in neoliberalism. He visualizes politics as more than technical problem solving by experts that eliminates the need for democratic discussion of values. While communicative action offers a theoretical alternative to the instrumental rationality Habermas sees in the neoliberal public arena and lifeworld, it is unlikely to replace it. As Flyvbjerg (2000) observes, communicative action is an ideal, governmentality describes a reality. The instrumental rationality found in governmentality with its focus on what works is likely to continue to dominate in higher education. But communicative action with its emphasis on discussion, participation in decision-making by consensus according to agreed criteria also provides an action framework for student engagement in higher education.

Underpinning Habermas' communicative rationality is a theory of knowledge that opens for closer inspection and critique the elective affinity between neoliberalism and student engagement. Habermas (1987) identified three main cognitive areas in which human interests generate knowledge. Technical interests include rational and operational behaviours leading to personal independence. Research evidence is factual, often relying on statistical knowledge. Communicative interests offer conceptions that are extra-rational. They engage with emotive, imaginal, spiritual and intuitive knowledge often discovered in groups. Research offers interpretative qualitative evidence leading to understanding rather than explanation. Emancipatory interests encourage research into all aspects of society and culture.

They are holistic in scope and critical in purpose. They mandate critiques of oppression, power imbalances and undemocratic practices. They offer a critical consciousness that encourages social and political action. Habermas' theory of knowledge supports communicative action in a number of ways. It enables us to judge how technical, communicative and emancipatory knowledge contributes to an understanding of validity claims in the construction of a consensus. It helps us see how neoliberal interests limit access to knowledge that is not technical, practical or work related. It offers us insights into how we are controlled, disciplined and self-disciplined in the pursuit of a technical rationality and how this prevents learning empowering us in social and political struggles (Welton 2001). It shows that all three cognitive areas need to be included in curricula and that engagement should not be restricted to pedagogy.

Brookfield (2005) claims that Habermas' defence of the public sphere, civil society and the lifeworld involves a theory of adult learning that supports a learning democracy. It is true that this claim can only be inferred from Habermas' work. But both Habermas' communicative action and his theory of knowledge help to take student engagement beyond its elective affinity with neoliberalism. The use of communicative action can lead to more democratic practice. It highlights the power of dialogue, of testing criteria and agreeing on processes to enable rational decision-making in classrooms. This opens the way for research to support students to engage with and critique political and social processes and their own private lifeworld; to think beyond education as just a means to well-paid employment. Mainstream student engagement research does not engage with these ideas. His theory of knowledge enables students to recognize the paradigmatic differences between human cognitive interests (Stuckey et al. 2014); and makes them aware of the limitations of technical knowledge without the opportunity to fully engage with communicative and emancipatory interests. In short, Habermas' work can be aligned with engagement research. Mainstream engagement research, focusing on 'what works' and the discovery of fact-totems (de Santos 2009) fits comfortably into the technical and neoliberal paradigm. Research on engaging relationships, integration and belonging fits into the communicative paradigm. Engagement research in the emancipatory paradigm focuses beyond the mainstream where it is both holistic in its compass and critical of what is.

Paulo Freire and Critical Pedagogy

According to Mayo (1999) Freire is widely regarded as a leading theorist and practitioner of critical pedagogy, the educational practice of critical theory. He speaks to educational practices that might address social differences, social justice and social transformation. Originally focusing on adult literacy in non-formal settings in Brazil, Freire's work has enjoyed a much wider impact on all forms of education including higher education. Here I use his work to begin filling the theoretical space left by governmentality and mainstream student engagement's focus on practical knowledge, performativity and accountability. Freire's work is valuable because it enables us to question Foucault's analytical grid of governmentality and how it explains how the conduct of conduct works in neoliberal times (Bye 2015); and how the elective affinity between neoliberalism and student engagement might change as a response to critical pedagogy's critique. Freire (1998) sees capitalism as producing fatalism among individuals and in societies. In his *Pedagogy of Freedom* (Freire 1998, p. 93), for example, he refers to "the fatalistic philosophy of neo-liberal politics". He thinks neoliberalism is a form of 'necrophilly', something that transforms feelings, thoughts and actions into mechanistic things. Necrophilly kills hope and destroys humanity's potential to dream. "Conformity in the face of situations considered to be irreversible because of destiny" (Freire 1998, p. 102) results. Freire saw education as offering hope for a transformation from the fatalistic acceptance of neoliberal ideas to a state of emancipation and freedom because humans are unfinished and in a process of becoming. They retain the means to create change in themselves and in society (Sutton 2015).

At its heart, Freire's critical pedagogy contains three elements. First is *conscientization*—the awakening of critical consciousness which is "learning to perceive social, political and economic contradictions and to take action against the oppressive element of reality" (Freire 1972, p. 73). With conscientization, Freire alerts teachers, learners, administrators and politicians of the need to deepen awareness of their sociocultural world and to realize that they have the capacity to transform that world because conscientization generates critique which offers passage to change (Door 2014). But conscientization is not a simple concept. Freire (1993) abandoned the use of the term for a number of years because people treated it simply as a magic pill. But conscientization is a complex stage theory, whose exact applications are not always obvious. It places people on a developmental continuum from semi-intransitive consciousness to fully critical transitive consciousness (Cobden 1998). Freire wanted the realization of full critical consciousness. He found a barrier to its development in 'banking education'. This barrier would only be overcome by 'problem-posing education'. According to Freire (1972, p. 56) "banking education treats students as objects of assistance; problem-posing education makes them critical thinkers". Banking education impedes conscientization and enables governmentality; problem-posing education supposes chinks in governmentality and offers a different view of elective affinity. Accordingly Cruz (2013) suggests that conscientization is relevant in neoliberal times because it can help students to understand how neoliberalism has shaped their lives and education.

The second element in Freire's critical pedagogy is *praxis*. By praxis he means "the action and reflection of men (sic) upon their world in order to transform it" (Freire 1972, p. 52). Praxis enables critical consciousness. It embodies two inseparable components: reflection and action (Coben 1998); knowing the world and working in the world. Without praxis reflection is mere activism; without action it is mere verbalism. Reflection involves the conscious analysis of reality; of the restraints and opportunities of life. Action enables learners to minimize these restraints and to maximize opportunities (Coben 1998). *Dialogue* is the third element in critical pedagogy for without dialogue praxis will not help learners to become critically conscious. It is "the encounter between men (sic), mediated by the world in order to name the world" (Freire 1972, p. 62). Coben (1998) suggests that in Freire dialogue means more than communication. She likens it to an almost spiritual process involving communion between leaders and people, teachers and students which is only possible when there is love, hope, faith, trust and humility. In education "dialogue between teachers and students does not place them on the same footing professionally; but it does mark the democratic position between them" (Freire 1995, pp. 116–17). Dialogue enables education to be democratic. Even with the limitation of professional distance between teachers and students, dialogue allows spaces to be created in mainstream engagement for individual and social change. Consequently fate and conformity as prescribed in governmentality can be challenged and changed (Sutton 2015).

Problem-posing pedagogy is the process that enables conscientization through praxis and dialogue. It is the launching pad for change and underpins Freire's critical pedagogy. It makes both teachers and students critical agents in changing the world by specifying that knowledge is not deposited by the teacher into a student but is created through dialogue between the two. He sees problem-posing pedagogy as a process in which students

> are increasingly posed with problems relating to themselves in the world and with the world, will feel increasingly challenged and obliged to respond to that challenge. Because they apprehend the challenge as interrelated to other problems within a total context not as a theoretical question, the resulting comprehension tends to be increasingly critical and thus constantly less alienated (Freire 1972, p. 54).

As pointed out earlier, this stands opposed to "banking education which regards men (sic) as adaptable, manageable beings" (Freire 1972, p. 47). However, Coben (1998) detects a major problem in problem-posing pedagogy. While Freire decries authoritarianism, he nevertheless assigns the teacher authority in deciding which knowledge is correct. This is an issue in Freire's work. Despite this, problem-posing pedagogy offers a way for students, teachers and administrators to move beyond being adaptable, manageable beings. Governmentality is akin to banking education and enables the elective affinity between neoliberalism and student engagement to make students in higher education compliant. Problem-posing pedagogy creates spaces for questioning and change.

bell hooks: Transgression, Feminism, Antiracism and Critical Pedagogy

bell hooks is an American critical theorist who considers the state of her society and higher education as unjust. Neoliberal education expects teachers and students to be disciplined and self-disciplined in the pursuit of success in the market. hooks counters this view. She (1994/2006) praises transgressions of political, cultural and social norms as a way out of a crisis of engagement in universities and society at large. Contributing to this crisis are factors such as the commodification of knowledge, unquestioned belief in individual achievement and the rise of a dominator culture fuelled by gender and racial injustice that limits learning.

> Dominator culture has tried to keep us all afraid, to make us choose safety instead of risk, sameness instead of diversity. Moving through that fear, finding out what connects us, revelling in our differences; this is the process that brings us closer, that gives us a world of shared values, of meaningful community (hooks 2003, p. 197).

To overcome this fear she argues that it is for all to challenge knowledge that is claimed to be objective, unbiased and therefore true. hooks (2003, p. 3) refers to the importance of "decolonisation of (such) ways of knowing" by valuing ideas and practices that counter dominator culture such as those drawing on feminism, anti-racism and critical pedagogy. Her call to transgress the norms of dominator culture is very important in finding alternative spaces for student engagement to those afforded by neoliberalism.

As a feminist, hooks targets sexism as one feature of dominator culture. But her feminism differs from the 'lean in' feminism described by Rottenberg (2014) as a creature of neoliberalism. hooks' feminism does not aspire for women to rise to material wealth in capitalist hierarchy. Hers is inclusive of all who suffer domination. Indeed, she sees men as potential members of the feminist movement as sexism victimizes men as well as women. She also recognizes the part played by class in the inequality between women and men. hooks' main argument is that capitalism supports oppression and being a feminist should not exclude others fighting against its domination. Capitalism and classism hurt everyone and feminism should be part of a broader anti-oppression ideology that opposes capitalist materialist values that do not liberate women economically. The class interests of minorities, particularly of minority women have pride of place in hooks' feminist advocacy. Minority women must be won to feminism as they often reject the views of white bourgeois feminists who themselves want to be members of the dominator culture (hooks 2003). To achieve an inclusive feminist society and education, hooks suggests a revolutionary feminist pedagogy that must

> … relinquish our ties to traditional ways of teaching that reinforce domination. To have a revolutionary feminist pedagogy we must first focus on the teacher-student relationship and the issue of power (hooks 2015, p. 29).

Such pedagogy enriches student engagement by offering ideas and practices to take people beyond the neoliberal dominator culture.

Another feature of hooks' analysis of dominator culture is her anti-racist work. This makes a valuable contribution to the search for spaces beyond neoliberalism. According to Robbins (2009) neoliberalism sees itself as colour blind, without racial prejudice. Everyone can succeed regardless of race or class. hooks disagrees. Her personal experiences as a black woman lead her to suggest that racism is alive in neoliberal society. It is a divisive force separating people from each other as they pursue economic gain. Yet, she finds that neoliberal ideas are wiping out class and race consciousness. People, including feminists, are socialized to be racist, classist and sexist, in varying degrees. hooks (2003) quotes personal classroom experiences where students claim that there is no racism shaping their lives. They affirm the neoliberal doctrine that "we are just people" who will succeed on merit, not according to our race. She reports that these claims are empty when

I ask if they were about to die and could choose to come back as a white male, a white female, a black female, or a black male, which identity would they choose. Each time I do this exercise, most individuals, irrespective of gender or race invariably choose whiteness, and most often male whiteness. Black females are the least chosen (hooks 2003, p. 26).

She argues that it requires a huge effort by all races to challenge a legacy of negative socialization. In hooks' view, capitalism is not colour blind but socializes people into thinking that it is. This calls for developing critical consciousness about racism and actively questioning the colour-blind myth.

hooks searches for a practical model of social change to challenge class, sexist and racist domination. She finds such a model in the critical pedagogy of Paolo Freire (Burke 2004). She lists critical consciousness, praxis and dialogue as crucial components of a pedagogy that confronts domination and neoliberalism. She uses the term 'engaged pedagogy' to theorize her approach to teaching. This involves building learning communities that act as critical action points to undermine the socialization that preserves domination.

Progressive, holistic education, "engaged pedagogy" is more demanding than conventional critical or feminist pedagogy. For, unlike these two teaching practices, it emphasizes well-being. That means that teachers must be actively involved (and) committed to a process of self-actualization that promotes their own well-being if they are to teach in a manner that empowers students (hooks 1994, p. 15).

Feelings of well-being enable greater freedom not only to teach/learn, but also to share in the intellectual and spiritual growth of students and "to teach in a manner that respects and cares for the souls of our students…" (hooks 1994, p. 13). She visualizes a classroom where there is a sense of freedom but also struggle; where teachers and students work together to overcome the alienation that has become the norm in the university. This view of a holistic revolutionary education reaches far beyond what is practiced in neoliberal classrooms.

Linda Tuhiwai Smith et al.: Decolonizing Research and Teaching Methodologies

Linda Tuhiwai Smith (Ngati Awa and Ngati Porou) is a Māori theorist from New Zealand who like hooks wants to roll back the power of dominator culture. The culture under her critical gaze is western colonialism and its scientific research methodologies. She argues that indigenous people such as Māori have been rendered largely invisible or reduced to 'other' by such methodologies. For Smith (2005, p. 86) indigenous people "remain as minorities in lands in which they were once sovereign" at least partially because their research is made invisible or not validated. Smith's work and that of other indigenous researchers (e.g. Keskitalo 1997; Little Bear 2000) is important to the argument in this chapter because mainstream student engagement has gained its prominence on the back of an extensive research programme that aligns with dominator culture in its insistence on scientific, preferably quantitative methodologies. By exposing a methodological gap between mainstream and indigenous research Smith opens a potential theoretical space for engagement research beyond the mainstream. She is critical of neoliberal positions such as the way knowledge is commodified for the market, scholarship is positivist with alternative approaches ignored and oral histories of indigenous people are dismissed as 'other'. Smith (1999, p. 2) identifies and theorizes "a significant site of struggle between the interests and ways of knowing of the western mainstream and the interests and ways of knowing of the Other".

According to Smith (1999) mainstream western methodologies involve the imposition of a single world view on people with alternate views who are led to believe that their views do not count. Scientific methodologies, including those favoured under neoliberalism

> have little tolerance for public debate, have little patience for alternative views, and have no interest in qualitative richness or complexity. Rather, they are nostalgic for a return to a research paradigm that, like life in general, should be simple (Smith 2005, p. 85).

Consequently indigenous people do not see themselves represented in mainstream western research. They do not see themselves in student engagement research either. Here Smith hints at an important gap in mainstream student engagement research because indigenous people and their research methodologies are largely absent in student engagement scholarship. Harper and Quaye (2009) for example, in their substantial book supposedly dedicated to engaging diverse populations, do not really acknowledge the existence of Indigenous Americans. But Smith goes beyond being critical of western scientific research by affirming the merit and worth of emerging indigenous research (Smith 2005). She notes indigenous research that escapes the scientific gaze by avoiding its epistemic basis and developing counter hegemonic methodologies and practices. She suggests that critical theory holds out the promise that such research could lead to emancipation and social justice for oppressed groups. She wants an indigenist approach to research that is formed around three principles: *resistance, political integrity* and *privileging* indigenous voices. Such principles might also be valuable guides in researching engagement beyond the mainstream.

Smith (2005) therefore makes clear that she writes from indigenous historical, political and moral spaces rooted in resistance to colonialism, but in support of political activism and goals for social justice. Māori researchers in New Zealand name their decolonizing research methodology Kaupapa Māori research. According to Smith (2005, p. 90)

> there are strong reasons for such a naming, as the struggle has been seen as one over Māori language and the ability by Māori as Māori to name the world, to theorize the world, and to research back to power.

Kaupapa Māori research, like other indigenous methodologies, sets out to make positive differences for indigenous people. It is based on a model of social change that *resists* the scientific standard for naming the world; achieves *political integrity* within local communities by demonstrating empathy with their world views, but also assures quality such as trustworthiness, credibility, transferability, dependability and confirmability (Lincoln and Guba 1985); and *privileges* indigenous ways of organizing, conducting and evaluating research. Translating and adapting such methodologies to engagement research creates new spaces beyond the current elective affinity between neoliberalism and student engagement. Examples of such spaces include resisting the lure of scientific engagement research and its delivery of fact-totems. Political integrity is achieved by engagement with and gaining understanding in communities outside the academy and not being complicit with neoliberalism. Scientific research would continue, but knowledge of engagement would also be sought in alternative domains and afforded a privileged voice in specific communities.

Smith's primary purpose is to change western scientific research methodologies. It is not focused on pedagogies resulting from such change. Pedagogies are usually aligned with specific research methodologies and in Chap. 1 I suggested such alignments for mainstream student engagement. Here I summarize a pedagogy that could align with the requirements of indigenous research methodologies and take student engagement beyond neoliberal expectations. From a literature review, Madden (2015) found four pedagogical pathways that meet, interconnect and also separate. The first is based on traditional ways of learning and teaching such as learning from oral traditions and longstanding connections with land. It is grounded in community and relationships between people. The second pathway involves twin goals: deconstructing the past as seen in colonial texts and reconstructing a new set of understandings that are inclusive of indigenous theories of knowledge and practice. The third pathway deconstructs the way indigenous and racialized people are portrayed in mainstream education. In treading this pathway teachers' interpretations will be the dominant narrative. So they must encourage alternative and counter narratives to be heard to avoid oppression. The final pedagogic pathway leads to places indigenous people regard as home. Place-based approaches bring teachers and their students into relationships with situated indigenous knowledges that emerge from and through place. These pathways take engagement beyond the classroom into communities. They validate different ways of engaging learning and offer a critical even radical dimension to learning not usually present in mainstream engagement research and practice.

Theodore Brameld: Education for the Future

Brameld was an American philosopher who is now largely neglected, even forgotten. Despite this, the impact of his ideas on this chapter is significant. His critical theory is utopian and offers a future vision of higher education that takes us well beyond neoliberal governmentality and an elective affinity between student engagement and neoliberalism. Like Habermas' philosophy, Brameld's is rooted in crisis. In his view

> crisis connotes a major dislocation – a dislocation of the fundamental institutions, habits, practices, attitudes of any given culture or any section of a culture. When a point is reached in which the major functions, the major structures, the major purposes of a culture or subculture are thrown out of joint, then its members find themselves bewildered, lost uprooted (1965/2000, pp. 51–52).

Like other critical theorists he wanted a future in which crisis is overcome by the transformation of the existing social order from individualism to a collective struggle to democratize the economic, political and cultural spheres of society. Education would spearhead this transformation (Stone 2003). Brameld (1947, p. 52) wrote that educators and students "must solve our problem, not by conserving, not merely by modifying, nor by retreating, but by future-looking, by building a new order of civilization under genuine public control...". This call to action counteracts the (self) disciplining response so evident in the conduct of conduct found in governmentality. Student engagement occurs in the reconstruction of society, not with the success indicators favoured in the neoliberal state.

Like that of other critical theorists, Brameld's futures orientated writing is informed by Marxism as well as a number of other philosophical positions such as pragmatism, logical positivism and existentialism (Brameld 2000). During the cold war his work was dismissed by some theorists as dangerously political, an educational radicalism neither intellectually satisfying nor politically potent (Zepper 2003). The focus of their displeasure was his adoption of social reconstructionism. He identified four philosophic positions in education: essentialism, perennialism, progressivism and reconstructionism. Brameld argued (2000, p. 73) that they should not be seen only as philosophies of education "but as alternatives through which education ... attempts to bring itself into vital relationship with cultural transmission and cultural modification". While there are overlaps between these philosophies, the first two represent cultural transmission and conservation; the second pair envisages cultural change and rebuilding. As the name suggests, reconstruction advocates fundamental change in education and cultural value in response to the crisis in society. Brameld (2000, p. 75) writes

> ...reconstruction is above all ... a philosophy of values, ... of ends, ...of purposes. It believes that you and I as teachers and citizens, have the obligation to analyse critically what is wrong with the values that we have been holding and then to decide about the values that we should be holding.

By advocating widespread reconstruction of values in education, he opens a space for critiques of neoliberalism in economics, politics, education and cultural life.

Brameld sees education, including higher education, as the means for achieving a democratic transformation of the existing social order (Nash 2000). He (2000) advocated a 'bi-polar' philosophy of democratic education in which students engage both constructively in policy-making at all levels of the political system, while also knowing when and how to dissent from policies and practices, even when they are supported by a majority. He saw social transformation and recon-struction as an educational as well as a political process. In particular, he wanted learning, teaching, the curriculum and the whole context of education decon-structed; their cultural assumptions, power relationships, and historical influences exposed, critiqued and altered. He wanted "to transform education into a powerful means for social change toward world civilization" (Brameld 2000, p. 82). Educators and their students should lead in achieving this reconstruction of values. Included in an agenda for change were reconstructing iniquitous relations between races and genders, the dominance of corporate business in the business of gov-ernment, the emphasis on performance based accountability, the reliance on objective science in learning programmes, the aversion to ideas dealing with class and Marx and the focus on national identity at the expense of world order. Without critical scrutiny of such ideas and practices inequities, historical and current forms of oppression would remain. The very purpose of education to develop individuals into active and questioning citizens would be suppressed. Engagement would be with technical and instrumental values.

A question hovers over whether Brameld's pedagogy of reconstructivism is actually democratic. This is because he expected reconstructionist educators to be social change activists in the classroom and the world; to present constructionist ideas positively to students. Brameld (1957) used the phrase 'defensible partiality' to describe the way teachers should present reconstructionist ideas and practices in their work. Zepper (2003) reports numerous critics claiming 'defensible partiality' to be no more than indoctrination and therefore undemocratic. Brameld rejected this criticism because he insisted that teachers should never avoid or obscure the fair and intelligent analysis of opponents of reconstructionism.

> The teacher who holds convictions without indoctrinating them is one who expresses them for the precise purpose of heightening critical sensitivity to them, provides maximum opportunity for study –of evidence and arguments opposed to as well as in favour of his convictions and to hold alternative ones and encourages consensuses of conviction that are attained only as a result of the preceding process (Brameld 1957, p. 327).

While the reconstructivist educator favourably presents and defends views to students not in the mainstream, she does not prevent them from accepting and affirming mainstream views, such as those in neoliberalism. Students are expected to use their own minds, ask questions and critique social reconstructivist views if warranted. The notion of defensible partiality is important in helping to create a viable theoretical space beside neoliberalism and so potentially weaken the elective affinity with student engagement.

Looking Forward: Ten Proposals for Action

This chapter has offered a range of theories that have the potential to take student engagement research and practice *beyond* the mainstream of neoliberalism and its elective affinity with student engagement. Together, the ideas of the five critical theorists discussed offer varied spaces for developing student engagement in ways not currently covered in the mainstream literature. The following 10 *proposals for action* could take student engagement beyond the mainstream:

1. pursuing change at the local level using critique (e.g. Habermas, Freire, hooks, Smith);
2. developing critical consciousness about dominator culture (e.g. Habermas, Freire, hooks, Smith, Brameld);
3. introducing a problem posing pedagogy (e.g. Freire, Brameld);
4. engaging with issues raised by feminism, anti-racism and class in curricula (e.g. hooks, Smith);
5. learning the importance of place in engagement to help counter the one size fits all mentality (e.g. Smith, Freire);
6. engaging in political action in communities to work with social justice issues (e.g. Freire, hooks, Smith, Brameld);
7. developing a theory of knowledge beyond the instrumental (e.g. Habermas, Smith);
8. practising discourse ethics based on reason and consensual decision-making that include student voices (e.g. Habermas);
9. valuing emotion and spirituality when thinking about engagement (e.g. Freire, hooks, Smith, Brameld);
10. developing visions for challenging and reconstructing current cultural norms and practices (e.g. Brameld, Smith, hooks).

These 10 *proposals for action* contain a fundamental critique of neoliberalism, and by extension mainstream student engagement. Together they suggest a coherent set of practices built on shared values and purposes with potential to change thinking about and practice of student engagement. They visualize a student engagement that is more democratic, critical, lifelong and life wide, problem posing, inclusive of the 'other', orientated to communicative action over individualism. Yet, these proposals are not white knights without flaws. They too can be critiqued. One criticism could be that fundamental change brings with it the dangers of authoritarianism. The ideas of Freire, Smith and Brameld, for example, could lead to the continuation of teacher power while diluting the power of student voice. Another is that the 10 *proposals for action* can be considered utopian and impractical, a bridge too far. This critique might particularly address Habermas' consensus through communicative action and Brameld's idea of total reconstruction of education. They might also be criticized for their Marxist orientation as Habermas, Freire, hooks and Brameld have been at times under its influence. Then, the control of education by indigenous people and minorities could lead to a splintering of educational provision that may curtail a coherent policy approach to higher education and so disadvantage minorities even further. Finally, the proposals for action could be critiqued as too hard to implement by teachers and students used to less theoretical and political approaches to learning.

Critiques such as these cannot just be swept under the carpet. They serve as warning how even positive ideas for change in higher education could turn out to have undesirable and destructive effects. But the dangers of change cannot take away from the necessity of changing student engagement from neoliberal hegemony to one that has the potential to be more democratic, learner focused and outgoing. In the next three chapters, I develop emergent and generic propositions from the proposals for action synthesized from the five critical theorists discussed in this chapter.

References

Brameld, T. (1947). Philosophies of education in an age of crisis. *School and Society, 65*, 452–460.

Brameld, T. (1957). What is indoctrination? *School and Society, 85*, 326–328.

Brameld, T. (1965/2000). *Education as power: A re-issue by the Society of Educational Reconstruction*. New York, NY: Holt, Rinehart & Wilson.

Brookfield, S. (2005). *The power of critical theory: Liberating adult learning and teaching*. San Francisco, CA: Jossey Bass.

Burke, B. (2004). Bell Hooks on education. *The encylopedia of informal education*. Retrieved from http://infed.org/mobi/bell-hooks-on-education/

Bye, J. (2015). Foucault and the use of critique: Breaching the self-evidence of educational practices. *International Journal of Qualitative Studies in Education, 28*(4), 394–414.

Coben, D. (1998). *Radical heroes: Gramsci, Freire and the politics of adult education*. New York, NY: Garland Publishing.

Cruz, A. (2013). Paulo Freire's concept of conscientizacao. In R. Lake & T. Kress (Eds.), *Paulo Freire's intellectual roots: Towards historicity in praxis* (pp. 169–182). London, UK: Bloomsbury.

de Santos, M. (2009). Fact-totems and the statistical imagination: The public life of a statistic in Argentina 2001. *Sociological Theory, 27*(4), 466–489.

Door, V. (2014). Critical pedagogy and reflexivity: The issue of ethical consistency. *International Journal of Critical Pedagogy, 5*(2), 88–99.

Flyvbjerg, B. (2000). *Ideal theory, real rationality: Habermas vs Foucault and Nietzsche*. Paper presented at the Political Studies Association 50th Annual Conference, London, UK. http://projekter.aau.dk/projekter/files/39624900/Projekt%20-%202-10-10.pdf

Foucault, M. (2000). Questions of method. In J. Faubion (Ed.), *Michel Foucault: Power. Essential works of Foucault 1954–1984* (Vol. 3, pp. 223–238). New York, NY: The New Press.

Freire, P. (1972). *Pedagogy of the oppressed*. Harmondsworth, UK: Penguin Books.

Freire, P. (1993). *Pedagogy of the city*. New York, NY: Continuum.

Freire, P. (1995). *Pedagogy of hope: Reliving pedagogy of the oppressed*. New York, NY: Continuum.

Freire, P. (1998). *Pedagogy of freedom: Ethics, democracy and civic courage*. Oxford, UK: Rowman & Littlefield.

Habermas, J. (1984). *The theory of communicative action, Volume 1: Reason and the rationalization of society*. Boston, MA: Beacon Press.

Habermas, J. (1987). *Knowledge and human interests* (J. Shapiro, Trans.). Oxford, UK: Polity Press.

Harper, S., & Quaye, J. (2009). *Student engagement in higher education: Theoretical perspectives and practical approaches for diverse populations*. New York, NY: Routledge.

hooks, B. (1994). *Teaching to transgress: Education as the practice of freedom.* New York, NY: Routledge.

hooks, B. (1994/2006). *Outlaw culture: Resisting representations.* New York, NY: Routledge.

hooks, B. (2003). *Teaching community: A pedagogy of hope.* New York, NY: Routledge.

hooks, B. (2015). *Talking back: Thinking feminist, thinking black.* New York, NY: Routledge.

Keskitalo, J. (1997). Sami post-secondary education: Ideals and realities. In H. Gaski (Ed.), *Sami culture in a new era: The Norwegian Sami experience* (pp. 155–171). Kárájohka, Norway: Davvi Girji.

King, M. (2009). Clarifying the Foucault-Habermas debate: Morality, ethics and normative foundations. *Philosophy and Social Criticism, 35*(3), 287–314. doi:10.1177/0191453708100232

Lincoln, Y., & Guba, E. (1985). *Naturalistic inquiry.* Beverly Hills, CA: Sage.

Little Bear, L. (2000). Jagged worlds colliding. In M. Battiste (Ed.), *Reclaiming indigenous voice and vision* (pp. 77–85). Vancouver, Canada: University of British Columbia.

Madden, B. (2015). Pedagogical pathways for Indigenous education with/in teacher education. *Teaching and Teacher Education, 51,* 1–15. doi:10.1016/j.tate.2015.05.005

Mayo, P. (1999). *Gramsci, Freire and adult education: Possibilities for transformative action.* London, UK: Zed Books.

Nash, R. (2000). Introduction. In T. Brameld (Ed.), *Education as power: A re-issue by the Society of Educational Reconstruction* (pp. 7–36). New York, NY: Holt, Rinehart & Winston.

Robbins, C. (2009). Racism and the authority of neoliberalism: A review of three new books on the persistence of racial inequality in a color-blind era. Retrieved from http://www.jceps.com/wp-content/uploads/PDFs/02-2-09.pdf

Rottenberg, C. (2014). The rise of neoliberal feminism. *Cultural Studies, 28*(3), 418–437. doi:10.1080/09502386.2013.857361

Shor, I. (1992). *Empowering education: Critical teaching for social change.* Chicago, IL: University of Chicago Press.

Smith, L. (1999). *Decolonizing methodologies: Research and indigenous peoples.* London, UK; Dunedin, New Zealand: Zed Books and University of Otago Press.

Smith, L. (2005). On tricky ground: Researching the native in the age of uncertainty. In N. Denzin & Y. Lincoln (Eds.), *The Sage handbook of qualitative research* (3rd ed., pp. 85–108). Thousand Oaks, CA: Sage Publications.

Stone, F. (2003). *Theodore Brameld's educational reconstruction: An intellectual biography.* San Francisco, CA: Caddo Gap Press.

Stuckey, H., Taylor, E., & Cranton, P. (2014). Developing a survey of transformative learning outcomes and processes based on theoretical principles. *Journal of Transformative Education,* 1–18. doi:10.1177/1541344614540335

Sutton, P. (2015). A paradoxical academic identity: Fate, utopia and critical hope. *Teaching in Higher Education, 20*(1), 37–47. doi:10.1080/13562517.2014.957265

Welton, M. (2001). Civil society and the public sphere. *Studies in the Education of Adults, 33*(1), 20–34.

Zepper, J. (2003). Brameld: Architect of confusion, gadfly or prognosticator. In F. Stone (Ed.), *Theodore Brameld's educational reconstruction: An intellectual biography* (pp. 275–281). San Francisco, CA: Caddo Gap Press.

Chapter 8
Towards a Critical Pedagogy of Engagement

Abstract This chapter has two objectives. The first is to develop proposals for classroom practices based on principles outlined by selected critical theorists. Here I provide living examples of how teachers already practice in a critical pedagogy of engagement to achieve four purposes: exposing ideological dominance, developing critical consciousness, fostering empowered learners and acting to change society. The second objective is to develop proposals for classroom practice beyond the mainstream bringing together suggestions for practice from both critical theory and mainstream student engagement. This merging process changes the purposes outlined for a critical pedagogy to a mixed engagement pedagogy beyond the mainstream built around learner agency, learner success, learner well-being and learning fairness.

Translating theory into practice is challenging. But such a translation is the purpose of this chapter. In the previous chapter, I used ideas from selected critical theorists to sketch a vision for society that would take higher education and student engagement beyond the neoliberal mainstream. In this chapter, I translate this vision into an emergent critical pedagogy of student engagement and ideas for practice. The word *praxis* comes to mind when considering transitions between critical theory and practice (Freire 1972). For Freire praxis is made up of two inseparable parts: critical reflection and action. Critical reflection raises consciousness about the reality of the educative process; about the restraints and opportunities offered by education. According to Cruz (2013) it enables students and teachers alike to obtain a clearer understanding of the forces that shape their lives including learning, teaching and student engagement. Critical reflection offers pathways to action; to methods and processes that help implement findings from critical reflection. Such actions include both learning and teaching in ways not considered by the mainstream. Sutton (2015) suggests that action can result in a pedagogy *in* itself; one that is contained within the neoliberal mode of knowledge production. But praxis leads to a pedagogy *for* itself; one that is committed to unveiling possibilities beyond the mainstream with opportunities for individual and social transformation. According to Barnett and Coate (2005) a pedagogy *for* itself opens up new ways of being, knowing and doing.

The chapter unfolds in three stages. It first critically reflects on the theories discussed in the previous chapter to sketch directions for practice beyond the mainstream. Second, it translates five critical reflections into actions by developing a pedagogy *for* itself that is focused on engaged learning beyond the mainstream. Finally, it synthesizes the mainstream propositions developed in Chap. 3 with the critical tasks proposed in this Chapter to suggest a pedagogy *for* and *in* itself. This offers ways in which teaching practice can honour mainstream student engagement research and practice while also enabling engagement to move beyond it.

Critical Reflections Leading to Action

Critical reflection does not reveal objective facts. Rather, it harvests insights that can lead to action. In this section, I critically reflect on the content of Chap. 7 and harvest this for potential action. Such insights are of course contestable. Not only is the critical theory in Chap. 7 open to different interpretations, the insights discussed here are not completely discrete. They meet and interweave with others and so lay a complex foundation for the pedagogy that follows. Together though these critical reflections describe an agenda for action to move student engagement beyond the mainstream.

Student Engagement Occurs in a Specific Ideological Climate

This reflection confirms the obvious. In the early twenty-first century, the ideological climate is dominated by neoliberalism which has been depicted as a hegemonic force in daily life; in society, economics, politics and education (Laclau and Mouffe 2001). hooks (2003) thinks this climate is so strong that she recognizes in it a *dominator culture.* According to Jost et al. (2009) *elective affinities* can develop between a dominant political culture and the seemingly unrelated findings of researchers in higher education. Mainstream student engagement's elective affinity with neoliberalism is created by shared understandings of the purpose of higher education: that what is to be learnt is practical and economically useful in the market place; that learning is about performing in certain ways in order to achieve specified outcomes; and that quality is assured by measurable accountability processes. But a critical reflection on this neoliberal ideological climate suggests that it is restrictively narrow and requires reconstruction and opening up to new values, ends and purposes (Brameld 1965). It requires the emergence of a reconstructed ideological climate in which 'dominator culture' is challenged (hooks 2003) and alternative values, ends and purposes adopted into mainstream pedagogy. In this reconstructed ideological climate, student engagement widens its perspective to include critique of what is; analysis of economic and social injustices; and agenda for creating a more just society. Here student engagement will be active in and contribute to an ideological climate of critique, change and hope.

Student Engagement Visualizes a Pedagogy of Hope

Sutton (2015) follows Freire in identifying the need for a pedagogy of hope in neoliberal times. He argues that neoliberal pedagogy is fatalistic and without hope, a mass production of individual performances. He calls for a utopian strand in pedagogy that enables higher education to achieve individual and social transformations through a sense of hope. His reading of hope synthesizes reason and passion, determinism and freedom. It enables working within 'dominator culture' (hooks 2003) while at the same time transcending it. Sutton cites the work of Halpin (2003) as a valuable resource for reframing teaching, learning and engagement as a pedagogy of critical hope. Halpin (2003, p. 30) argues "teaching is premised on hope—that is, on the possibility that it will realise improvement of one kind or another". Such improvement may be in technical performances or in considering and learning towards alternative values, ends and purpose. Hope then is "a way of living prospectively in and engaging purposefully with the past and present" (Halpin 2003, p. 14). His notion of a pedagogy of critical hope has students and teachers able "to live without certainty and yet without being paralyzed by hesitation" (2003, p. 6). A pedagogy of critical hope is not based in blind opposition, but in a belief that achieving change is possible and alienation avoidable. Students engaging in such learning reframe what and how they learn by donning critical glasses that enable fresh understandings of their past, present and futures.

Student Engagement Has an Emancipatory Sociocultural Ecological Meaning

Chapter 7 showed how critical theorists perceived education as holistic, encompassing technical, communicative and emancipatory cognitive interests (Habermas 1987). Reflecting on this suggests that learning and teaching should not be restricted to technical skills, objective facts and a pedagogy based on what works. It should include the political and be change seeking. Lawson and Lawson's (2013) sociocultural ecological perspective on student engagement provides one framework for how student engagement could become holistic. They place student engagement within an ecology of social relations. "Guided in part by social-ecological analysis and social-cultural theory, engagement is conceptualized as a dynamic system of social and psychological constructs as well as a synergistic process" (Lawson and Lawson 2013, p. 432). With this perspective the focus moves off the individual learner and teacher and their behaviours in classrooms to a much wider social context. But the Lawson and Lawson framework seems more a forerunner to, than an example of student engagement beyond the mainstream. It shows little awareness of emancipatory cognitive interests and so lacks a coherent approach to reconstructing the future (Brameld 1965). A reconstructive approach broadens the scope of learning from a narrow prescribed curriculum and technical pedagogy to one that engages learners in the cultural and ecological politics that provide the context for higher education (McLaren 2003). Engagement now includes learning about the history, politics and ways of being of indigenous people (Smith 1999) and other minorities (hooks 2003). It also encourages students to expand understandings of social justice by including ecological perspectives when learning (Furman and Gruenewald 2004).

Student Engagement Validates Emancipation

A fourth critical reflection is that mainstream and critical views of engagement have different educational purposes. To elaborate this reflection, I again draw on Habermas' (1987) technical, communicative and emancipatory paradigms of human cognitive interests. The technical paradigm includes rational operational behaviours leading to personal independence. Evidence here is factual, often relying on statistical knowledge. The communicative paradigm offers conceptions that are extra-rational. It engages with emotive, imaginal, spiritual and intuitive knowledge often discovered in or generated by groups. This paradigm offers interpretative qualitative evidence leading to understanding rather than explanation. The emancipatory paradigm encourages learning that is holistic in scope and critical in purpose. It mandates critiques of oppression, power imbalances and undemocratic practices. According to Stuckey et al. (2014) it offers a critical consciousness that encourages social and political action. Student engagement in this paradigm uses critical reflection and action to combat inequities and achieve greater social justice for all including indigenous people (Smith 1999), oppressed minorities (hooks 2003) and other members of disadvantaged groups. Habermas' three human interests and knowledge can be aligned directly with engagement. Mainstream engagement focuses on the discovery of 'fact totems' (de Santos 2009) and fits comfortably into the technical paradigm. Engaging with, integrating into and belonging to the academy and making collective decisions suit the practical paradigm. Engagement in the emancipatory paradigm develops understanding of power, its imbalances and injustices and encourages critical insights into how to create change.

In Student Engagement One Size Does not Fit All

Arguably the critical theorists discussed in Chap. 7 are crisis theorists, Habermas and Brameld explicitly so. But the others too—Freire with banking education,

Hooks with dominator culture and Smith with the way indigenous culture is made invisible—recognized a crisis in mainstream education. Their ways for dealing with crisis were not the same. But each theorist included in their solution an understanding that diversity must be accepted, valued and included. One size does not fit all. Yet, student engagement research and practice by and large build on a one size fits all approach by putting energy into producing generic and often quantified engagement indicators. These give educational administrators, politicians and the public a feeling of certainty, security in knowing that things are going well. Engagement indicators enable performance to be measured, recorded, reported and valued. High achievers on such measures become leaders to be followed on questions of quality teaching and learning. Their success secures conformity to their practices, leading to authoritarian behaviours that put substantial pressures on people to perform in certain approved ways (Fielding 2006). Such measures become a technology of control that limits the way student engagement is conceptualized and practised. Reflection on the work of critical theorists suggests it does not need to be this way. An engagement pedagogy that invests time and effort to identify injustices and restrictive ideologies; that develops agenda to correct them and encourages action to implement change for minorities will help to take student engagement beyond the mainstream.

Four Emancipatory Purposes Characterize Student Engagement

A final reflection concerns the credibility and appropriateness of the 10 *proposals for action* drawn from the work of the five theorists discussed in Chap. 7. These proposals emerged from my personal reading of the writings of these selected critical theorists. Two questions about their selection must be addressed to help in the construction of a believable critical engagement pedagogy. They are: first, when considering the whole body of critical theory, are these proposals credible and representative? And second, to what extent are they appropriate in the construction of a critical pedagogy? There are numerous publications dealing with critical theory and pedagogy (for example Brookfield 2005; Shor 1992). While their ideas do not always map exactly to the 10 *proposals for action*, their intent is similar. Brookfield, for example, sets out seven learning tasks in critical theory: recognize and challenge ideology, counter hegemony, unmask power, overcome alienation, pursue liberation, reclaim reason, practise democracy. Table 8.1 shows how proposals for action distilled from the literature in Chap. 7 match Brookfield's learning tasks.

The second question asks how well the proposals for action sketch a critical engagement pedagogy. The answer to this question is complex. The proposals themselves offer approaches for teaching and learning beyond the neoliberal mainstream as they mirror the reflections on the critical theory literature canvassed in Chap. 7. They picture a distinct ideological climate, offer a pedagogy of critical hope, canvass a critical ecology of social relations, promise emancipation and reject the idea

Table 8.1 Mapping *Proposals for Practice* to Brookfield's *Learning Tasks*

Proposals for action (Chap. 7)	Brookfield's learning tasks
1. Pursuing change at the local level using critique	Recognize and challenge ideology
2. Developing critical consciousness about dominator culture	Counter hegemony Recognize and challenge ideology
3. Introducing a problem posing pedagogy	Recognize and challenge ideology
4. Engaging with feminism, anti-racism and class in curricula	Counter hegemony Unmask power
5. Learning the importance of place in engagement to help counter the one-size fits all mentality	Overcome alienation
6. Engaging in political action in communities to work with social justice issues	Unmask power Pursue liberation
7. Developing a theory of knowledge beyond the instrumental	Reclaim reason
8. Practising discourse ethics based on reason and consensual decision-making	Reclaim reason
9. Valuing emotion and spirituality when thinking about engagement	Overcome alienation
10. Developing visions for challenging and reconstructing current cultural norms and practices	Pursue liberation Practise democracy

that one size fits all. Together they commit to an overarching political goal to help students build a democratic, cooperative and social justice seeking society (Brookfield and Holst 2011). Yet, the 10 proposals seem more like a collection of emergent good ideas than the basis for a coherent emancipatory pedagogy. As they were abstracted from the work of different theorists this is not really surprising. They lack organizing purposes to transform them into a coherent pedagogy like that offered in mainstream education. By drawing on complexity theory and the notion of emergence (Davis and Sumara 2008), a set of critical purposes emerge from the writings discussed in Chap. 7. Together they offer a coherent platform for developing a critical pedagogy of student engagement. Table 8.2 attempts to show this by consolidating the 10 critical tasks for learning and teaching into four critical purposes.

Proposals for Critical Practice

There are many possible practical ideas to implement the four critical purposes— exposing ideological dominance, developing critical consciousness, fostering empowered learners, acting to change society—that would take engagement beyond the mainstream into emancipatory practice. One chapter cannot do justice to them all. So I have selected a number of examples from current critical pedagogy praxis to show how the four emergent critical purposes could be achieved. Some of

Table 8.2 Four purposes for a critical student engagement pedagogy

Critical purposes	Critical proposals for action	Critical theorist source
Exposing ideological dominance	• Develop visions for changing and rebuilding current cultural norms • Develop a theory of knowledge beyond the instrumental	Brameld, Smith, hooks Habermas, Smith
Developing critical consciousness	• Grow critical consciousness about dominator culture • Practice discourse ethics based on reason and consensual decision-making	Habermas, Freire, hooks, Smith, Brameld Habermas
Fostering empowered learners	• Use a problem posing pedagogy • Correct the absence of feminism, racism and class in engagement • Value emotion and spirituality when thinking about engagement	Freire, Brameld hooks, Smith Freire, Hooks, Smith, Brameld
Acting to change society	• Encourage change at the local level using critique • Recognize the importance of place in engagement • Include political action in communities to engage with social justice issues	Habermas, Freire, hooks, Smith Smith, Freire Freire, Hooks, Smith, Brameld

the examples share similarities with progressive and humanistic pedagogies (Brookfield and Holst 2011); others are more radical. A number have been or are currently being practised; some are still ideas. The examples may seem rather utopian, even subversive, but they are at present practised and/or thought about. Later in the chapter, I try to bring together emancipatory practices and mainstream ones into a pedagogy beyond the mainstream. But in this section, I canvas a genuine alternative to mainstream student engagement practice as a critical pedagogy of hope.

Exposing Ideological Dominance

In neoliberal times, the dominant ideological norm in higher education places power in classrooms into the hands of teachers. Even where the intent is to make student learning and engagement the focus of instruction, teachers plan, deliver, assess and therefore control what is learnt. They control the transfer from teachers to students of official knowledge and skills for the workplace (Apple 1993). Teachers are accountable for student success and therefore have a strong stake in controlling the learning process. I do not suggest that the vital role of teaching and teachers should diminish, but that it must change if the task of student engagement is to expose ideological dominance. Brookfield and Holst (2011) suggest five actions to support that change. The first is to enable students to expose power and hegemony at work in their lives. The second is to support learners to work towards a more democratic classroom and society. The third is to enable students to develop positions based on reason about particular struggles in education and society. The fourth is to help students use critical reflection and action (praxis), to enable them to strive to achieve success that is beyond mere competence. The fifth is to create classrooms that are negotiated spaces so that the voices of students are heard. Clearly, these five actions will not diminish the role of the teacher. They revolutionize it. They will also undermine the dominance of technical knowledge as the need for communicative and emancipatory knowledge grows in importance.

Examples of Practice

We are spoilt for choice when looking for examples of classrooms that expose the ideological dominance of neoliberalism and the role of the teacher within it. Brookfield and Holst (2011) and Shor (1992) provide examples of how such actions can be implemented in higher education classrooms. I will use the work of Neary (2013) on *Student as Producer* to illustrate how a dominant ideology may be exposed and reworked in classrooms. Neary (2013, n.p.) calls his approach "a pedagogy for the avant-garde". It uses avant-garde Marxist theory to change how intellectual labour is seen in the neoliberal notion of *Student as Consumer*. Instead of students being objects of education, *Student as Producer* focuses on them as subjects in the learning-teaching process. It achieves this by re-engineering the relationship between teaching and research. It uses the knowledge teachers bring to enable students to use their creativity in the process of academic research. This results in them learning about the ambiguities, tensions and complexities in academic work. They learn to see themselves as part of, not apart from, the academic production process of knowledge and meaning-making. From being the dominant force in learning, the teacher becomes a partner in academic work. This notion of *Student as Producer* is applied quite widely in the United Kingdom, even if not in Neary's radical guise. It has become part of the student engagement scene and a less radical version has been adopted in some higher education institutions as reported in Nygaard et al. (2013), for example.

Developing Critical Consciousness

If one consequence of dominant neoliberal ideology is to reinforce the position of the teacher in the transfer of technical knowledge, students' (and teachers') often unquestioning acceptance of this ideological dominance is another. All five critical theorists introduced in Chap. 7 made it a priority to change this acceptance by enabling people to develop a critical view of their world, how it is controlled, their place in it, the ways the status quo might be changed and how this might be achieved consensually using evidence. Freire (1972) called the various stages in this process 'reading the world', the development of a critical consciousness. Allman (2010) describes the conduct of a course based on Freire's work in which she and colleagues engaged learners to read and change their world. The course was based on generative themes chosen to express the everyday existence of participants' lives, particularly their working lives. Themes, supported by teachers' knowledge of resources were chosen through dialogue. Teachers participated in and guided this dialogue but the decision of what theme to study was made by the group consensually based on evidence. It took time to consider the evidence needed to reach a consensus, particularly when negotiating the first theme of the course. But the process of research and dialogue resulted in increased understanding of the context within which each lived and worked. This understanding enabled participants to learn what and how to critique and how to start changing their world.

Examples of Practice

Critical methods as reported by Allman are also central to those discussed by Shor (1996) in his story of teaching and learning about Utopia on a crumbling university campus in New York with some 35 largely white working class students. From the hierarchical arrangement and utilitarian design of desks in his basement room, to facing down a student rebellion when removing himself from the dominator position, he struggled with and eventually persuaded most learners to engage with Utopia and his methods in deep ways, Shor tells a stirring tale of his and his students' growing critical consciousness using power-sharing dialogue and consensual decision-making. Students initially resisted his attempts to share power. The negotiation for a power-sharing contract was quite torturous. While most students finally engaged with this pedagogy; it was not a straight forward process. He summarizes his approach using the work of Elasser and Irvine (1992) who described the classroom as a speech community. Shor developed his speech community using four key methods: he gave students the opportunity to use language they were comfortable with; negotiated learning content and processes with students; generated with students new knowledge for themselves and others; and conjointly with students initiated and supported actions which challenge inequitable power relations in the classroom and wider society. Reading his book left me with the feeling that out of struggle Shor and his students forged a democratic learning community based on dialogue engaged in an ethic of consensual decision-making.

Fostering Empowered Learners

Brookfield (2013) dubs Habermas' ideal speech situation *Powertopia*, a democratic classroom that fashions a rational consensus achieved through open dialogue; a consensus that enables compassion for diverse viewpoints and behaviours that confronts marginalization. It corrects the avoidance of feminist perspectives, class differences and discussions of racism that is part of the engagement mainstream by involving students with critical social and ecological issues in pursuit of social justice. Brookfield acknowledges that *Powertopia* does not yet exist, but like Shor wants to work towards it. It cannot be achieved without students and teachers being politically conscious and active; engaged with values and practices of diverse cultures including those of working class people; and comfortable with trying to meet the needs of people who by virtue of their physical, emotional and spiritual characteristics are not part of mainstream cultures and behaviours. To advance the ideal of *Powertopia*, Brookfield suggests a range of engaging teaching approaches: teaching critical thinking; using discussion, fostering problem-posing learning using the classroom as a learning community, democratizing the classroom and including the power of communication technologies. Without using the term, Fielding (2006) expands on Brookfield's idea of *Powertopia* by describing a person-centred classroom. This is not a classroom where the student is a consumer of knowledge for the market place. Rather it is a space where students can develop personally by engaging in relational dialogue in learning communities. Here the student's voice is heard, valued and acted on by other students, teachers and institution in formal and informal formal settings.

Examples of Practice

Indeed, the idea of student voice is central to fostering empowering learners. Smyth (2012) and Smyth et al. (2014) go further than merely advising educators that students be given opportunities to speak, to have a voice in the learning process. Smyth (2012) argues that engaged students learn to *speak back* to exclusion, oppression and social injustice. He offers an array of suggestions for teaching that engages students to speak back. Such teaching takes engagement beyond the neoliberal mainstream use of student voice by enabling them to take ownership of what they learn, encouraging them to be courageous, supporting them to participate in the delivery cycle including the assessment process. Smyth (2012) argues that unless students take ownership of their own learning they are not authentically engaged. Taking ownership means addressing real-life intellectual, emotional and social problems experienced in their own contexts. This requires courageous habits of mind that are able and willing to analyze, discuss and act on without fear problems faced not only in the classroom but in the community at large. To understand their learning and to take control of it they are consciously involved in planning how they will engage, when and with whom. They are also partners in designing assessment and evaluation processes. If students are involved in negotiating content and methods, even within often constraining official regulations, they learn to speak back. However, Smyth (2012) warns that unless classrooms are free of fear of failure and 'punishment' for challenging thinking and writing, students will not speak back.

Acting to Change Society

Currently neoliberalism holds the ideological and policy high ground for educational practice. It is difficult to find ways to combat, let alone overcome that advantage. Foucault (2000) offers a glimpse of how higher education generally, and so student engagement specifically, might be prised from its elective affinity with neoliberalism. He agrees that critique can help effect change at the local level. Local critique leads to change in mainstream thinking when students learn to be aware of, analyze and critique social injustices; when students are taught to think globally and act locally in their own spaces (Stucki 2010). Bishop (2003) sees this as asserting the right to determine one's own destiny. Such thinking is widespread among ethnic, cultural and gender minorities and is particularly visible in the work of indigenous educators around the world. Their work is important as it sketches a way out of neoliberal dominance. The work of Māori in Aotearoa New Zealand is an example of a political and cultural movement that seeks to establish its identity as being independent from, but not always in opposition to neoliberalism. For Māori the identity is found in the land once held by ancestors. But it can also be found in educational institutions and classrooms in practices that have a distinct Māori identity (Edwards 2010). A Kaupapa Māori philosophy (way of life) is founded on a number of principles: self-determination; validating cultural identity; a culturally based pedagogy that emphasizes collectivity over individualism; and a shared vision for the future (Bishop 2003).

Examples of Practice

These principles are realized by three Wānanga, post-school institutions established and funded by Government in New Zealand. All are designed to have distinctive Māori features while meeting normal accountability and performativity requirements. The joint requirement to be Māori while being accountable to western authority has led to tensions both for governments and Wānanga resulting in occasional standoffs and crises. But by and large Wānanga have successfully steered between the demands of Kaupapa Māori principles and western rule. This has enabled them to implement a Kaupapa Māori pedagogy at institutional and classroom levels, thereby showing that at the local level concerns for social justice can be actioned. Kaupapa Māori principles are used to reveal priorities at a strategic level. For one of the Wānanga priorities identified by research included quality teaching and learning based on Māori values and practices, second chance education for Māori and other learners, Maori management values and practices that achieve government requirements, a distinctive profile based on kaupapa Māori and social justice principles, and political activism to achieve the priorities (Zepke 2011). These priorities are implemented at the classroom level as illustrated by another research project involving the same Wānanga. Funded to implement a strategy for developing functional literacy, the Wānanga embarked also on teaching critical literacy to enable students to critique the status quo and cultural literacy to enable its graduates to function in the Māori world (Zepke 2011). Despite considerable debate, the Wānanga was able to implement all three literacies.

Classroom Applications and Experiences

While the critical purposes outlined in Table 8.2 synthesize the findings from Chap. 7, the proposals for action in Table 8.2 only provide a brief sketch of possible classroom activities. They do not pick up on the details of a possible critical engagement pedagogy. Table 8.3 attempts to do this. In the first column, it repeats the critical purposes discussed in the previous section. It translates the critical purposes into emancipatory classroom student engagement attitudes, knowledge and behaviours in the second column. This recognizes that in an emancipatory pedagogy student engagement requires knowledge, values and behaviours that have the potential to change them. In the third column, Table 8.3 provides examples of how students and teachers may experience engaging attitudes, knowledge and behaviours in learning and teaching.

Student Engagement Beyond the Mainstream: A Synthesis

Underpinning the argument in this book is a pessimistic assumption that neoliberal influences in higher education will continue into the foreseeable future. The elective affinity between neoliberalism and student engagement may be diluted but not broken. In short, the critical engagement pedagogy pictured in Table 8.3 is likely to attract opposition in neoliberal times. In a more affirming vein, I have also suggested that under its neoliberal umbrella, student engagement research and practice can exercise a positive influence on learning and teaching in higher education. Neoliberal ideas have already softened an approach to learning and teaching focused on content delivery to include recognition that active and deep involvement in learning is vital to student success. In short, mainstream student engagement cares for the agency of the learner, her success and personal well-being, and if not social justice, then certainly in creating a fairer world. So, mainstream student engagement has a very important part to play in the future of student engagement. The exact nature of its influence compared to emancipatory activity is open to debate. Table 8.4 represents my attempt to synthesize the contributions of mainstream and critical practice to learning and teaching and so give us student engagement beyond the mainstream.

Table 8.3 Classroom practice in a critical student engagement pedagogy

Critical purposes	Emancipatory tasks in student engagement	Applications and experiences
Exposing ideological dominance	Exercising Agency	• Engaging in critical reflection • Asking questions • Taking personal control over learning • Speaking back to injustice • Sharing intellectual labour
Developing critical consciousness	Reading the world	• Participating in planning learning processes including assessment of learning • Conducting discourse analyses and acting on results • Developing multiple frameworks of analysis • Learning in a critical learning community • Understanding that the world is fluid and uncertain • Engaging with troubling ideas • Uncoupling from the stream of cultural givens
Fostering empowered learners	Ensuring subjective well-being	• Building social, cultural and political capital for self and others • Engaging in consensual decision-making • Understanding own and others' positions in the world • Sharing in intellectual labour • Engaging in communicative action • Feeling engaged
Acting to change society	Learning social justice	• Engaging with others including 'the other' • Engaging constructively in cultural and political life • Recognizing and critiquing repressive tolerance • Challenging hegemonic discourses • Understanding and engaging with cultural politics • Recognizing and combating abuses of power • Acting constructively in the world • Acting as a catalyst for auctioning ideas

The first column lists the major tasks for a combined mainstream and critical student engagement practice. These tasks are softened versions for those in the second column in Table 8.3 headed emancipatory tasks. They are softened because the critical 'reading the world', which is largely political in aim, becomes 'learner success', which can be read as political success as well as personal success. 'Learning social justice' becomes 'learning equity' which again adds personal considerations to the sociopolitical. Another change in the first column is a changed focus to individual learners rather than focusing on learning processes. The second

Table 8.4 Combining mainstream and emancipatory engagement practices

Tasks for student engagement beyond the mainstream	Mainstream applications and experiences	Emancipatory applications and experiences
Learner agency	• Experiencing self-belief • Working autonomously • Building relationships • Feeling competent	• Engaging in critical reflection • Asking questions • Taking personal control over learning • Speaking back to injustice • Sharing intellectual labour
Learner success	• Rising to academic challenge • Engaging in deep learning experiences • Being active learners • Engaging in constructive learning interactions • Having constructive peer relationships • Using social skills • Using learning support services • Experiencing social and academic integration • Having success—e.g. completion • Participating in governance • Experiencing service learning • Working in learning communities	• Participating in planning learning processes including assessment of learning • Conducting discourse analyses and acting on results • Developing multiple frameworks of analysis • Learning in a critical learning community • Understanding that the world is fluid and uncertain • Engaging with troubling ideas • Uncoupling from the stream of cultural givens
Learner well-being	• Trusting in self and others • Belonging with others • Understanding emotions	• Building social, cultural and political capital for self and others • Engaging in consensual decision-making • Understanding own and others' positions in the world • Sharing in intellectual labour • Engaging in communicative action • Feeling engaged
Learning equity	• Accepting that rules apply to everyone • Being honest to self and others • Treating others as self wants to be treated • Affording and receiving equal learning opportunities in class	• Engaging with others including 'the other' • Engaging constructively in cultural and political life • Recognizing and critiquing repressive tolerance • Challenging hegemonic discourses • Understanding and engaging with cultural politics • Recognizing and combating abuses of power • Acting constructively in the world • Acting as a catalyst for auctioning ideas

column summarizes how these tasks may be applied in mainstream engagement. Items in column 3 repeat the applications that first appeared in column 3 of Table 8.3. They are intended to act as an organic catalyst: one that "stays attuned to the best of what the mainstream has to offer ... yet maintains a grounding for affirming and enabling sub cultures of criticism" (West 1993, p. 27). The column offers both a holistic sociocultural ecological view of engagement based on developing a critical consciousness that encourages an appetite for social and ecological justice. Thinking beyond the mainstream challenges what Brookfield and Holst (2011) call one-dimensional thought which is designed to make sure neoliberal ideas and methods work and that thinking about engagement stays within the present framework of discussion and research.

Discussion

Whether in its mainstream or emancipatory guise, student engagement seeks to enhance learner agency. This enables learners and teachers to look to both mainstream ideas of motivation and agency and to ideas and practices that help develop ideological critique. This requires that students learn to critically reflect on their experiences, ask questions about wider society, take personal control over their learning and speak back to what they consider to be social injustice. Barnett and Coate (2005) offer suggestions how this may be achieved. They, like McMahon and Portelli (2012) and Vandenabeele et al. (2011), want to supplement operational and instrumental aspects of engagement with an ontological view. This has three components. The first is that students learn to make legitimate claims in a world of uncertainty and respond to challenges to such claims. The second is that students engage and act constructively in the world. The third involves students becoming aware of themselves and their potential in a world that is open, fluid, contested and in need of courageous actions. Smyth (2012) goes further. He encourages students to learn to 'speak back'. In the pursuit of social justice they speak back to a lack of respect for the beliefs and practices of people not in the mainstream; to an absence of relational power that prevents achievement of collective group success; and to depleted credentials that condemn people into undervalued courses and occupations.

Achieving learner success is a key task for mainstream engagement. But success does not have to be defined conventionally as readiness for high achievement in formal education or the market place. It can also point to developing a critical consciousness through democratic participation in education such as working in partnership with teachers, institutions and other stakeholders to plan courses, learning activities and assessment of learning. It can lead to reading the world by engaging constructively with troubling ideas such as that the world is fluid, uncertain and unjust as well as questioning and uncoupling from prevailing ideological, political and cultural givens. Success can lead to skill sets fit for the market but also to enabling learners to unmask unfairness in mass and social media. Smyth (2012) offers a critical democratic engagement framework that provides a scaffold for critical engagement practice. The framework focuses on *learning*, *ideas* and *lives*, each with a number of engaging 'must dos'. In the *learning* element, engagement affords learners' ownership over their learning by involving them in planning learning experiences and developing courageous habits of mind by teaching them to develop analytic and reflective skills. The *ideas* element engages students in 'talking relationships' including in spaces that usually silence them. The *lives* element is about learning to work with others in conventional communities of learning and in emancipatory social movements striving for greater social justice.

It seems self-evident that engaged learning is linked to well-being. However, with the exception perhaps of Bryson and Hardy (2012) the importance of well-being in student engagement is not often discussed in the mainstream engagement literature. Yet, research on both individual and social well-being is full of the importance of engagement with positive emotional feelings, a satisfying life, vitality, resilience and self-esteem, autonomy and competence. Social well-being includes engaging in supportive relationships with family, friends and supporters such as teachers and peers; and trusting other people while enjoying respect and a sense of belonging (Forgeard et al. 2011). Beyond the mainstream engagement is critical learning that involves learners in building social, cultural and political capital for themselves and others, including the 'other'and taking part in consensual decision-making and engaging in communicative action (Stuckey et al. 2014). Forgeard et al. (2011) expects higher education to build a well-being culture that ensures that learners are aware of the world and their and others role in it, have clear goals for living in that world including a belief that their goals are achievable, and retain a sense of personal control over their learning. Beyond the mainstream, well-being encourages engagement in communities of learning seeking greater social justice. Field (2009) affirms that all forms of engagement enhance well-being.

I have labelled the fourth task for engagement 'learning equity'. In its main-stream guise this means to be fair-minded: to accept that rules of engagement apply to everyone equally; to be honest to self and others; to treat others regardless of background as we want to be treated; to afford others and to receive equal learning opportunities. Critical engagement translates equity into social justice. Sanders-Lawson et al. (2006) identify three understandings of social justice: dis-tributive justice determines the equitable distribution of resources; procedural jus-tice determines whose voices are heard and silenced; interactional justice determines how communication between different strata in a hierarchy is organized. Distributive justice involves learning that inequalities exist, requires the will to tackle them and the skills to act constructively in addressing them. Procedural justice asks for active engagement in cultural and political life, particularly engaging with 'the other' on the margins of mainstream society. It also involves engaging in critical active citizenship that challenges hegemonic discourses and combats abuses of power. Interactional justice involves engaged learners as inter-preter of different communication methods and messages including repressive tolerance. Brookfield (2007) is particularly intent to warn learners about repressive tolerance. He argues, following Marcuse, that repressive tolerance ensures that learners believing they live in a free and democratic society are in error because their conditioning "will always predispose them to choose what for them are common sense socially sanctioned understandings" (Brookfield 2007, p. 558).

End Note

In this chapter, I outlined pedagogies *in* and *of* themselves. A pedagogy *in* itself is of the mainstream, aligned to neoliberalism. The ideas presented in Chaps. 2 and 3 provide the practical ideas for such a pedagogy. Chapter 7 introduces important themes of a pedagogy beyond the mainstream for which this chapter introduced practical applications. This is a pedagogy *of* itself. Together, the pedagogies *of* and *in* themselves offer a comprehensive engagement pedagogy that furthers learner agency, success, well-being and learning equity/social justice. But no matter how change is orientated, a pedagogy alone is no guarantor for change. Curriculum, evaluation and leadership must align with such a pedagogy. These will be the focus of Chaps. 9–11.

References

Allman, P. (2010). *Critical education against global capitalism. Karl Marx and revolutionary critical education*. Rotterdam, The Netherlands: Sense Publishers.

Apple, M. (1993). *Official knowledge: Democratic education in a conservative age*. New York, NY: Routledge.

Barnett, R., & Coate, K. (2005). *Engaging the curriculum in higher education*. Maidenhead, UK: Society for Research into Higher Education and Open University Press.

Bishop, R. (2003). Changing power relations in education: Kaupapa Maori messages for 'mainstream' education in Aotearoa/New Zealand. *Comparative Education, 39*(2), 221–238.

Brameld, T. (1965/2000). *Education as power: A re-issue by the Society of Educational Reconstruction*. New York, NY: Holt, Rinehart & Wilson.

Brookfield, S. (2005). *The power of critical theory: Liberating adult learning and teaching*. San Francisco, CA: Jossey Bass.

Brookfield, S. (2007). Diversifying curriculum as the practice of repressive tolerance. *Teaching in Higher Education, 12*(5&6), 557–569.

Brookfield, S. (2013). *Powerful techniques for teaching adults*. San Francisco, CA: Jossey Bass.

Brookfield, S., & Holst, J. (2011). *Radicalizing learning: Adult education for a just world*. San Francisco, CA: Jossey Bass.

Bryson, C., & Hardy, C. (2012). The nature of academic engagement: What the students tell us. In I. Solomonides, A. Reid, & P. Petocz (Eds.), *Engaging with learning in higher education*. Faringdon, UK: Libri Publishing.

Cruz, A. (2013). Paulo Freire's concept of conscientizacao. In R. Lake & T. Kress (Eds.), *Paulo Freire's intellectual roots: Towards historicity in praxis* (pp. 169–182). London, UK: Bloomsbury.

Davis, B., & Sumara, D. (2008). *Complexity and education: Inquiries into learning, teaching and research*. London, UK: Routledge.

de Santos, M. (2009). Fact-totems and the statistical imagination: The public life of a statistic in Argentina 2001. *Sociological Theory, 27*(4), 466–489.

Edwards, S. (2010). *The academic addiction: The western academy as an 'intimate enemy' of Matauranga Wananga*. Unpublished paper.

Elasser, N., & Irvine, P. (1992). Literacy as commodity: Redistributing the goods. *Journal of Education, 174*(3), 26–40.

Field, J. (2009). *Well-being and happiness: Inquiry into the future for lifelong learning. Thematic Article 4*. Retrieved from Leicester, UK:

Fielding, M. (2006). Leadership, radical student engagement and the necessity of person-centred education. *International Journal of Leadership in Education, 9*(4), 299–313.

Forgeard, M., Jayawickreme, E., Kern, M., & Seligman, M. (2011). Doing the right thing: Measuring wellbeing for public policy. *International Journal of Wellbeing, 1*(1), 79–106.

Foucault, M. (2000). Questions of method. In J. Faubion (Ed.), *Michel Foucault: Power. Essential works of Foucault 1954–1984* (Vol. 3, pp. 223–238). New York, NY: The New Press.

Freire, P. (1972). *Pedagogy of the oppressed*. Harmondsworth, UK: Penguin Books.

Furman, G., & Gruenewald, D. (2004). Expanding the landscape of social justice: A critical ecological analysis. *Educational Administration Quarterly, 40*(1), 47–76.

Habermas, J. (1987). *Knowledge and human interests* (J. Shapiro, Trans.). Oxford, UK: Polity Press.

Halpin, D. (2003). *Hope and education: The role of the utopian imagination*. London, UK: Routledge.

Hooks, B. (2003). *Teaching community: A pedagogy of hope*. New York, NY: Routledge.

Jost, J., Federico, C., & Napier, J. (2009). Political ideology: Its structure, functions and elective affinity. *Annual Review of Psychology, 60*, 307–337.

Laclau, E., & Mouffe, C. (2001). *Hegemony and socialist strategy: Towards a radical democratic politics* (2nd Ed.). London: UK: Verso.

Lawson, M., & Lawson, H. (2013). New conceptual frameworks for student engagement research, policy and practice. *Review of Educational Research, 83*(3), 432–479.

McLaren, P. (2003). *Life in schools: An introduction to critical pedagogy in the foundations of education* (4th ed.). New York, NY: Allyn and Bacon.

McMahon, B., & Portelli, J. (2012). The challenges of neoliberalism in education: Implications for student engagement. In B. McMahon & J. Portelli (Eds.), *Student engagement in urban school: Beyond neoliberal discourses* (pp. 1–10). Charlotte, NC: Information Age Publishing.

Neary, M. (2013). Student as producer: A pedagogy for the avant-garde; or, how do revolutionary teachers teach? Retrieved from http://josswinn.org/wp-content/uploads/2013/12/15-72-1-pb-1.pdf

Nygaard, N., Brand, S., Bartholomew, P., & Millard, L. (2013). *Student engagement: Identity, motivation and community*. Faringdon, UK: Libri Publishing.

Sanders-Lawson, R., Smith-Campbell, S., & Benham, M. (2006). Wholistic visioning for social justice: Black women theorizing practice. In C. Marshall & M. Oliva (Eds.), *Leadership for social justice: Making revolutions in education* (pp. 31–61). Boston, MA: Pearson.

Shor, I. (1992). *Empowering education: Critical teaching for social change*. Chicago, IL: University of Chicago Press.

Shor, I. (1996). *When students have power: Negotiating authority in a critical pedagogy*. Chicago, ILL: University of Chicago Press.

Smith, L. (1999). *Decolonizing methodologies: Research and indigenous peoples*. London, UK; Dunedin, New Zealand: Zed Books and University of Otago Press.

Smyth, J. (2012). When students 'speak back': Student engagement towards a socially just society. In B. McMahon & J. Portelli (Eds.), *Student engagement in urban school: Beyond neoliberal discourses* (pp. 73–90). Charlotte, NC: Information Age Publishing.

Smyth, J., Down, B., McInerney, P., & Hattam, R. (2014). *Doing critical research: A conversation with the research of John Smyth*. New York, NY: Peter Lang Publishing.

Stuckey, H., Taylor, E., & Cranton, P. (2014). Developing a survey of transformative learning outcomes and processes based on theoretical principles. *Journal of Transformative Education*, 1–18. doi:10.1177/1541344614540335

Stucki, P. (2010). *Maori pedagogy, pedagogical beliefs and practices in a Maori tertiary institution.* (Doctoral thesis), Massey University, New Zealand. Retrieved from http://mro.massey.ac.nz/bitstream/handle/10179/2329/02_whole.pdf?sequence=1&isAllowed=y

Sutton, P. (2015). A paradoxical academic identity: Fate, utopia and critical hope. *Teaching in Higher Education, 20*(1), 37–47. doi:10.1080/13562517.2014.957265

Vandenabeele, J., Vanassche, E., & Wildemeersch, D. (2011). Stories of/on citizenship education: A case of participatory planning. *International Journal of Lifelong Education, 30*(2), 171–185.

West, C. (1993). *Keeping faith: Philosophy and race in America.* New York, NY: Routledge.

Zepke, N. (2011). Navigating between Maori particularism and economic universalism in adult literacy provision in Aotearoa New Zealand: The case of a Wananga. *Discourse: Studies in the Cultural Politics of Education, 32*(3), 431–442. doi:10.1080/01596306.2011.573259

Chapter 9
Towards a Critical Curriculum for Engagement

Abstract What is a critical curriculum for engagement? Such a curriculum overlaps with the prescriptions of a mainstream curriculum but takes learning beyond this. A critical curriculum includes all relevant purposes, knowledge and values leading to awareness of self, society and the ecosystem. It enables critique of mainstream knowledge, values and practices and works for greater social justice. The chapter introduces the notion of a 'big E' critical curriculum, which features student engagement as a catalyst for critical learning. While theoretical supports for a 'big E' critical curriculum are canvassed, so are practical applications.

Discussion so far has centred on *how* teachers engage students in a pedagogy of student engagement. We have focused on pedagogy because pedagogy has been and largely continues to be the focus of mainstream student engagement research and practice. While pedagogy is a necessary aspect of student engagement, it is not sufficient. Mainstream engagement pedagogy focuses on techniques of teaching and learning mainly in classrooms. It is concerned with behaviours, skills and attitudes without explicitly considering the varied contexts within which these can occur. According to McFadden and Munns (2002, p. 360) what is critically important in getting to grips with student engagement "is an understanding of how students respond socially and culturally to their educational circumstances, including the teaching paradigm used". They want student engagement to be more than pedagogy and call for a 'big E' engagement curriculum. They adopt Bernstein's view that education comprises three domains: curriculum, pedagogy and evaluation. According to Bernstein (1996) these operate together as three interdependent message systems through which knowledge is realized. Curriculum identifies valid knowledge; pedagogy determines how students engage with that knowledge; and evaluation judges whether knowledge is validly realized. Mainstream student engagement research and practice focus on what works, rendering largely invisible wider concerns of curriculum such as its purposes, knowledge and values. Priestley (2011) argues that pedagogy overshadows curriculum because of neoliberal ideology. He contends that where mentioned at all, a mainstream curriculum is dominated by behavioural outcomes, generic skills, capacities and key competencies. This view of curriculum is narrow instrumentalism based on economic priorities focused on skills required for the workplace.

This view has been widely critiqued as limiting designs for teaching and learning (Yates 2009), and hence for student engagement. Yates visualizes pedagogy as a subset of curriculum offering only a partial understanding of students' learning. She argues that curriculum is concerned with the knowledge being conveyed (or intended to be conveyed), and about the values and processes that are not simply derivable from "evidence of what works". Knowledge, purposes and values are at the core of the curriculum. How these are then present in diverse disciplines, cultures and contexts determines the curriculum at work. Whatever its context of application or purposes such a curriculum cannot be neutral. According to Apple (2012, p. xiv) "it is fundamentally valuative" and involves an act of selection by someone about what should count as appropriate purposes, knowledge and values. In the mainstream selection of these is shared by politicians, administrators and teachers. It conveys instrumental purposes, knowledge and values to build work readiness. A critical curriculum does not replace mainstream learning. Rather, it extends a mainstream curriculum, pushing learning beyond the mainstream. It offers opportunities to complement and challenge the mainstream to build a more just future for all. It occurs within a political, cultural, ecological, institutional and personal framework of values that is shaped in a wider social context (Ramsden and Callender 2014). The knowledge conveyed, the purposes chosen and the values held require students and teachers to become conscious of themselves, their place in the scheme of things and to critically engage with the world (Freire 1972).

This chapter raises two intertwining questions: what critical purposes, knowledge and values are conveyed by a curriculum; and what is an engaging critical curriculum anyway? I suggest that a critical curriculum conveys, first, valid knowledge that includes all relevant Type 1 and 2 knowledge but with an emphasis on critique. Barnett (1997) identifies four levels of critical knowledge: discipline specific critique; critical reflection on one's own knowledge; critical interpretation of existing knowledge; and the transformation of existing knowledge. A 'big E' curriculum covers all levels within specific disciplines and outside them as part of the ethos and culture of the learning environment. Engaging with this array of critical knowledge enables 'big E' engagement (McFadden and Munns 2002, p. 360) where students are active members of a critical discourse community and culture that can engage with mainstream knowledge but also challenge it. Such a 'big E' curriculum must, second, have critical purposes and values. Biesta (2011) draws on the work of the German education theorist Hans Groothoff to describe a continental European conception of education (Erziehung) that could act as proxy for the purposes and values of a critical engagement curriculum. This would enable students to become self-aware as human beings, interact positively with others, become critical learners, understand contemporary social life and actively help shape its future, understand and engage with the ends and means of higher education and act constructively within different contexts and institutions. Such a conception of purposes, knowledge and values offers some specifics for 'big E' engagement in a critical curriculum.

In introducing the idea of a 'big E' curriculum, McFadden and Munns (2002) describe some of its features and effects, but leave blank spots and do not engage specifically with critical learning. Au (2012) fills some of these blanks. In the process he provides a more complete description of what a critical 'big E' engagement curriculum might look like—from here called a 'big E' critical curriculum. He visualizes it as a complex environmental design that seeks to selectively make discipline and critical knowledge available to different students as part of a broader process of shaping self-consciousness and consciousness of the wider world in critical and liberating ways. Au makes clear that such a curriculum is not just another set of generic 'to dos' because the critical specifics differ between contexts, populations and disciplines. The chapter now turns to discuss some of the specifics of a 'big E' critical curriculum. It is organized around *purposes, knowledge and values*. Although it treats them separately, they are related and even overlap. Under *purposes* we examine how knowledge, performativity and accountability, the three anchoring ideas for a neoliberal mainstream curriculum are reframed into a critical one that centres on student engagement with the world. The focus in the *knowledge* section is on criticality within different knowledge classifications. The *values* section acknowledges the traps in considering values generically but uses the work of Groothoff and the theorists discussed in Chap. 7 to provide a sketch of critical value clusters underpinning a 'big E' critical curriculum. Each section concludes with some thoughts on how critical purposes, knowledge and values may underpin practice.

Purposes

Subject fields seek to codify their own purposes, knowledge and values for students in a written, implied or hidden curriculum. The way these are codified is political as the purposes of curricula are shaped within dominant ideologies (Apple 2012). Currently they are shaped in the image of neoliberal norms and expectations. One purpose of a 'big E' critical curriculum is to help students' develop a critical awareness of neoliberal purposes and expectations in higher education. There are two aspects to this. First, such a curriculum enables students to identify and critique such dominant ideological norms and practices (Au 2012). In identifying and critiquing dominant neoliberal purposes, a 'big E' critical curriculum opens students to possibilities for learning that lie beyond the mainstream. Practical knowledge, performativity and accountability, the three anchoring ideas for neoliberal norms and expectations are exposed for examination and critique. A 'big E' critical curriculum expects students to know both what to critique and how to do so. For example, the limits of what works in a subject area are investigated and analyzed for problems. The neoliberal version of performativity is discussed critically as potentially authoritarian and self-limiting. Other criteria for evaluating performance are critically examined. The narrow neoliberal application of accountability is recognized and critiqued and more critical forms of accountability are examined.

The curriculum emerging here is strongly committed to developing in students both a consciousness of the neoliberal hegemony shaping their learning and ways of critiquing and perhaps changing it (Brookfield 2005).

The second aspect of developing critical consciousness in students is to reframe neoliberal norms and expectations by developing a critical awareness of what is possible (Au 2012). A 'big E' critical curriculum does this by engaging students in learning that offers a deeper and wider understanding of the world than is afforded in a mainstream curriculum. In particular it encourages students to develop, argue and defend positions based on reason (Brookfield and Holst 2011). Reason opens students to perceiving the world beyond neoliberal constructions of knowledge, performativity and accountability. While technical and interpretative knowledge is also part of a critical curriculum, the focus is on critical knowledge. This privileges criticality and dialogue to strive for agreement (Habermas 1987). Such a curriculum also introduces the notion of paradigm change in which new knowledge is constantly discovered and old discarded (Kuhn 1999) and the concept of fallibility is made accessible to students (Popper 1992). In a curriculum where even well-established empirical knowledge is seen to be fallible, the hold of neoliberal hegemony weakens. The meaning of taken for granted performance standards such as course completion and winning employment change to include self-set standards for successful learning such as how to set standards, question own consciousness and explore how the persistence of official knowledge might affect the future (Au 2012). The meaning of accountability changes from a technical understanding that stresses compliance with externally set quality standards to a collegial practice of quality enhancement requiring mutual responsibility (Charlton 2002).

It is common for educators and others to argue that democratic principles should underpin an engaging education and curriculum. Indeed, Brookfield (2013) claims that whenever discussions about curriculum occur, the mention of democratic curriculum goals provides an uncritical seal of approval. But the meaning of democracy is malleable; it is not uncontested and has neoliberal as well as critical purposes. One thing is certain though, whatever meaning is used, democratic curriculum goals call for students' active engagement in learning, decision-making and wider society. Biesta (2006) suggests that a mainstream view of a democratic curriculum is that it is instrumental in producing democratic citizens who participate as individuals in society. This view is favoured in neoliberal times as it suits neoliberal instrumental purposes. Another view is that democratic principles require social and political activity in which students are expected to learn about working together for a greater good in the classroom, wider community and society. Such social activity is not critical in itself. To be critical a curriculum requires collective participation in the construction, maintenance and transformation of social and political life (Bernstein 1996). A 'big E' critical curriculum achieves this participation in democratic practice *through* democracy. This requires that curricular require students to know and experience democratic principles directly within everyday democratic classroom structures and cultures. Such engagement has a positive by product. It provides students with the purpose to learn about and engage actively with democratic principles and so foster a democratic culture (Biesta 2006).

Another key purpose of a democratic and critical curriculum is to enable students to understand and practice power democratically in the world. But power, also has multiple meanings and a curriculum must be clear what it intends. I support Cervero and Wilson's (2001) view that all power exercised in a classroom is political and is ever present in relationships. Its purpose in a curriculum is to enable students to understand the politics of the classroom and wider society. Cervero and Wilson identify three strands of political power in higher education. These are important because they clearly differentiate between uses of power in a mainstream and a critical curriculum. The first two strands are well suited to a curriculum constructed along neoliberal lines. The first strand Cervero and Wilson label *political is personal*. This is about the power of the independent learner who is motivated and equipped to identify their own learning needs and who commands the political and social capital to meet them. The second strand, which overlaps the first, is that the *political is practical*. Such a curriculum emphasizes instrumental applications of power with politics focusing on the ability to get things done; to acquire and command whatever resources are needed to achieve goals. The third strand is critical although it can include the first two strands. Here the curriculum stipulates that the *political is structural* and is involved in the redistribution of power to groups who are under-capitalized politically, socially, culturally and economically.

A further purpose of a 'big E' critical curriculum is to give voice to those lacking the necessary capital to engage with what a mainstream curriculum offers. Numerous authors have addressed this issue. hooks (2003), for example, consistently exposes the lack of power of women, people of colour and members of the working class while recognizing many others considered 'diverse' by the mainstream but who lack personal, practical and structural power to benefit from mainstream education. Diversity is recognized in mainstream curricular but in a way that considers people who are different as lacking something that must be fixed; they must be made into something else (hooks 2003). In a 'big E' critical curriculum all students are accepted on their own terms, by valuing who they are and what they bring. It adopts a standpoint that challenges hegemonic views about the power of western cultural norms, avoids forcing people who are different to conform to those norms by valuing their knowledge, skills and attitudes (Au 2012). An example of applied standpoint theory can be found in Madden (2015). While writing about indigenous people, her four pedagogic pathways serve as proxy for a 'big E' critical curriculum conscious of the standpoint of minorities. She identifies: respect for minority knowledge and approaches to education; integration of content that is relevant to, and builds upon minority students' views of human, natural, and spirit worlds; reciprocal teaching and learning relationships that disrupt a teacher/student hierarchy; and teaching that employs knowledge to develop responsibility to one's relations, including future generations.

Developing engaged citizens is a central purpose of a mainstream curriculum. Through learning, individuals are expected to demonstrate the will and skills to do everything possible to get fit for the race that leads to market place success. Hence, the mainstream curriculum constructs engaged students as skilful and active rather than as feeling and thinking beings. In short, students are expected to conform, respond and adapt to the world as it is (Allman 2010). This version of an engaged student is challenged in a 'big E' critical curriculum. Students must have the will to engage in more than their personal success. Engagement now is about coming to understand consciousness of self, others and the world; to look critically at the way the self, the classroom and the wider world are structured and controlled; to identify ways in which structures might be improved; and to act knowingly in order to achieve their own and society's critical ends. The knowledge required to realize these purposes of a critical curriculum lies in critical theory and the diverse fields of study available in higher education. Barnett (2009) summarizes some of the general purposes of a 'big E' critical curriculum. It is sufficiently demanding to promote 'resilience'; offers contrasting insights and perspectives, so that 'openness' to even troubling ideas can develop; requires from teachers and students a continual presence and commitment, through course regulations, for example, to develop 'self-discipline'; contains sufficient space and spaces, so that 'authenticity' and 'integrity' are likely.

Table 9.1 Critical purposes in a 'big E' critical curriculum

Critical Purposes	Focus	Curriculum learning tasks
Learning to critique	Critiquing ideological domination	• Identify dominant ideologies • Critically reflect on their meaning personally and for others • Critique dominance
Awareness of possibilities	Expanding knowledge	• Recognize the 'fallibility' of knowledge • Critique and reframe 'fact totems' used in performativity and accountability
Practicing democracy	Active engagement in classroom decision-making	• Work, listen to and debate with others • Listen and negotiate • Make decisions for themselves and others
Understanding power	Power is everywhere and is political	• Recognize that power is political • Use personal power to meet own learning needs • Apply practical power to get things done • Critique the distribution of structural power
Valuing difference	Inclusion of knowledge and beliefs of groups not in the mainstream	• Recognize and critique disadvantage • Learn what is relevant to minorities • Respect minority views of their human, spiritual and natural worlds
Fostering active citizenship	Developing engaged citizens	• Look critically at how the classroom is structured • Participate in democratic processes • Identify and critique undemocratic practices

Critical Purposes in Practice

A basic assumption of a 'big E' critical curriculum is that it is embedded in different ways in disciplines, cultures and ways of thinking. This does not mean that there are uncountable numbers of curriculum designs without anything in common. Rather, critical purposes in a 'big E' critical curriculum feature in every curriculum but may be applied differently in different contexts. Table 9.1 attempts to summarize the purposes embedded in 'big E critical' curricula.

Knowledge in a 'Big E' Critical Curriculum

Without valid knowledge there is no curriculum. But the meaning of valid knowledge is contested. The contest is mainly between those who claim it as objective and representational of reality and those who see it as subjective and socially constructed. To me neither position convinces. I assume that there is real valid knowledge, but it may not be known at a given time or it changes. This fallibilist view of knowledge is widely supported. Kuhn's (1999) work on scientific paradigm change lends credibility to the view that knowledge can be and is constantly challenged and changed. Writers in the hermeneutic tradition like Hirsch, Gadamer, Habermas and Derrida perceive the truth value of knowledge to be open to a wide variety of interpretations (Kinsella 2006). Feminist writers have long questioned the truth of what they consider to be male constructions of reality (hooks 2003). Writers asserting the knowledge claims of first peoples challenge the hegemony of western knowledge claims (Smith 2005). A realist like Popper (1992) seems to accept that even in its strong objective form, knowledge consists of theories and arguments, not incontrovertible truth. Curriculum knowledge then depends on multiple factors for its validity. It is theorized through many intellectual, cultural and social filters based on gender, ethnicity or class; and on the power exercised by political and disciplinary 'official knowledge' (Apple 2012). Valid knowledge in a curriculum is real but is always challengeable as it is only a best attempt to make sense of the world and explore possibilities (Young 2014).

A 'big E' critical curriculum challenges official knowledge as the only valid real knowledge and so offers alternative possibilities to the neoliberal mainstream. Its defining characteristic is criticality. According to Brookfield (2000) critical curriculum knowledge has four functions. One he calls ideological critique. This holds that certain belief systems such as neoliberalism impose one way of thinking. This creates inequities in education and society at large. Another is rooted in humanist psychology. According to this, people want to develop themselves to their full potential. To achieve this, they must be able to examine their experiences critically. A third function is philosophical. This holds that we do not learn effectively unless we know how to identify and refute false arguments. We do this when we examine the factual and logical bases of meanings and when we critically reflect on ideologies and our own assumptions. A fourth function flows from fallibilism; that valid knowledge is changeable but offers clear accounts of what knowledge is justifiable at a given point in time. Subject fields as well as diverse ethnic, socioeconomic, gender and religious traditions construct views of what knowledge is justifiable. Overarching such functions is criticality which must be learnt as a vital and problem identifying and solving part of any curriculum. Yet criticality is often neglected in mainstream engagement. In a 'big E' critical curriculum, engagement involves active involvement in critical thinking about knowledge of the self, the ideological standpoints represented in a curriculum and underlying issues with disciplinary and social knowledge.

According to Freire (1972) at the heart of a critical curriculum is *conscientization*. This is awakened by knowledge enabling self-awareness in students of who they are, what they know, their place in the world and what they must yet know and do to meet the requirements of their field of study. Self-awareness also enables them to gauge the effects on themselves and others of social, political and economic conditions in the world. To become more self-aware students are taught to critically reflect. Critical reflection embedded in a critical curriculum helps students identify faulty facts or logic in the thinking and reflection of others, recognize and challenge ideas that ensure the dominance of certain ideologies, examine their own reflections and assumptions about the world in the light of how others explain theirs, and actively work to improve to reach their potential. But students do not automatically become self-aware or critically conscious. To achieve this requires students to be fully engaged in their learning. Barnett and Coate (2005) visualize three interrelated curriculum tasks for gaining self-awareness. The first enables students to know how to make legitimate claims in a world of uncertainty and to negotiate challenges to such claims. The second helps them know how to act constructively in the world. The third task grows self-awareness how to affect a world that is open, fluid, contested and in need of courageous knowledge acts. In short, knowing how to critically reflect leads to understanding of how democratic practices can lead to changing what is.

Barnett and Coate's overlapping curriculum projects inspire students' engagement with the world beyond themselves. Through critical reflection *conscientization* provides students with knowledge how to act to affect their sociocultural world (Door 2014). Barnett and Coate identify four levels of criticality in a curriculum: critical skills, reflexivity, refashioning of traditions and transformative critique. Each level requires students to acquire different knowledge that achieves different effects in the world. Critical skills enable problem solving that is deeper and wider than non-critical skills do. Reflexivity provides opportunities to critically reflect and act on students' own perceptions, experiences and actions in order to create change in their sphere of interest. Refashioning traditions requires students to challenge their own thinking and flexibly transfer this to traditions such as those in their subject field. Transformative critique in a curriculum sees students question the validity of existing knowledge in order to reconstruct aspects of their sphere of influence. These curriculum projects require students to engage in critical reflection as a matter of course. This will make an important contribution to a 'big E' critical curriculum, one that is foreshadowed in Habermas' (1987) critical domain of cognitive interests. Such a curriculum encourages students to engage with aspects of society and culture that are germane to a field of study. But, because it is holistic in design and critical in purpose a 'big E' critical curriculum enables students to think beyond their spheres of interest and influence. It mandates critiques of oppression, power imbalances and undemocratic practices and engagement in social and political action.

Personal and political conscientization demands a 'big E' critical curriculum that prioritizes thinking outside the boundaries defined by text. This requires a curriculum that teaches to deconstruct written, oral or symbolic messages (Derrida 1967/ 1978). Engagement with such thinking is needed whatever subject area a curriculum addresses. A critical curriculum ensures that students know what it is to think in this way. Minimally, they are taught four key principles: to identify faulty facts or logic in the thinking and reflection of others (Cottrell 2011); to recognize and challenge ideas that ensure the dominance of certain ideologies (Brookfield and Holst 2011); to examine their own reflections and assumptions about the world in the light of how others explain theirs (Barnett 1997) and to actively work to improve self so they can reach their potential (Rogers 1969). These principles have two applications. They require, first, being able to find fault. Being deconstructive in this sense is to spot a problem with an idea, fact, structure or action; analyze, research and reflect on the problem and argue solutions convincingly. Deconstruction may identify acceptable alternatives to the faulty one. Second, a critical curriculum teaches students to recognize and challenge ideas that ensure the dominance of certain ideologies; to examine their own reflections and assumptions about the world in the light of how others explain theirs; and to work actively to improve themselves so that they reach their potential. The first application provides the knowledge to learn a process; the second transforms them into critical beings (Barnett 1997).

McFadden and Munns (2002, p. 357) quote the following aphorism from the work of Bernstein: "if the culture of the teacher is to become part of the consciousness of the child, then the culture of the child must first be in the consciousness of the teacher". This implies that if curriculum knowledge is to be accepted as valid by students, the curriculum must demonstrate consciousness of and give voice to their world views and understanding of what is valid knowledge. The aphorism addresses the ongoing challenges faced in higher education when students from underrepresented or even oppressed (not white, male, western, middleclass, heterosexual and able bodied) populations reject knowledge and learning offered in mainstream education. A 'big E' critical curriculum recognizes that for students from such backgrounds mainstream knowledge comes from nowhere they can identify with or recognize as including their own previous knowledge and experience. To meet this challenge, the standpoints of such students as offering valid knowledge to the field of study are highlighted. Au (2012) draws on standpoint theory to sketch how an inclusive standpoint curriculum can be developed. He argues that it carries with it acceptance and application of knowledge not of the mainstream; challenges and possibly changes the hegemony of that knowledge by developing a consciousness of inclusion; develops as a result a consciousness of opposition to the status quo; and offers a new approach to knowledge production. The inclusion of diverse standpoints in a curriculum enables all students to see that knowledge comes from somewhere familiar.

The application of standpoint theory in the curriculum expands students' consciousness of the world. It enables them to engage with knowledge well beyond the technical favoured in a neoliberal curriculum. In any field of study becoming conscious of diverse standpoints develops political literacy (Douglas 2002). This is not a priority in most mainstream curricular. Indeed knowing how the world works in a wider political sense is often excluded from them. A 'big E' critical curriculum on the other hand expects political literacy even beyond appreciating diverse standpoints. Political literacy of how and why education and society work the way they do becomes important. On a macro-level such a curriculum includes materials relevant to a field of study. It investigates how policies affecting the field and the students being socialized into it are made, why they are made, what is right and wrong about existing policies and what students can do to change them. Students working in the field are tasked with questioning why ideals transmitted in the classroom may not be evident in the field. On a micro-level the political literacy component of a curriculum explains how power, relationships and practices circulate in the classroom. Specifically, such a curriculum makes visible the politics of the classroom. For example, different approaches to teaching, specific curriculum inclusions and exclusions and evaluation techniques are openly and perhaps critically discussed. Political literacy also enables meaningful exploration of the hidden applications of power in the classroom. In particular, these relate to questions about whose voices are heard and whose are not.

Possibilities for the future are more assumed than discussed in a mainstream curriculum. Where they are investigated explicitly as part of the curriculum, the future is mainly concerned with preparing students for employment, explaining skill and attitudinal requirements and adapting flexibly to foreseeable changes in students' chosen field of study. The future is seen in economic terms and the curriculum is focused on identifying and maximizing trends in employment opportunities. Where the future is seen as problematic, solutions focus on developing flexibility and adaptability. A critical curriculum also is committed to enabling students develop understanding about the future of work. But additionally, it expects students to acquire knowledge and courage to critique givens and identify opportunities to influence and even sometimes tweak them. Such a curriculum teaches students about the future in more critical terms. This involves thinking about the past and present of a subject and exploring the multiple pathways the past and present may open. Learning includes speculating about personal, educational and occupational futures and engaging in, what Toffler calls the politics of the preferable (Voros 2003). Here students develop ideas about preferred policies and educational strategies based on their values, assumptions, preferences and debate

Table 9.2 Critical knowledge in a 'big E' critical curriculum

Critical Knowledge	Focus	Learning tasks
Fallibility of knowledge	The truth value of knowledge is not stable	• Consider how special interests help shape curriculum knowledge • Recognize knowledge held by special interests • Question such knowledge
Official knowledge	The curriculum is shaped by knowledge that supports the dominant ideology	• Critique ideologies • Seek knowledge that is justifiable true belief • Examine experiences critically • Identify and refute false arguments
Conscientization	Students are self-aware of social, political and economic conditions in the world	• Critical reflection on own beliefs • Critical reflection on how to act constructively in society • Contribute to refashioning invalid knowledge traditions • Engage in transformative critique
Deconstruction	Identify faulty facts, logic and bias in knowledge	• Question dominant ideologies • Examine own reflections in the light of such questioning • Actively work to improve self in response to own and others' reflection
Value diverse standpoints	Knowledge held by underrepresented and oppressed groups is valuable	• Critically reflect on knowledge not of the mainstream • Challenge mainstream knowledge by developing a consciousness for inclusion • Develop a new approach to knowledge production
Political literacy	How and why policies are made	• Identify strengths and weaknesses of policies • Critique weaknesses • Analyze how official knowledge and power circulates in the classroom and society
Future focus	Speculating about a preferable possible future in discipline, culture and diverse contexts	• Identify trends in own discipline and society generally • Construct a possible desirable discipline and personal future • Critique trends and their possible consequences

these in open classroom and other forums as a basis for developing self and social consciousness. Engagement in this form of future thinking helps students to develop a sense of critical realism about knowledge and teaches students about its conjectural nature (Bell 1998).

Critical Knowledge in Practice

Although knowledge is at the core of a curriculum, its nature is widely debated. To make a claim for 'one true' knowledge seems dangerous and I do not make it. Different disciplines and cultures make different truth claims for knowledge. This section in this chapter on critical knowledge is designed to bypass the debate about the truth values of disciplinary and cultural knowledge by suggesting that critical knowledge is external to that debate and should be central to every curriculum. Table 9.2 offers a picture of critical knowledge in a 'big E' critical curriculum.

Values

Curriculum values underpin purposes, norms, standards, rules and expected behaviours of students in a teaching–learning environment (Halstead and Taylor 2000). Whether they learn in large or small groups, are similar or diverse, student values are shaped by explicit or implicit patterns of principles in a curriculum. Explicit values are those conveyed through a discipline and are at the curriculum's core. They apply wherever and whenever the discipline is studied. Their continuity and change are in the hands of experts. Implicit curriculum values are principles and beliefs from outside the subject field. They are part of the learning–teaching environment that surrounds and overlaps the explicit values of the subject area studied. They may convey broader academic values such as literacy, but also express political, cultural and ethical values introduced by policy makers, teachers and also students. As they engage with a curriculum, students help develop, contribute to and maintain cultural practices through explicit and implicit values that fit together to form coherent value clusters or patterns of principles and beliefs. These coherent value clusters prevent a curriculum from becoming a collection of ill-fitting parts (Messenger 2015). The influence of implicit curriculum values determines as much as the subject matter whether a curriculum is mainstream or critical. Individual employability, competence, enterprise and compliance are values underpinning the mainstream curriculum. Political action based on beliefs about criticality, democracy, collegiality and change describes the values of a 'big E' critical curriculum.

Barnett's (1997) description of four levels of critical knowledge suggests that critical values are present in all curricular, regardless of whether they are explicit in the subject matter or implicit in the teaching–learning environment. But values are not uniform in subject fields as some disciplines are more open to critical values than others. For example, a discipline replete with empirically informed facts that have to be rote learnt is perhaps less open to accommodate critical, democratic and collegial values than disciplines that are more interpretative or speculative. It would be unwise, therefore, to assign generic or universal critical values across disciplines. Values are not uniform in diverse learning–teaching environments either. But implicit curricular are generally more open to influence from critical theory. For example, the utopian cluster of values in Brameld's (1965/2000) work may strike root implicitly in the curriculum as it forms around disciplines rather than in the disciplines themselves. Reconstructionism is a philosophy made up of value clusters that envisages the creation of a radical democratic society in which teachers and students analyze critically what is wrong with current educational values and work towards values that shape a more democratic future. Administrators, teachers and students together shape this implicit curriculum by infusing critical values into the teaching–learning environment. I do not claim that such values emerge without struggle or opposition and certainly not uniformly as neoliberal values remain strongly embedded in curricular. Nevertheless it is the learning–teaching environment that enables a critical 'big E' curriculum to flourish and that is the focus for the remainder of this section.

Other critical value clusters present in a 'big E' critical curriculum highlight dialogue. Dialogue demands engagement by all members of a learning–teaching community in problem solving, developing self and social awareness, interacting positively with others, becoming critical learners and understanding contemporary social life (Groothoff, cited in Biesta 2011). The work of Habermas and Freire (see Chap. 7) is crucial in dialogue becoming a key value in a critical environment. For Habermas (1987) dialogue, in the form of communicative action, counters the instrumentalism that is built into neoliberalism. It is a form of dialogue that aims for consensus based on a debate about validity claims. Dialogue here is conceived as a reciprocal and courteous debate in which two or more relatively equal individuals address a problem by asking questions and replying to them. The participants do not seek to win the discussion or argument, but aim for a consensus about truth and how to proceed. Where evidence is convincing agreement is possible. While the possibility of dialogue actually achieving consensus by rational means is questionable, the potential value of consensus seeking dialogue in education is not. In a slightly different way Freire (1972) also cites dialogue as a critical value in a curriculum. It is a multi-faceted value. It rejects banking education which shapes students as compliant and information absorbing learners and supports problem posing education which creates active learners engaged in praxis. Praxis values both reflection and practice; it promotes both studying and acting in the world by means of conscientization.

Standpoint theory provides the foundation for another important cluster of values in a 'big E' critical curriculum. This espouses values opposed to the generically oriented neoliberal mainstream, develops a culture of inclusion of a variety of values and offers a new approach to knowledge production. For the purpose of this chapter hooks and Smith (see Chap. 7) provide inspiration for inclusion as a critical curriculum value. Hooks (1994/2006) opposes the rise of a dominator culture fuelled by gender and racial injustices that limit learning. She rejects political, cultural and social norms and advocates transgressions against them as a way of challenging dominator culture. Challenge can free students as well as teachers from fear, help them to value difference and help build a world of shared values. Challenging dominator culture makes space in a curriculum for alternative values held by the currently powerless like women, the poor and ethnic minorities to achieve respect. Smith (1999, 2005) focuses on indigenous research and the dominance of western scientific methodologies at the expense of indigenous ones which are considered to be 'other. This dominance trades qualitative richness and complexity for scientific simplicity. If accepted, her analysis leads to curricula that acknowledge indigenous values as equal to mainstream ones. Smith (2005) makes clear that she writes from indigenous historical, political and moral spaces rooted in resistance to colonialism, political activism and goals for social justice. In a critical learning–teaching environment positive outcomes in this struggle could lead to an acceptance of alternative value clusters.

The neoliberal curriculum in higher education is hegemonic. A 'big E' critical curriculum contests this and anticipates change to a post neoliberal future for engagement. Instead of focusing on the future of the engaged individual, it spotlights the whole ecosystem in which the individual plays but a part. Engagement is to create change. This orientation to the future reveals another cluster of values informing a 'big E curriculum'. Whereas the future in a mainstream curriculum is assumed to be stable and a continuation of the present; in a 'big E' critical curriculum it is fluid, uncertain and contestable. Students and graduates believe they have opportunities to change the status quo and to create a more democratic, inclusive and socially just future for themselves and others. Student engagement becomes an agent of change and hope by diluting its elective affinity with neoliberalism. Freire (1972) and hooks (2003) both call for a pedagogy of hope. Such a pedagogy is sponsored in a curriculum that enables students to become self-aware as human beings, interact positively with others, become critical learners, understand contemporary social life and actively help shape its future, understand and engage with the ends and means of higher education and act constructively within different contexts and institutions (Groothoff, cited in Biesta 2011). Such a curriculum accepts that engagement is political and full of strife; that students in addition to their studies in a discipline learn how to read and change the world. The complexity that is engagement is accepted, even embraced.

Critical Values in Practice

Disciplines, cultures and contexts have their own explicit sets of values embedded in curricula. Critical values about purposes and knowledge are also held and promoted within these specific curricula. Table 9.3 attempts to show how such values may be developed in practice.

Table 9.3 Critical values in a 'big E' critical curriculum

Critical values	Focus	Learning tasks
Reflecting on curriculum values	Explicit and implicit curriculum values	• Criticality • Democracy • Collegiality • Change
Dialogue	Speaking, listening, debating	• Interacting positively • Hearing student voice • Listening • Social awareness
Alternative standpoints	Learning about and respecting standpoints not of the mainstream	• Learning about domination • Critique dominator culture • Challenge dominator culture
Change	Engagement for a different future	• Understand the neoliberal future • Learn ways to challenge this • Aspire to democratic change

An Example of a 'Big E' Critical Curriculum in Action

In this chapter I have outlined theoretical and practical aspects of a 'big E' critical curriculum. Such a curriculum centres on purposes, knowledge and values in engagement that are beyond the mainstream and pedagogy. It leads students to a growing awareness of self, society and the ecosystem; and enables them to critique mainstream knowledge, values and practices in pursuit of greater social justice. A 'big E' critical curriculum is not just another generic and universal recipe for curriculum design. The nature of subject matter, composition of learning groups, their geographical location and cultural dispositions, their ideological orientations and levels of instruction ensure that 'Big E' critical curricula are diverse.

One question remains: how might a 'big E' critical curriculum play out in practice? This chapter concludes with a glimpse of a living curriculum beyond the neoliberal mainstream. It draws on the work of Susan Deeley (2015) who describes what students may learn through a critical service-learning curriculum. Deeley describes one learning experience from a service-learning curriculum of a female student in Thailand. One part of the course asked students to report and reflect on learning from critical incidents (pp. 114–115). A critical incident is a learning event that is disorienting. It is critical because it leads to change by forcing us to question and change our actions, adjust our knowledge and critically inspect our values. Critical incidents are a common feature in a curriculum and are applied via pedagogy. The incident reported here involves critical reflection, critical thinking and critical action just as envisaged by Freire.

The student's service placement required the visit to a Buddhist temple. She was accompanied by a monk. She knew to keep an appropriate distance from the monk as they entered one of the grand temples. She asked the monk to be the subject of a photograph for which he posed happily. Then she tried to hand him her camera to photograph her in the temple. He refused. She was disorientated and questioned her knowledge of social and religious behaviour in a Buddhist setting. Reflecting, she realized that monks could not take anything directly from a woman. So she laid the camera on the ground. The monk picked it up to take her photograph. The important learning for her occurred during a critical reflection on the experience. She realized that her knowledge of Thai culture was incomplete so that her purpose of the monk taking her photograph could not be achieved. She also realized that the values she lived by as a modern western woman were not shared by Buddhist monks. Wanting to have a record of herself and the monk in this exotic setting led her to make an error of judgement. She was very hard on herself in her critical reflection, concluding "this incident reveals a level of my ethnocentrism....[M]y subsequent reflections will lead me to acting in a more ethnorelative manner" (Deeley 2015, p. 115).

References

Allman, P. (2010). *Critical education against global capitalism. Karl Marx and revolutionary critical education*. Rotterdam, The Netherlands: Sense Publishers.

Apple, M. (2012). Introduction. In M. Au (Ed.), *Critical curriculum studies: Education, consciousness and the politics of knowing* (pp. xii–xv). New York, NY: Routledge.

Au, M. (2012). *Critical curriculum studies: Education, consciousness and the politics of knowing*. New York, NY: Routledge.

Barnett, R. (1997). *Higher education: A critical business*. Buckingham, UK: The Society for Research into Higher Education and Open University Press.

Barnett, R. (2009). Knowing and becoming in the higher education curriculum. *Studies in Higher Education, 34*(4), 429–440. doi:10.1080/03075070902771978

Barnett, R., & Coate, K. (2005). *Engaging the curriculum in higher education*. Maidenhead, UK: Society for Research into Higher Education and Open University Press.

Bell, W. (1998). Understanding the futures field. In D. Hicks & R. Slaughter (Eds.), *Futures education: World yearbook of education*. London, UK: Kogan Page.

Bernstein, B. (1996). *Pedagogy, symbolic control and identity: Theory, research, critique*. London, UK: Taylor and Francis.

Biesta, G. (2006). *Beyond learning: Democratic education for a human future*. London, UK: Paradigm Publishers.

Biesta, G. (2011). Disciplines and theory in the academic study of education: A comparative analysis of the Anglo-American and continental construction of the field. *Pedagogy, Culture and Society, 19*(2), 175–192.

Brameld, T. (1965/2000). *Education as power: A re-issue by the Society of Educational Reconstruction*. New York, NY: Holt, Rinehart & Wilson.

Brookfield, S. (2000). The concept of critically reflective practice. In A. Wilson & E. Hayes (Eds.), *Handbook of adult and continuing education* (pp. 33–50). San Francisco, CA: Jossey Bass.

Brookfield, S. (2005). *The power of critical theory: Liberating adult learning and teaching*. San Francisco, CA: Jossey Bass.

Brookfield, S. (2013). *Powerful techniques for teaching adults*. San Francisco, CA: Jossey Bass.

Brookfield, S., & Holst, J. (2011). *Radicalizing learning: Adult education for a just world*. San Francisco, CA: Jossey Bass.

Cervero, R., & Wilson, A. (2001). *Power in practice: Adult education and the struggle for knowledge and power in society*. San Francisco, CA: Jossey Bass.

Charlton, B. (2002). Audit, accountability, quality and all that: The growth of managerial technologies in UK universities. In S. Prickett & P. Erskine-Hill (Eds.), *Education! Education! Education! Managerial ethics and the law of unintended consequences* (pp. 18–28). Exeter, UK: Imprint Academic.

Cottrell, S. (2011). *Critical thinking skills: Developing effective analysis and argument* (2nd ed.). Basingstoke, UK: Palgrave MacMillan.

Deeley, S. (2015). *Critical perspectives on service-learning in higher education*. London, UK: Palgrave Macmillan.

Derrida, J. (1967/1978). *Of grammatology* (G. Spivak, Trans.). Baltimore, MD: John Hopkins University Press.

Door, V. (2014). Critical pedagogy and reflexivity: The issue of ethical consistency. *International Journal of Critical Pedagogy, 5*(2), 88–99.

Douglas, A. (2002). Educating for real and hoped for political words: Ways forward in developing political literacy. Retrieved from http://www.citized.info/?r_menu=res_art&strand=4

Freire, P. (1972). *Pedagogy of the oppressed*. Harmondsworth, UK: Penguin Books.

Habermas, J. (1987). *Knowledge and human interests* (J. Shapiro, Trans.). Oxford, UK: Polity Press.

Halstead, J., & Taylor, M. (2000). Learning and teaching about values: A review of recent research. *Cambridge Journal of Education, 30*(2), 169–202. doi:10.1080/713657146

Hooks, B. (1994/2006). *Outlaw culture: Resisting representations*. New York, NY: Routledge.

Hooks, B. (2003). *Teaching community: A pedagogy of hope*. New York, NY: Routledge.

Kinsella, E. (2006). Hermeneutics and critical hermeneutics: Exploring possibilities within the art of interpretation. *Forum: Qualitative Social Research, 7*(3). Retrieved from http://www.qualitative-research.net/index.php/fqs/article/view/145

Kuhn, T. (1999). *The structure of scientific revolutions* (3rd ed.). Chicago, IL: Chicago University Press.

Madden, B. (2015). Pedagogical pathways for Indigenous education with/in teacher education. *Teaching and Teacher Education, 51*, 1–15. doi:10.1016/j.tate.2015.05.005

McFadden, M., & Munns, G. (2002). Student engagement and the social relations of pedagogy. *British Journal of Sociology of Education, 23*(3), 357–366.

Messenger, H. (2015). The identification of a value-based pedagogical pattern promoting 'development of the person' in higher education. *Teaching in Higher Education, 20*(7), 738–749. doi:10.1080/13562517.2015.1069267

Popper, K. (1992). *Unended quest: An intellectual autobiography*. London, UK: Routledge.

Priestley, M. (2011). Whatever happened to curriculum theory? Critical realism and curriculum change. *Pedagogy, Culture and Society, 19*(2), 221–237.

Ramsden, P., & Callender, C. (2014). *Review of the national student survey: Appendix A: Literature review*. Retrieved from London, UK: http://www.hefce.ac.uk/pubs/rereports/year/2014/nssreview/#alldownloads

Rogers, C. (1969). *Freedom to learn: A view of what education might become*. Columbus, OH: Charles Merrill.

Smith, L. (1999). *Decolonizing methodologies: Research and indigenous peoples*. London, UK; Dunedin, New Zealand: Zed Books and University of Otago Press.

Smith, L. (2005). On tricky ground: Researching the native in the age of uncertainty. In N. Denzin & Y. Lincoln (Eds.), *The Sage handbook of qualitative research* (3rd ed., pp. 85–108). Thousand Oaks, CA: Sage Publications.

Voros, J. (2003). *The generic foresight process: Expanding the frame of futures enquiry and practice*. Paper presented at the Professional Development Forum, Australian Foresight Institute, Swinburn Institute of Technology, 11 November. http://hdl.handle.net/1959.3/40020

Yates, L. (2009). From curriculum to pedagogy and back again: Knowledge, the person and the changing world. *Pedagogy, Culture and Society, 17*(1), 17–28.

Young, M. (2014). What is a curriculum and what can it do? *The Curriculum Journal, 25*(1), 7–13. doi:10.1080/09585176.2014.902526

Chapter 10
Supporting Engagement Through Critical Evaluation

Abstract This chapter comprises four interrelated sections. The first asks whether student engagement can sensibly be connected to evaluation at all; and whether and how neoliberalism influences mainstream evaluation theories and practices. The second section outlines key features of mainstream evaluation in neoliberal times so that its weaknesses can be critiqued in the third. The fourth section discusses how a critical approach to evaluation might take evaluation beyond the mainstream.

We now examine *evaluation*, the third of Bernstein's (1996) interdependent educational message systems. This assesses how ably students learn taught knowledge and how well pedagogic and curriculum goals are achieved. Pedagogy and curriculum, the other two message systems were explored in Chaps. 8 and 9. As with many educational concepts, *evaluation* is more complex than appears at first sight. One reason is that evaluation is part of pedagogy and curriculum, not apart from them. A number of principles and ideas are intertwined in and shared by all three message systems; the central role of learning outcomes, for example. Another reason is that its purposes are understood in different ways. Crooks (1988) identified eight purposes for assessment: (i) admission to and placement in programmes and learning activities; (ii) motivating students to succeed through feedback; (iii) focusing learning by making clear to students what is important to learn; (iv) consolidating and structuring learning in clear ways; (v) guiding and encouraging learning through dialogue; (vi) deciding whether students are ready to move to the next step; (vii) certifying or grading whether students have achieved required learning; and (viii) evaluating teaching and programmes. Another complicating factor is that different labels are used to discuss evaluation. *Assessment* is often employed to label purposes that have to do with judging the quality and success of student learning; *evaluation* for activities that judge the quality of a programme or teaching. In this chapter, we discuss both types of purposes under Bernstein's label *evaluation*.

The chapter first asks whether and how student engagement is connected to evaluation; and whether and how neoliberalism influences mainstream evaluation. It outlines, second, key features of mainstream evaluation in neoliberal times so

N. Zepke, *Student Engagement in Neoliberal Times*,
DOI 10.1007/978-981-10-3200-4_10

that, third, its weaknesses can be exposed and critiqued. Finally, the chapter discusses how a critical approach to evaluation might take evaluation beyond the mainstream.

Connections

At first sight connections between (i) evaluation and engagement and (ii) evaluation and the neoliberal mainstream may not be obvious. Yet to lend creditability to the argument in this chapter, such connections must be made. The connection between evaluation and engagement is strong. The 'approaches to learning' construct (Marton and Säljö 1976), for example, introduced in Chap. 2 identified surface, strategic and deep approaches to engagement in learning. Whichever of these approaches to learning students engage in affects purposes for evaluation. For students adopting a surface or reproducing approach the purpose is just to meet course requirements. Consequently engagement focuses on memorizing facts and procedures and treating knowledge as bits of information assembled for the evaluation in order to pass. As a result engagement in examinations, tests and assignments is superficial. The intention of students using a strategic or organizing approach is to achieve the highest possible grades by strategically choosing between surface and deep learning to achieve their goals. Engagement is designed to achieve the best possible results with the least effort (Entwistle 2005). Entwistle also suggested that learners using the deep or transforming approach want to understand ideas for themselves. Key features of deep learning include a deep and active engagement with the evaluation process for its own sake.

Additionally, student engagement is considered to be a useful predictor of success in learning and evaluation (Kuh et al. 2008). Wyatt (2011) notes a positive correlation between student engagement and student success, including success in formal evaluations. Students who engage in learning are more likely to succeed in evaluation tasks than those who do not. This does not just apply to engagement in cognitive activities that link, analyse, synthesize and evaluate ideas. Kuh et al. (2006) have also connected aspects of engagement not associated with cognitive tasks such as motivation, interest, curiosity, responsibility, determination, perseverance, positive attitude, work habits, self-regulation and social skills to success in performances on tests, examinations and other forms of evaluation. In short, student engagement is strongly associated with evaluation as it helps to develop intellectual, emotional, behavioural, physical and social functions that lead to successful evaluation outcomes. Whether at a surface, strategic or deep level, students who engage in learning are more likely to succeed in evaluations than those who do not.

Connections between neoliberal influences, engagement and evaluation are also strong. As discussed in Chap. 5 they share an *elective affinity*. Elective affinities can develop between political ideologies and seemingly unrelated ideas and practices such as engagement in higher education (Jost et al. 2009). That does not mean that student engagement is a creature of neoliberalism as interest in engagement preceded the high tide of neoliberalism. But engagement research and practice have embraced and incorporated neoliberal beliefs and practices as a result of major and widespread ideological change in Western societies generally. The same is true of evaluation which has assumed a dominant role in neoliberal education. Yet, while evaluation policies, research and practices have adopted and even enforce neoliberal norms and language, evaluation theory and practice also maintain their own trajectories. They welcome but are not dependent on their elective affinity with neoliberalism. Consequently evaluation practices rely on their own academic traditions as well as on neoliberal norms. For example, learning objectives, a concern for validity and reliability, the use of alternative evaluation methods such as formative and ipsative evaluation have always been of interest to evaluation theorists (Scott 2016). But traditional evaluation approaches have been reshaped and sharpened to fit the neoliberal evaluation paradigm. Three key neoliberal assumptions share this elective affinity with engagement and evaluation: that what is to be learnt is practical and economically useful in the market place; that learning is about performing in certain ways in order to achieve specified outcomes; and that quality is assured by measurable accountability processes.

Evaluation of knowledge is traditionally based on disciplines. But neoliberalism has added its own requirements of evaluation by expecting that graduates are fit to serve markets as workers. This limits the scope for evaluating knowledge to competence in technical and operational workplace knowledge. According to Stuckey et al. (2014) this focus on the technical limits evaluation of knowledge to Habermas' technical domain while his interpretative and critical knowledge domains are neglected. Evaluation in neoliberal times is also very concerned with performativity: the measurement of performance using largely quantitative methods that determine whether students, programmes and teachers have met narrowly specified leaning outcomes and other performance criteria. Performativity as measured by statistics is widely expected, not only in evaluation, engagement and higher education but also in social life generally. Such measurements take on a life of their own as 'fact totems' (de Santos 2009) which can decide the future of students, programmes and institutions. Accountability is a third key neoliberal assumption that shapes both evaluation and engagement. The neoliberal use of accountability in evaluation means that performances can be audited publically (Charlton 2002). To be accountable is to be able to demonstrate that prespecified outcomes have been achieved. Such outcomes may be learning outcomes set for students, targets required of programmes or performance criteria set for teachers. According to Biesta (2004) an audit culture emerges that is keyed to an outcome orientated pedagogy, curriculum and evaluation.

Evaluation in the Neoliberal Mainstream

There is no official neoliberal model for evaluation just as there is no one prototype for student engagement. An elective affinity between evaluation and neoliberalism emerges only once shared understandings of evaluation between mainstream higher education and neoliberalism become clear. I use *Outcome-based Education* (OBE) as a proxy to reveal the elective affinity between neoliberalism and evaluation. OBE is a suitable surrogate because it contains in a single package an integrated approach to evaluation attractive to both neoliberalism and mainstream higher education. OBE was championed by the first President Bush in the USA to make education more accountable for public money spent on it (Schrag 1995). For a variety of perceived advantages involving coherence, accountability and transparency, OBE was adopted in school sectors in numerous countries such as Australia, New Zealand and South Africa (Jansen 1998). Under different names, such as competency and standards-based education, variations of OBE have also been accepted as desirable by neoliberal governments and higher education agencies throughout the Western world (Kuh et al. 2006). OBE has been adopted in 29 neoliberal oriented countries in Europe under the Bologna Declaration (Cumming and Ross 2007). The European Commission (2012) adopted OBE to address key problems in education in Europe such as chronic unemployment. Non-government bodies such as the International Engineering Alliance (2012), active in many countries adopted OBE under the provisions of the Washington Accord, a foundation stone for neoliberal international policy agreements.

So OBE ticks the policy boxes for acceptable evaluation practices in mainstream neoliberal higher education. It offers governments and institutions control of the whole educational process. The focus on diverse discipline-based content knowledge is largely replaced by practical and generic Type 2 knowledge. Type 1 knowledge is no longer the main focus for evaluation or, indeed for the learning, teaching and evaluation process. Measurable learning outcomes have assumed that role. These provide transparent evidence of accountability and performativity by showing whether outcomes have been achieved. Most mainstream higher education programmes are built on learning outcomes achieved as a result of engaging with planned educational experiences including evaluation. For teachers learning outcomes provide a clear picture of what is important to teach, how they can teach and evaluate it to prepare students for a complex and ever changing workplace. For students, learning outcomes enable a clear understanding of what is to be learnt, how they need to engage and what standards they need to achieve in order to succeed. According to Spady (1994, p. 1) "Outcome-Based Education means clearly focusing and organizing everything in an educational system around what is essential for all students to be able to do successfully at the end of their learning experiences". It focuses on and documents behavioural statements "the substance of what students have actually learned and can do, and gives educators and future employers an accurate picture of students' capabilities" (Spady 1994, p. 38).

Learning outcomes give engagement and evaluation a clear focus. They spell out the knowledge, behaviours and attitudes that enable students to demonstrate that they are able to meet the standards set by the learning outcomes. According to Spady (1994) such direct links between outcomes and evaluation create a level-playing field that enables evaluations to be fair and reliable; to measure achievements of every member of the learning community by the same criteria in the same way. Biggs and Tang (2007) suggest a holistic and constructivist design for learning to advance this tight tie between outcomes and evaluation. They propose constructive alignment to shape the whole learning process. This formalizes the connection between learning outcomes, planning engaging learning activities and evaluation. The intended outcomes indicate the activities students are to engage in to achieve the outcomes. Whether the outcomes are achieved is then determined through devising and grading evaluation tasks. Outcome statements are developed around verbs such as describe, define, explain, construct, demonstrate, evaluate in order to specify how something is to be learnt and what is to be assessed. Such verbs set standards that enable judgements to be made about whether the learning outcomes have been achieved. There are two forms of standards-based evaluation. One is competence based and compares students' performance with a standard and reports the performance as competent or not yet competent. The other is achievement based and recognizes excellence by including levels of achievement on a set standard such as letter or numerical grades.

According to Spady (1994) OBE reflects the complexities of real life now and for the future. Learning outcomes from the OBE stable therefore are both sensitive to the specific requirements of different subjects and learning contexts and also generic. For example, one generic process has developed around what Killen (2005) calls key competencies. These identify knowledge, skills and attitudes people need to live, learn, work and contribute to as active citizens. Generated in an OECD (2005) project involving 12 member countries, key competencies are organized into three overarching and generic clusters: using tools such as technology and language; interacting in heterogeneous groups; and acting autonomously. But these key competencies also accommodate numerous specific context and subject bound outcomes that can be evaluated using OBE methods. Biggs and Tang (2007) outline a taxonomy to recognize both the specific and generic nature of learning outcomes. They observed that linking learning outcomes purely to competencies neglected structural complexities involved in learning. They wanted learning outcomes to be evaluated according to the level of competency students demonstrate when their achievements are evaluated. Their *structure of the observed learning outcomes* (SOLO) provided a taxonomy of learning outcomes that enables qualitative as well as quantitative evaluation. They identified five ascending levels of evidence for learning in the SOLO taxonomy. These range from outright misunderstanding through surface to deep approaches to learning. Each level is established by dedicated verbs that describe the outcome level. Such levels enable learning outcomes and evaluation results to be carefully calibrated.

Evaluation that determines whether students have met the level of performance required by learning outcomes is summative or evaluation *of* learning. It is a judgement of the level a student has performed on in meeting the learning outcomes and decides between success and failure. This performativity and accountability view of evaluation has been softened by a shift to evaluation *for* learning. This shift is facilitated by OBE, constructive alignment and the SOLO taxonomy where evaluation is but a part of an integrated system of complex learning comprising outcomes, engagement in learning activities and evaluation (McDowell 2012). In evaluation *for* learning the emphasis shifts from summative to formative evaluation by providing valuative feedback on the quality of learning. This provides students with ongoing information on how they are currently performing on meeting learning outcomes. Brown and Race (2013) suggest seven ways to align both formative and summative evaluation with engagement in learning: evaluation that (i) helps students who want to learn rather than create anxiety; (ii) ensures learning outcomes are in constant view of learners; (iii) gives students ample practice in generating evidence that they can meet learning outcomes; (iv) provides useful feedback on the work students do in class; (v) gives quick and useful feedback on assignments and tests to help students understand what they can and cannot currently do; (vi) encourages students to coach peers on outcomes they are competent in; and (vii) deepens general competence by enabling students to assess their own learning.

But evaluation is not only about student learning. In neoliberal times performance qualities of universities, their programmes and teachers are also evaluated. Quality can be measured variously: for example, as value for money, fitness for purpose and as a process leading to student transformation (Harvey and Green 1993). Student success indicators such as retention, progression, completion, satisfaction and engagement can be appraised on all three measures of quality. For example, institutions that graduate a specified proportion of their students can be judged to provide value for money, be fit for purpose and possibly even to provide transformative experiences. Such evaluations usually include summative and formative elements that can lead to publication of both negative and positive outcomes. Results of summative evaluations can affect public perceptions, the future of programmes and the prospect of career advancement. Formative evaluations offer feedback including commendation and suggestions for improvement (Spady 1994). At least two broad accountability approaches can be identified: post course surveys and nationally conducted institutional evaluations. The former involves mainly students to provide feedback on teaching performance but can also draw in the views of interested outsiders such as employers. Such surveys are usually formative but can be monitored by managers to discipline teachers who come up short in student' evaluations (Yorke and Longden 2004). The second method revolves around institutional and programme evaluations conducted by external agents that visit universities on a regular basis. They report on the performance of institutions on a wide array of criteria, usually involving OBE criteria. Such reports are published and provide a powerful accountability mechanism.

Critique

It seems almost churlish to critique neoliberal understandings of evaluation. Its OBE, standards and performance-based proxies certainly seem to package all aspects of learning into coherent yet complex outcomes linked to an engaging pedagogy and evaluation methods. Learning outcomes indicate expectations of significant learning and so OBE can prepare students to be competent in life at work and in the community using transparent, fair and reliable evaluation methods. It enables institutions to provide value for money, be fit for purpose and maybe transformative. In short, OBE in neoliberal times seems to have the potential to make constructive contributions to individual and institutional performance; to ensure quality in engagement and learning. Yet, this positive interpretation neglects the debates and criticisms surrounding OBE and other competency and standards-based models of education and evaluation. In the main the debates take opposing positions on whether OBE's reliance on learning outcomes, constructive alignment and approaches to learning restricts and narrows learning into a purely technical process that fits graduates into the neoliberal workplace (Jansen 1998). In this section we examine some of the limiting impacts of OBE and similar mainstream systems on student engagement and evaluation. I focus the critique on learning outcomes concerned with competence rather than knowledge and values; the positivist meaning given to competence and the neglect of humanist and critical interpretations; the strong emphasis on political and economic meanings of accountability and performativity and the neglect of other views (Macfarlane 2016); the linking of fairness and reliability with sameness; the overlooked connection between evaluation and culture; and the audit approach to quality assurance processes.

A first important critique of OBE and allied competency and standards-based evaluation approaches is that it leads to a technical and reductionist view of evaluation that is narrowly focused on accountability and performativity of employment-related skills (Macfarlane 2016). Evaluation's goal here is to identify what students can do as a result of learning, not what they know or value. Under the influence of neoliberal policy OBE has become a funnel for channelling learning into operational competencies rather than into exploring knowledge and values. While this restricted evaluation approach is probably different to Spady's (1994) original transformational vision for OBE, it does satisfy the requirements of the mainstream neoliberal mindset. Rather than being holistic indicators of significant learning, learning outcomes and their evaluation focus on operational 'how to' competencies that demote knowledge and values to what is absolutely necessary for efficient behaviour. Biggs and Tang's (2007) description of constructive alignment and SOLO taxonomy further operationalize evaluation by tying learning outcomes to verbs like identify, enumerate, compare, contrast, theorize, evaluate. Such verbs restrict the ability to assess knowledge for its own sake and almost void opportunities to evaluate values. Barnett (1994) observed that of his three models of competence—academic, operational and critical—only operational competence

flourishes in neoliberal times. Academic competence, centred on Type 1 proposi-
tional knowledge regresses to a mere commodity supporting operational competence. Barnett's critical competence model, focused on values around democratic
dialogue, reflection and consensus, is largely replaced by a neoliberal reading of
citizenship in OBE.

Another critique is that OBE and similar models are closely tied to behaviourist
psychology. As discussed in Chap. 6 behaviourist psychology is part of what Walsh
et al. (2014) argue belongs to a natural-scientific paradigm. This holds to an ide-
alized view of science in which facts are value free, established by empirical
evidence and correct ways of seeing the world. Evaluation is objective, validated by
following clear criteria, methods and processes (Scott 2016). Scott observes that
there are other evaluation models that are not behaviourist or value-free and
objective. He identifies interpretivist, critical and postmodern views that render the
natural-scientific psychological model contestable. Interpretive and critical thinkers,
for example, look for alternative evaluation models of learning, teaching and
institutional performance that reject meanings of success reduced to a set of prespecified, behavioural and measurable learning or administrative indicators. To
them learning success cannot be determined by prespecified learning outcomes,
externally set indicators or criteria. Scott provides a useful summary of such
alternative evaluation models. In an interpretative model the meaning of success is
negotiated by all actors engaged in classroom practice such as students, teachers
and managers, not predetermined by outsiders. Critical theorists look for action in
evaluation that is informed by reading the world for a sense of social, economic and
ecological justice that gives voice to traditionally marginalized people and so
subverts the agendas of those with ideological power. In both alternative models
evaluation relates to the world and not just to work.

Another critique considers the influence of political and economic reason on
OBE and evaluation. As discussed earlier, the elective affinity between engagement
and neoliberalism is strongly influenced by an agenda to commodify knowledge
and achieve performativity and accountability. Learning outcomes guiding
OBE-type evaluations promote and enforce this agenda. As suggested above,
academic competence represented by Type 1 knowledge is largely absent from this
agenda. Instead learning outcomes, engaging learning activities and evaluations are
set up to show that students have acquired knowledge for economic success.
Quality learning requires learners to gain such useful knowledge in pedagogically
suitable ways (Entwistle 2003). But this view focuses narrowly on technical and
instrumental human interests ignoring knowledge that might be emancipatory.
Learning outcomes also help evaluate learning in ways that measure and report
student, teacher and institutional performance. Summative and formative evaluation
becomes a technology of control that judges, compares and often publicizes performances and so creates feelings of emotional compliance that pressure students to
perform in certain ways (Fielding 2006). Accountability in turn supports a culture
of teaching, learning and evaluation that Biesta (2004) dubs an audit culture.
Evaluation ensures that appropriate learning outcomes and evaluation protocols
conform to politically and economically desired outcomes. The education systems

created by OBE and its competency and standards-based cousins remind of *governmentality* which refers to the way conduct is normalized within societies by forging a consensus about what is important—in this case higher education (Lemke 2007).

A fourth critique focuses on the way fairness and equity are conceptualized in mainstream evaluation. OBE informed evaluation theory and practice under neoliberalism tries to balance two contrasting views of fairness and equity (McArthur 2015). On the one hand the demands of accountability and performativity require that what students produce in evaluations should be judged in the same way according to the criteria set in learning outcomes. Evaluations reflecting this view are primarily concerned with judging the product of learning consistently, transparently and free of value judgements according to the same standards regardless of subject, context and characteristics of students. McArthur (2015) argues that accountability, performativity and consistency win out because recognition of difference or individuality is constrained to what the learning outcomes require. Consequently "the ways in which fairness is often understood rest(s) on procedural notions of justice: ensuring the right procedures will ensure students are assessed fairly" (McArthur 2015, p. 3). This view of fairness is supported by students who often view themselves as customers with consumer rights to fair and equitable treatment. This leads them to favour sameness over difference in treatment. For example, they want institutions to assess in ways that enables them to compare themselves to others by judging the quality of their own education against other universities based on published evaluation results (Medland 2016).

A fifth critique of OBE-type evaluation again tackles fairness and equity. But now it concerns the way neoliberal social and cultural beliefs and practices avoid evaluation practices that recognize differences in culture. Medland (2016) argues that the evaluation culture that rules higher education favours monocultural Western assumptions and educational practices of fairness and equity. Employers, national quality assurance agencies and the general public assume that graduates have met common standards governed by Western cultural norms. That students themselves not only support but demand adherence to this culture, suggests that sameness will continue to be the dominant meaning of fairness and equity into the future. Leathwood (2005) argues that sameness in evaluation is so important because it is closely interwoven with relations of power. It sidesteps the unequal distribution of power between educators and students because teachers and graduates have run the same race, faced the same difficulties and shown their mettle in successfully finishing the evaluation race. This monocultural view of evaluation is unfair as neoliberal governments have sought to attract diverse cultural groups, yet deny that they are different when it comes to evaluation. But diverse cultures are not just about ethnicity as there are many cultures in higher education. As Madden (2015) found in her literature synthesis of the educational needs of first peoples in Canada, one way will not do justice to diverse cultures in higher education. Fairness and equity structured around predetermined learning outcomes and constructive alignment cannot deal justly with cultural differences (McArthur 2015).

A final critique broached here centres on the performativity and accountability processes employed to judge whether teachers and universities as well as students meet the quality standards established by governments and other stakeholders. Such processes often require numeric evidence about dodgy engagement indicators such as student attendance and in-class participation. Students, teachers and institutions must engage with such indicators in the expectation that they will demonstrate quality performance (Macfarlane 2016). Raban (2007) questioned that an accountability culture can lead to quality enhancement. He argues that audit accountability leads to a relative lack of interest in quality enhancement. An avoidance of risk, stifled innovation and suppressed desire for change results. Moreover, he suggests, that audit systems focused on public comparative performance statistics are weakly integrated into the educational purposes of higher education and also engagement. Jennings (2007) reinforces this general critique by arguing that quality audits are primarily focused on measuring institutional performance and student outputs/outcomes against external standards, not on how to enhance the quality of institutional research, teaching, learning, community engagement and the student learning experience. Scott (2016) observes that accountability systems are generally based on a mixture of central control to assure that government priorities are met and consumer interests, where the requirements of stakeholders, particularly employers, are added to government priorities. While Scott does not discuss neoliberalism, his analysis suggests that audit accountability serves technical interests and governmentality. This kind of evaluation seeks objectivity, rationality, empirical evidence and operational usefulness; precisely the qualities valued in neoliberal times.

Towards a More Critical Approach to Evaluation

Critique requires a response that rebuts criticism or offers an alternative. We will take the latter approach but not to scuttle mainstream practices altogether. This alternative assumes that it is possible to reshape neoliberal approaches to evaluation into more critical ones. But what does that mean? Evaluation is part of learning, not apart from it and therefore shares assumptions and practices with pedagogy and curriculum which were discussed in Chaps. 7–9 as a critical alternative to mainstream engagement. The ideas in these chapters, such as Freire's *conscientization,* transfer to evaluation. With pedagogy and curriculum focusing students on building critical self-awareness of their own and others' lives, a critical evaluation judges students' awareness of social, political and economic conditions in the world as well as their readiness for the job market. A critical evaluation assesses students' ability to critically reflect on their own learning, be actively engaged in the evaluation process, identify faulty facts and logic, recognize and challenge ideas of dominant ideologies, actively work to improve their own well-being and that of others and work to achieve social justice beyond the procedural notions of fairness. Au (2012) echoes Bernstein in outlining a critical approach to evaluation: (i) its *purpose* is to assess students' capabilities to operate within yet change a complex world; (ii) to make sense of operational, discipline and critical *knowledge*; and (iii) to *value* engagement that is broad, deep and builds consciousness of the wider world in critical and liberating ways.

Purposes

As we observed previously, learning outcomes are at the heart of mainstream evaluation. They are used currently to stand for what students are expected to know and do at the end of their course of study. They are the latest in a long line of terms and concepts used to capture how the purposes for learning and evaluation should be expressed. Allan (1997) suggested that learning outcomes could represent an inclusive way to express purposes. They do not have to, as in neoliberal evaluation practice, signify a very narrow range of standards and behaviours that students must demonstrate to show readiness for the workplace. Allan observed an ever firming linkage to behaviourism over time, but suggested that learning outcomes do not have to be behaviourist, narrow, explicit and absolute. They have tacit and contextual qualities that cannot be captured by a verb describing a behaviour. Eisner (1996, p. 103) suggested that "outcomes are essentially what one ends up with, intended or not, after some form of engagement". While recognizing the usefulness of behavioural objectives in evaluation, he added problem-solving and expressive objectives to the purposes of education. These latter purposes add tacit and unplanned personal learning objectives to behavioural ones. Eisner cannot be called a critical theorist but his two types of personal objectives connect with what critical theorists would consider to be important evaluation purposes. They recognize the importance of including a critical awareness of self and others in society to the purposes of evaluation.

In mainstream evaluation students have little part in planning its purposes and procedures. Student participation in decision-making about evaluation practices would undermine the unrestricted power currently exercised by teachers and industry through neoliberal governmentality. A more critical approach aims to be more democratic, creative, tacit and outward looking. This is possible with more power sharing with students. But we cannot assume that student participation would immediately negate the elective affinity between neoliberalism and student engagement in evaluation. Governmentality suggests that inserting students into a planning process will not change the consensus that the conduct of relationships in classrooms be determined by those in authority. Student habits of self-regulation undermine power sharing and lead to retention of the status quo (Lemke 2002). Teachers, planners and students wanting evaluation to be more democratic must trigger a change in self-regulation, in governmentality. This requires disrupting constructive alignment which binds learning outcomes, learning activities and evaluation (Hudson et al. 2015). A first step is changing the conduct of learning activities by encouraging students to engage safely and actively in consensus building communicative action (Habermas 1984) about their and others' learning. Such activities address set learning outcomes but implicitly widen them to include critical reflection, problem raising and solving about how they affect society and the world. By expanding the scope of learning activities, student–teacher partnerships also work to expand the instrumental focus of evaluation practices.

Achieving fairness is a key purpose for evaluation in neoliberal times. But as McArthur (2015) points out, fairness is couched largely in procedural terms—if the procedures are fair then so is the evaluation. The use of constructive alignment, for example, is an important indicator of procedural fairness. So is meeting set standards, particularly when they represent national or international measures of quality. The image here is that fairness is blind and impartial, neglectful of notions of equity and social justice. Yet equity requires that multiple and overlapping individual and group differences with the potential to affect evaluation results are recognized. Such differences are many and include gender, ethnicity, sexuality, health and socio-economic background. McArthur (2015, p. 2) suggests that social justice "is a two-pronged concept: it refers both to the justice of assessment within higher education, and to the role of assessment in nurturing the forms of learning that will promote greater social justice within society as a whole". Both equity and social justice are served by more democratic evaluation processes that recognize and accommodate differences in individuals and groups. These are also honoured when constructive alignment is disrupted by divergent learning activities and ideas (Hudson et al. 2015), more formative evaluation accompanied by timely and constructive feedback is practised; and peer and self- evaluation are valued (Brown and Race 2013). Perhaps most important in furthering equity and social justice is teaching students explicitly about evaluation processes as a key purpose of engagement and evaluation.

Knowledge

Knowledge is power—Francis Bacon's aphorism highlights the centrality of knowledge in evaluation. Without the ability to demonstrate that they command the 'right' kind of knowledge, students are rendered powerless. In neoliberal times the 'right' knowledge is technical and operational, necessary for success. Mainstream evaluation recognizes only technical knowledge as necessary in the market place, for well-being and the potential for influencing events (Barnett 1994). Hence knowing about technical operations and how to use them minimizes the need for other knowledge. But Habermas (1987) identified three kinds of knowledge, technical, practical and critical, as necessary components for a full range of human interests. An evaluation process that reinstates practical and critical knowledge as equal contributors to learning outcomes and evaluation widens the opportunity for successful students to exercise greater control over their lives. However, the importance of technical knowledge is not diminished in a more critical evaluation culture. This will continue to evaluate technical knowledge needed to perform work and life skills. But in addition evaluations change the nature of the technical knowledge that normally dominates mainstream evaluations. For example, analytic skills go beyond maintaining and fixing work processes, problems and enhancements. They include critical analysis of political situations affecting work, community life and the environment. While literacy and numeracy skills are recognized as very important in neoliberal consciousness, a more critical evaluation expands narrow requirements for reading, writing and arithmetic operations to critical content, textual and discourse analysis of information, media and political processes.

A more critical evaluation regime also assesses knowledge beyond the technical. It evaluates practical (academic) knowledge which is associated with Type 1 knowledge. Such knowledge is generated within academic disciplines and research traditions associated with a search for truth based on reason (Høstaker and Vabø 2005). Barnett (2009) draws on Bourdieu (1998) to offer a broader description of Type 1 knowledge, not as an alternative to technical (Type 2) knowledge, but as a partner in a more holistic representation. Type 1 knowledge has been built up over time in broad fields of intellectual effort by epistemic communities. Such fields have their own key concepts, truth criteria and modes of reason and judgement. They generate knowledge that is distinct from technical knowledge for the workplace. Where technical knowledge is generic and boundary-hops disciplinary fields, knowledge generated in disciplinary fields is distinct, but ever changing; at times new and transformative. It operates within its own boundaries and imposes its own standards. As part of the formal evaluation process, Type 1 knowledge expects students to make sense of their world. But with the ascendency of the technical Type 2 knowledge in neoliberal times, evaluation of Type 1 knowledge has declined to the point where a number of researchers suggest the need for an agenda to 'recover knowledge' in higher education and evaluation (Young 2008). They refer to Type 1 knowledge which would lead to a more critical evaluation regime because it helps students to interpret their world.

Of the knowledge triads identified by Habermas and Barnett, the third is critical. For Habermas (1987) such knowledge is about critical self-reflection to achieve a transformation of perspective that enables learners to identify false consciousness of what the world is like and their part in it. Critical knowledge has the potential to free students from personal, institutional and environmental forces that limit their control over their lives and enable them to see how they and others are controlled by political, technical, economic, sexual, racial and educational ideologies of domination. For Barnett (2009) critical knowledge brings a state of being he calls 'coming to know'; a freeing from illusion and ideology. It is critical because it develops dispositions that include a will to learn, to engage and to change. Such dispositions attract qualities such as courage, resilience integrity and openness. By coming to know, students achieve a transformation of being. Critical knowledge, while it informs pedagogy and curricular in some classrooms, is largely absent from evaluations. Learning outcomes and evaluation tasks that assess technical knowledge are normal, particularly when camouflaged as informing skills; disciplinary knowledge is acceptable when it is needed to develop skills and 'right' attitudes;

critical knowledge is dangerous because it leads to questioning the neoliberal consciousness. This makes it vitally important to feature in evaluation because such knowledge calls on a form of engagement not desired elsewhere in higher education because it enables students to act and effect change in the world.

Values

Changes in evaluation values do not occur in isolation. It is worth repeating that evaluation is part of pedagogy and curriculum, not apart from them. So changes from neoliberal to more critical values, result in a values transformation in all three of Bernstein's educational message systems—pedagogy, curriculum and evaluation. Such a transformation leads teachers, students and administrators to engage critically with what is suspect about current education beliefs and espouses values that help shape a more democratic future (Brameld 1965/2000) in both the classroom and wider society. It introduces a pedagogy (and curriculum) of hope in which equity and social justice can establish themselves against neoliberal culture (hooks 2003; Freire 1995). Transformation also leads to questioning values that focus knowledge on purely technical concerns, and teaching and learning on performativity and accountability; which according to Ball (2012, p. 19) "links effort, values, purposes and self-understanding to measures and comparisons of output". The current belief that all worthwhile effort must be countable and only what can be measured counts (Lynch 2010) holds sway no longer. Student engagement rather than being aligned with neoliberalism becomes a vehicle for change for a more democratic future. The influence of performativity and accountability diminishes and this leads to greater trust between actors in higher education. But, as I observed in Chap. 9, I do not expect such values to emerge without effort or opposition and certainly not uniformly as neoliberal values remain embedded in political and educational rationality. The transformation I write about will be hard won.

The values underpinning evaluation will probably change most reluctantly given the dominance of performativity and accountability underpinning evaluation thinking. Active engagement by students in evaluation develops only gradually. Learning outcomes, for example, continue to be set by educators and/or employers and remain prominent as signifiers of purposes and standards of quality and success. But they broaden out with emerging democratic values in pedagogy and curriculum to include tacit and expressive personal and critical objectives. Students learn to value being engaged as actors in, rather than as subjects of evaluation. Learning resulting from unplanned engagement in classroom activities is evaluated along with prespecified learning outcomes. With this expanded horizon for learning outcomes and activities, evaluation is less prescriptive than it is currently. It is evaluation's purpose to determine how well students meet official and tacit learning outcomes including reading and changing the world. Evaluation protocols are more democratic with increased student engagement in decision-making about everything from constructing learning outcomes to engaging in the evaluation process. They share, for example, responsibility for constructing and marking tests and assignments. Evaluation is less summative or high stakes and certainly less competitive as success is no longer confined to meeting narrowly confined standards controlled by the institution. Formative and self-referential or ipsative evaluation where students evaluate their own achievements over time, are valued (Hughes 2014). Fairness is not seen as sameness but as equity and social justice. Differences between people and contexts are not ignored but factored into the evaluation process.

Planning Criteria for Critical Evaluation

I have noted that critical evaluation will not be easy to achieve. Evaluation is a major bastion of power not only for teachers in higher education, but also for the preservation of neoliberal control of the education process. Evaluation is the main educational message system where neoliberal beliefs about the pre-eminence of technical skills and knowledge, performativity and accountability are made transparent and tangible. Nevertheless the question arises about *how* and *where* changes to mainstream evaluation can be achieved. I will address the 'how' question' in the next chapter. Answers to the 'where' question offer a number of possibilities. One place to challenge the neoliberal evaluation mainstream is initially in teacher, programme and institutional evaluation. Brookfield and Holst (2011) summarize a possible critical approach to evaluation in their section on *Criteria for Evaluating Programs* (p. 99). These criteria would make evaluation more democratic and more inclusive. They would ensure that student engagement becomes more agentic in evaluation and enable students to engage as full partners in planning of evaluation protocols and processes and teacher and programme evaluations. Such engagement would go beyond students offering opinions which can then be ignored.

Brookfield and Holst (2011) build their *criteria* around power and inclusion for working-class people, whom they call the dispossessed. I would agree that students from non-traditional backgrounds, including those from working-class families, are dispossessed of power in mainstream evaluation. But I am keen to see all evaluation processes become more critical and engaging, and therefore open to greater influence by the people being evaluated, be they students, teachers or institutions. Keeping this in mind, I adapt Brookfield and Holst's criteria which they framed as questions into normative statements for achieving greater democracy and inclusion in evaluation.

- Evaluation of students, teachers, programmes and institutions aim for social justice not just procedural fairness.
- Evaluation enables all people affected by evaluation processes to engage in deciding about quality.
- Evaluation recognizes that formal learning is interconnected with life and should lead to critical engagement in broader contexts.

- Evaluation ensures that political and educational ideologies guiding the educational process do not exclude the knowledge, skills and attitudes of any student.
- Evaluation ensures that graduates of programmes command the knowledge, skills and attitudes to exercise power.
- Evaluation ensures that students command the knowledge, skills and attitudes to lead.

References

Allan, J. (1997). *Curriculum design in higher education using a learning outcome- led model: Its influence on how students perceive learning.* A thesis submitted in partial fulfilments of the requirements of the University of Wolverhampton for the degree of Doctor of Philosophy. Retrieved from http://wlv.openrepository.com/wlv/handle/2436/30415 in January 2016.

Au, M. (2012). *Critical curriculum studies: Education, consciousness and the politics of knowing.* New York, NY: Routledge.

Ball, S. (2012). Performativity, commodification and commitment: An I-spy guide to the neoliberal university. *British Journal of Educational Studies, 60*(1), 17–28. doi:10.1080/00071005.2011.650940

Barnett, R. (1994). *The limits of competence: Knowledge, higher education and society.* Buckingham, UK: Society for Research into Higher Education & Open University.

Barnett, R. (2009). Knowing and becoming in the higher education curriculum. *Studies in Higher Education, 34*(4), 429–440. doi:10.1080/03075070902771978

Bernstein, B. (1996). *Pedagogy, symbolic control and identity: Theory, research, critique.* London: Taylor & Francis.

Biesta, G. (2004). Education, accountability, and the ethical demand: Can the democratic potential of accountability be regained? *Educational Theory, 54*(3), 233–250.

Biggs, J., & Tang, C. (2007). *Teaching for quality learning at University* (3rd ed.). Maidenhead, UK: Society for Research into Higher Education & Open University Press.

Bourdieu, P. (1998). *Practical reason.* Cambridge, UK: Polity Press.

Brameld, T. (1965/2000). *Education as power.* A re-issue by the Society of Educational Reconstruction. New York: Holt, Rinehart & Winston.

Brookfield, S., & Holst, J. (2011). *Radicalizing learning: Adult education for a just world.* San Francisco, CA: Jossey Bass.

Brown, S., & Race, P. (2013). Using effective assessment to promote learning. In L. Hunt & D. Chalmers (Eds.), *University teaching in focus: A learning centred approach* (pp. 74–91). London, UK: Routledge and ACER.

Charlton, B. (2002). Audit, accountability, quality and all that: The growth of managerial technologies in UK universities. In S. Prickett & P. Erskine-Hill (Eds.), *Education! Education! Education! Managerial ethics and the law of unintended consequences* (pp. 18–28). Exeter: Imprint Academic.

Crooks, T. (1988). *Assessing student performance.* HERDSA Green Guide No. 8. Kensington, Australia: Higher Education Research and Development Society of Australasia.

Cumming, A., & Ross, M. (2007). The tuning project for medicine—Learning outcomes for undergraduate medical education in Europe. *Medical Teacher, 29*(7), 636–641.

de Santos, M. (2009). Fact-totems and the statistical imagination: The public life of a statistic in Argentina 2001. *Sociological Theory, 27*(4), 466–489.

Eisner, E. (1996). Instructional and expressive objectives: their formulation and use in curriculum. In W. Popham, E. Eisner, H. Sullivan, & L. Tyler (Eds.), *Instructional objectives* (pp. 1–18). AERA monograph series on curriculum evaluation, no. 3. Chicago, Ill: Rand McNally.

Entwistle, N. (2003). *Concepts and conceptual frameworks underpinning the ETL project.* Occasional Report 3, Enhancing Teaching-Learning Environment in Undergraduate Courses. http://www.etl.tla.ed.ac.uk/docs/ETLreport3.pdf

Entwistle, N. (2005). Contrasting perspectives on learning. In: F. Marton, D. Hounsell, & N. Entwistle (Eds.), *The experience of learning: Implications for teaching and studying in higher education* (3rd (Internet) ed, pp. 3–22). Edinburgh: University of Edinburgh, Centre for Teaching, Learning and Assessment.

European Commission. (2012). *Commission presents new Rethinking Education strategy.* Press Release retrieved from Commission presents new Rethinking Education strategy, December 2015.

Fielding, M. (2006). Leadership, radical student engagement and the necessity of person-centred education. *International Journal of Leadership in Education, 9*(4), 299–313.

Freire, P. (1995). *Pedagogy of hope: Reliving pedagogy of the oppressed.* New York: Continuum.

Habermas, J. (1984). *The theory of communicative action vol. I, Reason and the rationalization of society.* Boston, MA: Beacon Press.

Habermas, J. (1987). *Knowledge and human interests.* Cambridge, UK: Polity Press.

Harvey, L., & Green, D. (1993). Defining quality. *Assessment & Evaluation in Higher Education, 18*(1), 9–34.

hooks, B. (2003). *Teaching community: A pedagogy of hope.* New York and London: Routledge.

Høstaker, R., & Vabø, A. (2005). Higher education and the transformation to a cognitive capitalism. In I. Bleiklie & M. Henkel (Eds.), *Governing knowledge: A study of continuity and change in higher education. A Festschrift in honour of Maurice Kogan* (pp. 227–243). doi:10.1007/1-4020-3504-7_14

Hudson, J., Bloxham, S., den Outer, B., & Price, M. (2015). Conceptual acrobatics: Talking about assessment standards in the transparency era. *Studies in Higher Education.* doi:10.1080/03075079.2015.1092130

Hughes, G. (2014). *Ipsative assessment: Motivation through marking progress.* London, UK: Palgrave Macmillan.

International Engineering Alliance. (2012). *International engineering alliance.* Retrieved from http://www.ieagreements.org/Washington-Accord/signatories.cfm, December 2015.

Jansen, J. (1998). Curriculum Reform in South Africa: A critical analysis of outcomes-based education. *Cambridge Journal of Education, 28*(3), 321–331. doi:10.1080/0305764980280305

Jennings, J. (2007). *The role of an independent quality assurance body in a climate of accountability: New Zealand at the crossroads.* Paper presented at the Asia-Pacific Quality Network meeting, Kuala Lumpur, 6th February.

Jost, J., Federico, C., & Napier, J. (2009). Political ideology: Its structure, functions and elected affinities. *Annual Review of Psychology, 60,* 307–337.

Killen, R. (2005). *Programming and assessment for quality teaching and learning.* Southbank, Vic: Thomson Social Science Press.

Kuh, G., Cruce,T., Shoup, R., Kinzie, J., & Gonyea, R. (2008). Unmasking the effects of student engagement on first-year college grades and persistence. *The Journal of Higher Education, 79* (5), 540–563. doi:10.1353/jhe.0.0019

Kuh G, J. Kinzie, J. Buckley, B. Bridges, and J. Hayek. (2006).*What matters to student success: A review of the literature.* Commissioned Report: http://nces.ed.gov/IPEDS/research/pdf/Kuh_Team_Report.pdf. [accessed July 2010].

Leathwood, C. (2005). Assessment policy and practice in higher education: Purpose, standards and equity. *Assessment & Evaluation in Higher Education, 30*(3), 307–324.

Lemke, T. (2002). Foucault, governmentality, and critique. *Rethinking Marxism,* 14(3), 49–64.

Lemke, T. (2007). An indigestible meal? Foucault, governmentality and state theory. *Distinktion: Scandinavian Journal of Social Theory, 15*(2), 43–64. doi:10.1080/1600910X.2007.9672946

Lynch, K. (2010). Carelessness: A hidden doxa of higher education. *Arts & Humanities in Higher Education, 9*(1), 54–67. doi:10.1177/1474022209350104

Macfarlane, B. (2016). The performative turn in the assessment of student learning: A rights perspective. *Teaching in Higher Education, 21*(7), 839–853. doi:10.1080/13562517.2016. 1183623

Madden, B. (2015). Pedagogical pathways for indigenous education with/in teacher education, *Teaching and Teacher Education, 51*, 1–15. 10.1016/j.tate.2015.05.005

Marton, F., & Säljö, R. (1976). On qualitative differences in learning: I outcome and process. *British Journal of Educational Psychology, 46*, 4–11.

McArthur, J (2015). Assessment for social justice: The role of assessment in achieving social justice, *Assessment & Evaluation in Higher Education*, doi:10.1080/02602938.2015.1053429

McDowell, L. (2012). Assessment for learning. In L. Clouder, C. Broughan, S. Jewell, & G. Steventon (Eds.), *Improving student engagement and development through assessment: Theory and practice in higher education* (pp. 73–85). London, UK: Routledge.

Medland, E. (2016). Assessment in higher education: Drivers, barriers and directions for change in the UK. *Assessment & Evaluation in Higher Education*. doi:10.1080/02602938.2014.982072

OECD. (2005). *Definition and selection of competencies: Executive summary*. Retrieved from http://www.oecd.org/pisa/35070367.pdf in December 2015.

Raban, C. (2007). Assurance versus enchancement: Less is more? *Journal of Further and Higher Education, 31*(1), 77–85.

Schrag, P. (1995). The new school wars: How outcome-based education blew up. *The American Prospect*. Retrieved from http://prospect.org/article/new-school-wars-how-outcome-based-education-blew in December 2015.

Scott, D. (2016). *New perspectives on curriculum, learning and assessment*. Heidelberg, De: Springer International.

Spady, W. (1994). *Outcome-based education: Critical issues and answers*. Arlington, VA: Association of School Administrators. Retrieved from http://files.eric.ed.gov/fulltext/ED380910.pdf

Stuckey, H., Taylor, E., & Cranton, P. (2014). Developing a survey of transformative learning outcomes and processes based on theoretical principles. *Journal of Transformative Education*, 1–18. doi:10.1177/1541344614540335

Walsh, R., Teo, T., & Baydala, A. (2014). *A critical history and philosophy of psychology: Diversity of context, thought, and practice*. Cambridge, UK: Cambridge University Press.

Wyatt, L. (2011). Nontraditional student engagement: Increasing adult student success and retention. *The Journal of Continuing Higher Education, 59*(1), 10–20. doi:10.1080/07377363. 2011.544977

Yorke, M., & Longden, B. (2004). *Retention and student success in higher education*. Maidenhead, UK: The Society for Research into Higher Education and Open University Press.

Young, M. (2008). *Bringing knowledge back in: From social constructivism to social realism in the sociology of education*. Abingdon: Routledge.

Chapter 11
Through Distributive Leadership
to Critical Engagement

Abstract This chapter poses the key question of how critical student engagement might be imported into the neoliberal mainstream. It argues that a radical form of distributive leadership provides an answer. This form of leadership brings with it changes to pedagogy, curriculum and evaluation that involve all participants, including students as leaders in educational decision-making and so remove sole leadership from teachers and managers. Key principles of radical distributive leadership are discussed in relation to student engagement. The principles are then examined in the light of current practice in three case studies from New Zealand, the United Kingdom and the United States.

By addressing two questions in this chapter, we pull together the many strands of the argument in the book:

1. How can we change student engagement from its neoliberal affinity to a more critical path?
2. How might critical student engagement be enacted?

The first question is weighed towards the theoretical; the second focuses more on action. The theory and practice embedded in these two questions are brought together by *praxis*, a concept used widely in educational, political and spiritual spheres by numerous philosophers and theorists. For example, we have met praxis before in the critical theories of Freire, Habermas and hooks. Praxis is the process by which we turn ideas into action (Arendt 1958). On one level this book has presented student engagement as an essential activity in learning and teaching in mainstream higher education. This gave student engagement an educational focus. But on another level I have challenged student engagement's elected affinity with a neoliberal agenda by suggesting theoretical and practical alternatives. Here the book is political and signifies the process by which theory can be enacted to achieve change. Chapters 6–10 developed engagement as critical theory and critical practice to retain the best of mainstream student engagement praxis, while contesting its 'sacred totems' such as Type 2 knowledge, performativity, audit accountability and

© Springer Nature Singapore Pte Ltd. 2017   187
N. Zepke, *Student Engagement in Neoliberal Times*,
DOI 10.1007/978-981-10-3200-4_11

the market economy. But how can we make the changes necessary to synthesize mainstream and critical visions of student engagement?

In response I offer a holistic and critical view of leadership that engages students, teachers and managers as active partners in a change process. I use the notion of distributive leadership to propose student engagement as a praxis that can undermine student engagement's elective affinity with neoliberalism and move it towards greater democracy and social justice. Woods and Roberts (2015) consider distributive leadership to be emergent, arising through complex interactive processes between all participants including students and so removes sole leadership in curriculum, pedagogy and evaluation from the control of teachers and managers. In previous chapters, I have argued that something similar can be said of student engagement. In a first section of this chapter, I outline how student engagement shapes up within distributive leadership. We will find that distributive leadership has a radical dimension that can encourage critical ways to engage students in concerted action towards common goals in leadership communities that enable them to share in the power of decision-making and to exercise their voice. The second section offers three case studies of student engagement through distributive leadership in action. These are drawn from New Zealand, the United Kingdom and the United States. They offer examples of how distributive leadership can support and develop student engagement both in a mainstream sense and as critical practices. The third section draws suggestions for future practice from the first two sections of the chapter.

Engaging Students in Leadership for Change

Over time leadership studies have offered many different theories and practices that have ebbed and flowed in influence. Most recently transformational leadership has been replaced by distributive leadership as the model of choice (Hartley 2010). Unfortunately, like engagement, distributive leadership suffers from a "buzzing confusion" of alternative perspectives (Leithwood et al. 2009, p. 270). There is little agreement or clarity about its core characteristics. Hartley accepts that distributive leadership can mean different things in different contexts. He draws on work by Burrell and Morgan (1979) to bring some clarity into the confusion by identifying four paradigms for distributive leadership (Table 11.1).

Table 11.1 Paradigms for distributive leadership adapted from Hartley (2010)

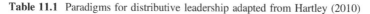

Radical Change

	Radical Humanism	Radical Structuralism	
Subjective Knowing	Interpretivism	Functionalism	Objective Knowing

Social Regulation

Of the two intersecting axes in Table 11.1, the vertical axis divides the two overarching views of the effects of distributive leadership: radical change and social regulation. Radical change presupposes that distributive leadership results in fundamental change by exposing domination and injustice; social regulation assumes maintenance of social order through cohesion, consensus and prosperity. The horizontal axis separates two opposing views of knowledge. One espouses subjectivism—the idea that knowledge is restricted to what we have experienced; the other objectivism—that knowledge is external to what we have experienced. The four paradigms emerge from the resulting quadrants. The *functionalist* paradigm sees distributive leadership as akin to the natural sciences and informed by objective facts. In the *interpretive* paradigm leaders take a hermeneutic approach by seeking mutual understanding of issues, people and operations. Leadership in *radical humanism* critiques a dominant ideology to challenge the false consciousness of individuals. In *radical structuralism* the purpose of leadership is to refocus individual consciousness to group effort that can change prevailing structures. According to Hartley (2010) the four paradigms reflect Habermas' view of human cognitive interests: the functionalist paradigm is similar to his technical—instrumental interests; the interpretive paradigm shares features with his practical interests and both radical humanism and radical structuralism are comparable to his critical interests. While according to Hartley the original Burrell and Morgan (1979) model shows the paradigms as discrete, Habermas' human interests suggest that human cognitive interest are not; all are able to contribute to the way distributive leadership is theorized and practiced.

The many meanings and uses of student engagement map readily onto these paradigms. Mainstream engagement has an affinity with neoliberalism, objective knowing and social regulation; critical engagement is aligned with subjective knowing and radical change. The transition from mainstream to critical student engagement is made possible by radical distributive leadership. Where such leadership in learning environments is radical, students are engaged as partners in a critical pedagogy, curriculum and evaluation. Both critical distributive leadership and student engagement belong to the radical dimension and its humanist and structuralist paradigms. Student engagement in distributive leadership involves concertive action with others to achieve common purposes by members of a community of practice. A community emerges either spontaneously or as a result of planning. Leadership is distributed because its members have skills and attributes needed to achieve the group's desired outcomes. Community processes and relationships are dynamic and fluid, with all community members active participants while engaging in different ways. This leads to a division of labour that takes account of the skills and attributes of community members and the requirements for leadership on specific aspects of a task. Members identify and engage with each other as a community for concertive action although they also work with their differences. Power in the community circulates among members as different knowledge and skills are needed to achieve the group's purposes. We now examine the symbiotic relationship between student engagement and distributive leadership in greater detail through the distributive leadership literature.

If the Burrell and Morgan model is rethought to recognize Habermas' view of cognitive human interests, then distributive leadership and student engagement can relate to all four paradigms. Leadership and engagement practices that seek to focus on maintaining effective social regulation in the functional or interpretive paradigms; leadership and engagement practices that want to achieve critical social change focus on radical humanism and structuralism. Critical distributive leadership has a number of characteristics, some are shared with distributive leadership generally, but some are distinctive. To adherents of social regulation distributive leadership was originally seen as an opportunity to lighten managing leaders' workload (Tian et al. 2016). But today distributive leadership is more than a delegation of tasks and responsibilities by managers or others highly placed in a policy hierarchy. Bennett et al. (2003, p. 7) identified three elements in distributive leadership theory that distinguish it from others. Most importantly, they labelled distributive leadership "as an emergent property of a group or network of interacting individuals". Another element is that the boundaries of leadership are undefined. This means that leadership can be distributed very widely, but it can also be restricted by and to leaders in managing positions. A third element holds that as expertise tends to be widely distributed in a group, so can leadership opportunities. In critical distributive leadership, leadership roles are inclusive of students who play similar leadership roles to teachers and managing leaders. They are engaged in leadership practices.

Gronn (2002) identified two possible distributive leadership processes. In one, leadership is additive, dispersed among multiple members of a group. Each member of the group can and often does take a leadership role in order to contribute to the group's function. In the other, leadership is exercised more holistically: "Here, the conduct which comprises the unit of analysis is concertive action, rather than aggregated behaviour" (Gronn 2002, p. 656). Gronn suggested that the concertive action process is the more significant. I agree as it seems more in tune with student engagement. Central to concertive action is that the purpose of leadership and engagement is to achieve shared goals. These can range from maintaining social regulation to achieving radical change. Gronn identified three patterns of concertive action in distributive leadership. In the first, spontaneous collaboration, people with different skills and attributes interact in productive relationships to complete a task of common interest. In the second pattern, role sharing, two or more people work constructively within implicit frameworks of understanding to achieve the shared purposes. In the third, formal relationships in agreed structures emerge to formalize working together, enabling leadership roles to be officially recognized. These three patterns in distributive leadership suit student engagement, particularly when it pursues radical change goals. Power is shared along with responsibilities among members of the community. Power is bottom-up and spontaneous, as when collaborating teams engage together to build networks within their communities and when working democratically on projects, with group members acting in communion.

The distributive leadership literature seems strangely moot on power. When the issue is raised, power is attributed interchangeably to dominant ideas and/or powerful agents within activity systems (Gronn 2002). But such attributions sit uneasily with the distributed cognition and activities in distributive leadership. Certainly a community pursues shared purposes, and powerful voices steer its actions from time to time. But common purposes and leading voices alone cannot explain the fluid nature of power relations. To do this, Foucault's work is useful. To Foucault, power is everywhere, not because it embraces everything, but because it comes from everywhere: "it is produced from one moment to the next, at every point, or rather in every relation from one point to another" (Foucault 1981, p. 93). In itself, power is neutral. It flows as in circuits, is episodic and its effects reside in how it is used in relationships. Yes, power can collect in disciplining regimes of truth in classrooms as well as in wider society. One such regime is that leadership should be exercised only by certain people such as teachers. But such regimes of truth may be challenged as in distributive leadership and student engagement power resides in relationships that recognize expertise in meeting a community's purposes. Power flows among leaders in pursuit of these purposes. In its radical form, distributive leadership recognizes the importance of student engagement in achieving a classroom community's purposes and so student engagement is central to power relations in the learning and teaching process.

Distributive leadership is not about the agency and power of individuals, but about "structurally conjoint agency, or the concertive labour performed by pluralities of interdependent organisation members" (Gronn 2002, p. 543). I use activity theory to emphasize that distributive leadership, like student engagement, is about agency and collaboration in pursuit of regulating and/or radical goals. There are numerous activity theories. In one, Engestrom et al. (1999) emphasized jointly performed activity with a division of labour, fluidity of relationships and freedom within the dynamics of an ever-changing social system. Bennett et al. (2003) summarized Engestrom's version of activity theory

> as a process of ever-moving relationships between technologies, nature, ideas (concepts), persons and communities, in which the focus of action circulates to one person, then another, according to the social and environmental context and the flow of action within this.

In another, Wenger (1998) suggests that activity theory happens in communities of practice—learning groups that engage active participants in achieving their aims and practices. Wenger did not mention distributive leadership or student engagement directly, but his communities of practice and situated learning map tidily onto the concertive action meaning of distributive leadership and engagement. Community members are competent to contribute to the goals of distributive leadership and engagement in the community, to work together to achieve those goals and to engage with the community as equals. Both activity theories would accept student engagement in learning communities as part of the conjoint leadership within the community.

According to Carey (2013) *student voice* is essential in student engagement. He lists a number of ways in which student voice is already a vital part of activity systems; in quality assurance and student feedback for example. But he suggests that such uses of student voice narrows student engagement to students speaking while not necessarily being heard. Fielding (2004) suggests that such restrictive uses of student voice can be expanded by distributive leadership in which students, teachers and managers act in partnership. Students do not just air their views; they expect them to be listened to with the potential for enactment. A major purpose of this more radical kind of distributive leadership is to achieve a more democratic student engagement aimed at achieving greater social justice. But such critical purposes are complex to achieve. They require concerted action involving students, teachers and administrators working together in their classroom communities to achieve tasks in emergent and fluid interplays of power relationships. Fielding looks to dialogue to work towards this; dialogue between all participants in the community of practice in order to speak with, not to and certainly not for others. Partnerships in the leadership of learning and research by all participants in a learning community foster engagement. Woods and Roberts (2015) agree that dialogic distributive leadership fosters inclusive engagement and growth as people experience social, cultural, ecological and spiritual connectedness in line with the concept of holistic democracy. Such distributive leadership creates the opportunity to enhance participative, cultural and developmental justice.

The four paradigms in Burrell and Morgan's (1979) model describe distributive leadership, but also student engagement. Critical distributive leadership and student engagement belong to the model's radical dimension and its humanist and structuralist paradigms. I have argued that the critical reading of distributive leadership is synergetic with critical student engagement and is therefore a suitable vehicle to progress critical engagement pedagogy, curriculum and evaluation as discussed in Chaps. 8–10. We now turn to three case studies to show how distributive leadership may facilitate critical student engagement.

Enacting Critical Student Engagement Using Distributive Leadership: Three Case Studies

In the previous section, I proposed that distributive leadership offers a way to transition mainstream student engagement into critical practice. Now we investigate the possibility for such change. To do this we consider three case studies from New Zealand, the United Kingdom and the United States. Each case interprets events and actions in a bounded context to outline how distributive leadership can influence the way student engagement is practiced. According to Stake (2000, p. 435), this kind of case study is less a method than "a choice of what is to be studied". Each case is set in a university and is told from personal experience or reporting of the case. The New Zealand case is my personal reflection of events from a record made by Viskovic (2006); the others are drawn from published reports. The United Kingdom case is from a report to a funding agency (Neary et al. 2014) and other writings by Neary (e.g. 2013). The case from the United States is drawn from work published by Bovill (2014) and Bovill et al. (2008). Neary et al. (2014) observe that student engagement via distributive leadership is not unusual in the United Kingdom. Bovill et al. (2008) report on eight similarly extensive case studies from different parts of the world. While each case study is unique in its use of distributive leadership and student engagement, each has footprints in all Burrell and Morgan's paradigms. Because of this spread, I suggest that distributive leadership is a suitable model for implementing critical student engagement.

New Zealand: Student as Partner

This case study is personal as I had a part in its creation and operation. It revolves around a partnership between a mainstream higher education provider—called WP here—offering degrees in adult education and a national federation of Māori private training providers offering Māori vocational and foundation training. The federation wanted its teachers to become qualified teachers of adults within a Māori cultural kaupapa (tradition). The partnership discussed here is historical as institutional requirements which led to on-line programme delivery ended the partnership which was committed to delivering the programmes face-to-face on marae and in other Māori settings. While alive between the mid-1990s and the mid-2000s the partnership was managed according to distributive leadership principles with student engagement in decision-making about curriculum, pedagogy and evaluation at its core. Māori providers, teachers and students worked together to make the partnership work. It did, although of course with numerous ups and downs. Originally, it was agreed that the content belonged to WP, the delivery process to Maori, with responsibility for evaluation shared. But over time learners and their organizations challenged this division of labour, expecting recognition of Maori knowledge in the curriculum in addition to Pakeha (European) knowledge. Concertive action took place (i) in formal meetings including both WP teachers and students' representatives; and (ii) in classrooms where negotiations about content and process were ongoing. Tensions were ever present and the description of this community's practice is 'smoothed' here, influenced by hindsight from my perspective.

The curriculum was negotiated between the national federation of Māori training providers and the teachers of WP. The eventual agreement was signed off by WP's top management. It contained three elements: (i) course content was in the hands of WP teachers to deliver the programmes according to nationally and WP approved requirements such as constructive alignment between learning outcomes and evaluation; (ii) delivery was face-to- face in Māori controlled settings such as marae; and (iii) pedagogy and evaluation were a shared responsibility but with due recognition of and engagement with Māori protocols. This curriculum underwent major changes over its lifespan. On the one hand, academic policies nationally saw a steady increase in neoliberal policy requirements about such things as performativity, accountability and the necessity for Type 2 knowledge. On the other hand students demanded a more visible Māori dimension in programme content. Each delivery site became a community of practice negotiating curriculum details for its own site. Students and teachers together reviewed issues and planned on concertive action to address them. Increasingly Māori cultural purposes became more important. In particular, Māori knowledge was increasingly recognized as an important element in the curriculum. Stories drawing on research and student cultural experiences and the Māori past became an important source for knowledge development. Such stories supplemented, illuminated and critiqued the content in European style required readings. Reflections and stocktakes were frequently necessary and each site raised and addressed its own challenges, not always to everyone's satisfaction.

Pedagogy was negotiated. Māori students and providers were assertive about this. As they worked in a western adult education dialogic tradition, WP teachers were happy about partnership and encouraged maximum student activity, input and decision-making. The original agreement provided for sessions beginning with a Māori mihi (greeting) and karakia (prayer) and ending with a poroporoaki (farewell) and karakia. Learning sessions varied in length but were often conducted over a day or a weekend. They were always held in a Māori setting, often on a marae to give prominence to Māori cultural voice. They also engaged students as leaders in the community's work programme. The way WP teachers worked with students varied from site to site but students did not permit traditional transmission pedagogy. In my own practice I attempted to have students make meaning about teaching and learning in their own context. I worked both deductively and inductively. For example, when working deductively students were given reading material, asked to relate this to their personal, cultural and classroom experiences and to share these with members of the group. When working inductively students identified a problem they faced in their own teaching and supported their solutions from readings or their cultural experiences. Students often chose to report back using an imaginative and engaging activity such as pictures or music. These tended to be highly critical of the readings because Māori experiences would not relate to them. I was often in a position of defending readings.

Evaluation created the most challenges for both students and teachers. Requirements for validity, reliability and transferability were stringent and we were all faced with the challenge of matching academic requirements with Māori kaupapa. I make no claim that the tensions in this cultural encounter were ever totally resolved. Both groups did their best to meet Māori and western academic requirements and the programme seems to have had sufficient credibility to earn respect from both cultural viewpoints. The principles guiding evaluation protocols were fourfold: (i) constructive alignment between learning outcomes and evaluation; (ii) an expectation that candidates have met similar requirements and been judged on similar criteria; (iii) evaluation tasks respect candidates social, educational and cultural contexts in transparent ways; and (iv) students have conjoint leadership in planning evaluation, formulating objectives, designing learning experiences and evaluating their own learning. The second and third principles require further explanation. The second principle assumes reliability or comparability, with each student demonstrating they have met specified or embedded standards. To assure reliability and comparability evaluation events were both internally and externally moderated. The third principle adopts Messick's (1989) classical formulation for consequential validity. To be consequentially valid, evaluations respect learners' cultural and educational contexts and consider the consequences of their use. Learning outcomes were set in programme documents and externally approved. But students had a role in planning learning experiences and evaluation tasks that were appropriate for their context. They could self-evaluate with moderation by teachers, and final judgments were aligned with the context students worked in.

The United Kingdom: Student as Producer

At the heart of this case study is the work of Mike Neary at the University of Lincoln and the idea, based on Marxist social theory, of *student as producer* of knowledge. This consciously opposes *student as consumer*, the role assigned students under neoliberalism. *Student as producer* is not a new idea, nor is it unique to Lincoln. In addition to Marxist social theory it draws on nineteenth century ideas about the purposes of a university that combine teaching and research as an essential part of a liberal humanistic university education. When applied to the university, it holds that (i) research and teaching should be independent of politics; (ii) students should produce knowledge in their communities of practice; and (iii) be engaged in a critical approach to learning and teaching. *Student as producer* gained traction as a project funded between 2010 and 2013 by the Higher Education Academy. The project was designed to be integrated across the university. While involvement by academics was not compulsory, the idea was taken up widely and is now well integrated into the teaching and learning model of the university. It is referred to as research-engaged learning involving undergraduate students being active in research and research-like forms of learning in collaboration with peers and teachers. Student engagement is necessary for *student as producer* to function. While distributive leadership is not mentioned specifically, the importance of student voice is emphasized and students are expected to assume leadership roles in classes, the institution and wider society.

Student as producer has created a language and framework for teachers and students to collaborate on curriculum design and development. In the main, curriculum design focuses on students engaging in formal research, problem-based or related inquiries that are suited to the normal conduct of research in their discipline. Research learning underpins undergraduate curriculum design for all programmes and at all levels across the university. Research-engaged teaching and learning has become its organizing principle and the central pedagogical process that informs other aspects of the university's strategic planning such as teacher education, spaces for teaching and learning and use of technologies. *Student as producer* aims to connect research and teaching in ways that enable students to learn by actively engaging in research processes and outcomes. Hence, student engagement is a key element in the university's curriculum strategy. It is planned for through active collaboration amongst and between students and teachers. Programmes are expected to name ways to develop student voice. There is an expectation that as part of the curriculum design and implementation process students will have responsibility for the management and delivery of their own learning and have the opportunity and ability to support the learning of other students. By encouraging student voice the curriculum recognizes that *student as producer* will engage in social and economic critique. In short, the curriculum is expected to encourage development of a community of learners and teachers that engages in critique but remains respectful of difference and dissensus.

Student as producer works to eight overarching principles; five of these speak directly to pedagogy. These are: (i) discovery—the key idea in research-based learning and teaching; (ii) engaging in digital scholarship using technology; (iii) providing a learning landscape that creates space suitable for *student as producer*; (iv) student voice—heeding student opinion and leadership; and (v) expert engagement with information. Research-engaged learning and teaching is the signature pedagogy of *student as producer*. Students are engaged in contributing new knowledge within a community of practice in their discipline, university or groups outside the university. Digital technology becomes very important in the collaborative production of knowledge. Research-engaged teaching changes the relationships between teachers and students. Teachers who were the providers of knowledge with students the recipients are now partners in generating knowledge. On-line technologies facilitate this turnaround. Web-based pedagogy such as information searching, collaborative activity and commons-based peer produced writings assists the learning process. Similarly growing in importance is the way space and furniture is organized. *Student as producer* requires suitable university facilities for students to better self-organize their learning. Hearing, responding to and acting on student voice are critical to the pedagogic success of *student as producer*. Student engagement and leadership within the community of practice gain in importance at all levels of the university. The pedagogy of *student as producer* requires up-to-date information and the skills to search for it. Library resources suited to meeting the requirements of research-based learning are considered crucial.

Evaluation is a sixth principle underpinning *student as producer*. But how it operates in detail is not discussed in the report informing this case study. What is mentioned is that evaluation tasks are expected to reflect the active discovery process involved in research-engaged learning. Students are to demonstrate their research skills, findings, outcomes and outputs within the compass of the design and content of their courses. Evaluation engages students in working with teachers in the design of evaluation tasks as well as in marking them using a variety of approaches including peer, group and self-assessment. Marking criteria are expected to judge evidence of the quality of research-engaged learning. Students participate in providing feedback on others' work. More detailed evaluation policies for undergraduate programmes within the university are set out under the university's regulations (University of Lincoln 2013). On inspection they seem remarkably mainstream; designed to establish national and international credibility of qualifications and so at odds with the notion of critical engagement. All assessments are graded according to the traditions and practices of individual subjects. Programmes have explicit learning outcomes which students must demonstrate they have met by meeting set criteria. There is an expectation that results fall within stated distributions of marks. While these regulations surprise, they must be understood in the context of national and international neoliberal accountability expectations. This should not detract from the ethos and implementation of *student as producer* which otherwise provides a good example of how student engagement can escape its elective affinity with neoliberalism.

The United States: Student as Course Planner

Elon University is a private four-year liberal-arts-science College in North Carolina. Its curriculum is organized around themes of leadership, inquiry, knowledge and communication. Classes are small; with a student to teacher ratio of 12–1. Traditionally Elon has involved its students in all aspects of governance, leadership and collaborative planning processes. It has a strong belief in students' experience, knowledge and desire to participate in course design teams. Student engagement in collaborative course design gives them the opportunity to exercise leadership; practise inquiry into curriculum, pedagogy and evaluation as a field of study; build their knowledge of key issues in their own subjects; and learn to communicate ideas effectively. While not all subjects in the university foster such engagement, it is spread quite widely in courses such as education, biology and philosophy. For example, a teacher–student team collaborated to redesign an education course in classroom management; a small group of students analysed and interpreted student feedback results on a first-year biology course and with teachers, decided on changes to be made; a small group of students who had passed a first-year introductory philosophy course were asked to research issues in philosophy and on the back of this research, take part in the redesign of the course. Student participation does not involve all students. Usually a small group of around seven students are selected to work with a small team of teachers. Sometimes selections are on merit, sometimes selection is deliberately of a diverse team.

Curriculum improvement is at the core of Elon's student engagement in distributive leadership. Institutional support is seen as essential to encourage innovations involving such student engagement. Curriculum innovations yield many insights into the collaborative design process. Purposes of collaborative projects include: helping students understand difficult and complex knowledge; fuelling teachers' understanding of how and why beginning learners struggle; and for both to grasp the complexities of the first-year undergraduate experience. By supporting such multiple forms of collaborative curriculum work, the university has learned much about student engagement. For example, the usefulness of a service centre such as the university's Centre for the Advancement of Teaching and Learning

(CATL) has been established; and the university has found that small payments and minimal academic credits to student participants have a motivating effects. The reworking of one first-year education course illuminates how a collaborative curriculum can work. Teachers in the course wanted to choose a new textbook and redesign the course around it. They interviewed and selected eight students; half had already studied the course and half were about to. With the help of the CATL, student and teacher partners identified 25 possible textbooks. They developed a rubric to assist the selection process. What gave the students power, was the agreement that the rubric showed the textbook written by one of the course teachers was unsuitable. The selection of the new textbook was key in designing the curriculum for the next iteration of the course.

Pedagogy is influenced by the university's desire to engage students in shared leadership in curriculum redesign. On one level, new students taking a course, particularly in education, biology and philosophy, know that course structure and resources have been critically examined and influenced by previous students' involvement in the design process. This has the potential to motivate them to engage in the course and to apply for participation in any redesign project in the following year. On another level, students who have been engaged in curriculum redesign can become more critically engaged in their own study during the following year. The university has found that by involving students in teamwork with teachers and peers in genuine projects engages them to research and learn and to affect changes at the university. Two examples from *Classoom Management* and *Introduction to Biology* illustrate how participation in course design influences pedagogy. For *Classroom Management*, an introductory education course, seven students and three teachers drafted new goals for the course, selected the text book and other resources, devised the topics to be studied and wrote assignments and grading policies for the course. The coordinator for *Introduction to Biology* took the lead in collecting evidence of student learning in the course from, for example, student interviews rating different learning experiences. The evidence was given to a group of students who had previously taken the course to propose what changes in learning activities should be made to it.

Information about students engaging to change evaluation protocols and practices is not as clear as is the general Elan University ethos of engaging students as leaders in curriculum and pedagogical design. The university's grading policy (Elon 2016) suggests that a mainstream approach based on summative and formative evaluation is used to determine grades and pass rates. Students are graded at the mid and end points of a semester but results from the mid-semester examination are not recorded and serve as formative evaluation to make students aware of their progress. Student initiative is fostered when they request challenge examinations to gain credit for a course without completing course requirements. They can achieve this credit if they can demonstrate that they have already met learning outcomes. There are suggestions that when redesigning courses students also exercise their voice to change evaluation processes. But the only example I could find applies to

Introduction to Biology where student collaboration with teachers in changing assessment tasks and criteria is acknowledged. This example suggests that students do engage with structuring evaluation processes.

Making Meaning

Both critical distributive leadership and student engagement are aligned with the radical dimension and its humanist and structuralist paradigms in Burrell and Morgan's (1979) model. When interpreted in the light of Habermas' cognitive human interests (Hartley 2010) they can also involve functional and interpretive activities in social regulation paradigms. Whether mainstream or critical, student engagement in distributive leadership involves concertive action in pursuit of common purposes by members of a community of practice who work actively to achieve them. A community emerges either spontaneously or as a result of planned initiatives. Leadership is distributed because its members have skills and attributes needed to achieve the group's desired outcomes. Community processes and relationships are dynamic and fluid, with all members active participants in a common work programme, but contributing in different ways. This leads to a division of labour that takes account of the skills and attributes of community members and the requirements for leadership on specific aspects of a task. Members identify and engage with each other as a community for concertive action although they also work with their differences. Power in the community circulates among members as different knowledge and skills are needed to achieve the group's purposes.

Both Neary et al. (2014) and Bovrill et al. (2008) observe that the educational practices reported in their case studies are repeated elsewhere. Such observations give credibility to the argument that distributive leadership can engage students in making decisions about their own and others' learning. In each case students acted as co-leaders in designing courses, learning activities and evaluations. Students' voices in decision-making about classroom activities were at the heart of how student engagement was practiced in every case. Student leadership was seen as taking place in a community of practice (Wenger 1998) pursuing concertive action (Gronn 2002) to develop dialogue between students and teachers (Fielding 2004). But there were significant differences too. The strength of student voice varied between cases and courses. Distributive leadership as a guiding concept for student engagement was deliberately applied in New Zealand but was not mentioned as such in the others. Student leadership in New Zealand was embedded in course design, pedagogy and evaluation, but particularly in daily negotiations about who was teaching and who was learning at any given time. In the United Kingdom students are co-leaders in the production of knowledge through their own research. This gives them the voice needed to influence their own and others' learning. It also encourages them to look critically at education and society more generally. Student leadership at Elon is constrained by the will of teachers who select student participants in redesign projects. While more limited in its distribution, student leadership nevertheless exercises considerable influence over course design, pedagogy and evaluation.

But is student engagement when mediated by distributive leadership in these case studies critical? In response, two observations can be made. First, all case studies offer some evidence of critical student engagement. This judgment is supported by Burrell and Morgan's (1979) radical structuralism paradigm and Habermas' (1987) critical cognitive human interests. In each case, students have agency to change the structure and culture of their engagement. Engagement results in knowledge that transforms their ways of thinking about and acting in education and society. Second, the form of emancipation is variable. In New Zealand the impact of students' voice was significant across all facets of their learning and affected programme structure and culture in major ways. Indeed student engagement drove change. In the United Kingdom, courses using research-based learning afford students opportunities to build their own knowledge in ways that develop a critical eye on their own education and society generally. In the United States critical-type engagement applies to those invited to participate. In New Zealand critical engagement was confined to one course. It did not impact on the wider institution in any way. In the other cases, the impact of critical engagement is spread more widely but unevenly across the whole institution. In both the UK and the US cases, critical student engagement is a choice made by course teachers and administrators. These choices can result in mainstream, social regulation and technical engagement. While evaluation processes in all cases involve students as co-leaders in the process, this remains limited by neoliberal norms about accountability and comparability.

Two lessons from these case studies are clear to me. First, it is possible to develop critical student engagement through radical structural and critical distributive leadership. Second, I question that this is either easy or can happen in a uniform way. Critical student engagement will remain partial and contextual with students and teachers slipping in and out of radical paradigms and critical cognitive interests. The opportunities and limits for change to a more critical engagement will be discussed in Chap. 12.

References

Arendt, H. (1958). *The human condition*. Chicago, Ill: Chicago University Press.

Bennett, N., Wise, C., Woods, P., & Harvey J. (2003). *Distributed leadership. A review of the literature*. Report for the National College for School Leadership, Nottingham.

Bovill, C. (2014). An investigation of co-created curricula within higher education in the UK, Ireland and the USA. *Innovations in Education and Teaching International, 51*(1), 15–25. doi:10.1080/14703297.2013.770264

Bovill, C., Morss, K., & Bulley, C. (2008). *Curriculum design for the first year. First year enhancement theme report*. Glasgow: QAA. http://www.enhancementthemes.ac.uk/docs/publications/the-first-year-experience-curriculum-design-for-the-first-year.pdf?sfvrsn=18. Accessed February 12, 2016

Burrell, G., & Morgan G. (1979). *Sociological paradigms and organisational analysis*. Aldershot, UK: Ashgate.

Carey, P. (2013). *Student engagement in university decision-making: policies, processes and the student voice*. Doctor of Philosophy Thesis, United Kingdom: Lancaster University.

Elon University. (2016). *General Academic Regulations: 2015–2016 Academic Catalog*. http:// www.elon.edu/docs/e-web/academics/catalog/09academicregs10.pdf Accessed February 20, 2016

Engestrom, Y., Miettinen, R., & Punamaki, R. (1999). *Perspectives on activity theory*. Cambridge, UK: Cambridge University Press.

Fielding, M. (2004). Transformative approaches to student voice: Theoretical underpinnings, recalcitrant realities. *British Educational Research Journal, 30*(2), 295–311. http://www.jstor. org/stable/1502226

Foucault, M. (1981). *The history of sexuality,* Vol. 1. London, UK: Penguin.

Gronn, P. (2002). Distributed leadership. In K. Leithwood, P. Hallinger, K. Seashore-Louis, G. Furman-Brown, P. Gronn, W. Mulford & K. Riley (Eds.), *Second handbook of educational leadership and administration* (pp. 652–696). Dordrecht The Netherlands: Kluwer.

Habermas, J. (1987). Knowledge and human interests (J. Shapiro, Trans.). Oxford, UK: Polity Press.

Hartley, D. (2010). Paradigms: how far does research in distributed leadership 'stretch'? *Educational Management Administration & Leadership, 38*(3). 271–285.

Leithwood K., Mascall B., & Strauss T. (2009). What we have learned and where we go from here. In K. Leithwood, B. Mascall & T. Strauss (Eds.), *Distributed leadership according to the evidence* (pp. 269–82). London, UK: Routledge.

Messick, S. (1989). Validity. In R. Linn (ed) Educational measurement (3rd Ed.). Washington, DC: American Council on Education.

Neary, M. (2013). *Student as producer: A pedagogy for the avant-garde; or, how do revolutionary teachers teach?* Retrieved from http://josswinn.org/wp-content/uploads/2013/12/15-72-1-pb-1. pdf. On October 11, 2014

Neary, M., Saunders, G., Hagyard, A., & Derricott, D. (2014). *Student as producer: Research-engaged teaching, an institutional approach.* Project Report. HEA. https://www. heacademy.ac.uk/sites/default/files/projects/lincoln_ntfs_2010_project_final_report_fv.pdf. Retrieved on February 12, 2016

Stake, R. (2000). Case study. In N. Denzin & Y. Lincoln (Eds.), *Handbook of qualitative research,* 2nd Edition (pp. 435–454). Thousand Oaks, CA: Sage.

Tian, M., Risku, M., & Collin, K. (2016). A meta-analysis of distributed leadership from 2002 to 2013: Theory development, empirical evidence and future research focus. *Educational Management Administration & Leadership, 44*(1), 146–164. doi:10.1177/1741143214558576

University of Lincoln. (2013). *Academic policy summary sheet: Marking and grading policy*. http://secretariat.blogs.lincoln.ac.uk/files/2013/08/Marking-and-Grading-Policy2.pdf. Retrieved February 18, 2016.

Viskovic, A. (2006) *A history of a degree for tertiary teachers*. Unpublished paper.

Wenger, E. (1998). *Communities of practice: Learning, meaning and identity*. Cambridge, UK: Cambridge University Press.

Woods, P., & Roberts, A. (2015). Distributed leadership and social justice: Images and meanings from across the school landscape. *International Journal of Leadership in Education.* doi:10. 1080/13603124.2015.1034185

Chapter 12
Achieving Change: Opportunities, Challenges and Limits

Abstract What are the opportunities for achieving the kind of changes canvassed in the book? This chapter addresses opportunities for making change and what that change might look like using selected examples of critical practice; it identifies challenges that must be faced to achieve that change; and outlines how these challenges may limit potential change. More specifically, the chapter summarizes the argument in the book, offers a practice framework for a critical approach to student engagement and supports the framework with stories that show what some university teachers have done to make the framework real. The chapter ends with a brief discussion of the challenges faced by teachers and students in achieving a change to critical engagement and discusses some of the limits on change faced by them by governmentality.

Making Change

One overarching question for this book is why student engagement is so important in higher education today. Two possible responses are canvassed. The first, detailed in Chaps. 1–3, suggests that there is a mainstream approach to student engagement that serves very well the purposes of a learning centred but teaching-led pedagogy. Diverse and complex, this pedagogy is thought to be a meta-construct (Fredricks et al. 2004), an umbrella term sheltering a number of different research and practice traditions. These include a focus on quantifiable and generic behavioural indicators of engagement; students feeling an emotional connection within supportive social and academic communities that nurture a sense of belonging; a cognitive dimension in which engagement results in a deep form of learning; and a holistic perspective which transcends the classroom and identifies social, cultural, ecological and spiritual precursors and consequences to classroom engagement. The book attempts to bring these diverse traditions together in 10 propositions for practice. These advance three purposes for student engagement. The first focuses on students and what they need to invest in learning to be engaged. The second examines what teachers and institutions must do to support engagement. The third examines the influences of the students' environment on their engagement.

The second response, discussed in Chaps. 4–6, becomes evident when the mainstream perspective is examined more deeply. Student engagement does not happen in a vacuum. It is part of and the consequence of beliefs, policies and behaviours in society more generally. It is embedded in and shaped by the politics of a time and place. I argue that the dominant political culture of the late twentieth and early twenty-first centuries is in the image of neoliberalism, a western economic theory with a strong shaping capacity likened to *governmentality* by Foucault (2008) and spread around the world via *globalization*. The dominance of neoliberalism has raised the importance of student engagement to its very high level in higher education. This is because student engagement research and practice has an *elective affinity* with neoliberal ideas, particularly around neoliberalism's central expectations of higher education: the importance of practical knowledge, performativity and accountability. This elective affinity is critiqued as leading to an instrumental approach to engagement that is more focused on what works to prepare students for employment in a capitalist economy than preparing students to be thoughtfully and actively engaged as citizens with critical awareness, compassion and a willingness to act in the world to achieve social justice.

The critique leads to a second overarching question for the book: what changes need to be made to mainstream engagement to develop engagement theories and practices that are critically aware of the world, enable democratic citizenship and pursue social justice? Addressing this question leads to a much broader critical reading of success and engagement. Chapters 7–11 develop this critical approach to student engagement. The work of Freire (1972), Habermas (1984), hooks (1994), Smith (1999) and Brameld (1965/2000) among others combine to help develop a critical theory of student engagement, one that impacts each of Bernstein's (1996) three educational message systems: curriculum, pedagogy and evaluation. An overview of a critical student engagement theory and practice emerges. Engagement here builds consciousness of self, others and society at large, critiques the mainstream, involves dialogue among equals, strives for communicative action, recognizes and acts to achieve social justice for others, especially 'the other' and exercises leadership in the production of knowledge. But an enthusiastic case for critical student engagement runs the danger of not addressing the practical issue' of how the changes envisioned in critical engagement might be achieved. In Chap. 11, the book offers a radical vision of distributive leadership (Hartley 2010) as a model for combining critical and mainstream engagement into a coherent, useful and dynamic approach to all facets of teaching and learning in higher education.

Towards a Practice Framework for Critical Engagement

We saw that a radical form of distributive leadership can help transition student engagement from the mainstream to a more critical application. Three case studies from New Zealand, the United Kingdom and the United States of America showed that distributive leadership involving students in a decision-making capacity in pedagogy, curriculum and evaluation already operates in varied institutions and programmes. To progress this to escape the neoliberal mainstream, teachers and administrators create conditions where students overcome their own limited consciousness about learning, education and society and engage in effecting radical changes in curriculum design, pedagogy and evaluation. But it has never been my intention to suggest that a critical form of student engagement can replace research and practice with an elective affinity to neoliberalism and the mainstream. There is much of value in this research and practice, which has been hard-won over many years. So the intent is to go beyond mainstream conceptions of student engagement with critical principles and practices. As a first step in achieving the transition between mainstream and critical engagement Table 12.1 presents a summary of the mainstream approach first discussed in Chap. 3.

In Chap. 9, we discussed what pedagogy in critical student engagement might look like. Table 12.2 attempts to summarize a critical approach.

But Tables 12.1 and 12.2 are not meant to oppose mainstream and critical student engagement. Not only has mainstream student engagement much to offer teaching and learning in higher education, but the elective affinity between neoliberalism and student engagement may be with us for some time. So, mainstream student engagement will continue to play an important part in the future of learning and teaching. The critical form will extend it and so over time dilute the elective affinity. Table 12.3 attempts to bring together the contributions of mainstream and critical engagement with the understanding that critical engagement is the goal; mainstream engagement is a necessary but first step on the way. The first column synthesizes the major tasks for both mainstream and critical student

Table 12.1 Emergence: a conceptual organizer of propositions and key concepts of engagement

Purposes	Proposition for practice	Examples of key concepts
Students' investment in learning	Student self-belief is vital for success Student motivation grows self-confidence Social and cultural capital enhance engagement Engaged learners are deep learners	Appreciative Inquiry Self-determination theory Social/cultural capital Deep learning
Teacher and institutional support	Quality teaching and institutional support enhance engagement Disciplinary knowledge engages students Quality teaching adapts to changing student expectations	Learner centred teaching Threshold concepts Social change
Enabling environments	Engagement occurs across the life span Engagement is supported by subjective well-being Active citizenship is important for engagement	Lifewide education Subjective well-being Student voice

Table 12.2 Classroom practice in a critical student engagement pedagogy

Critical purposes	Critical tasks in student engagement	Examples of critical practice
Exposing ideological dominance	Exercising Agency	• Engaging in critical reflection • Asking questions • Taking personal control over learning • Speaking back to injustice • Sharing intellectual labour
Developing critical consciousness	Reading the world	• Participating in planning learning processes including assessment of learning • Conducting discourse analyses and acting on results • Developing multiple frameworks of analysis • Learning in a critical learning community • Understanding that the world is fluid and uncertain • Engaging with troubling ideas • Uncoupling from the stream of cultural givens
Fostering empowered learners	Ensuring well-being	• Building social, cultural and political capital for self and others • Engaging in consensual decision-making • Understanding own and others' positions in the world • Sharing in intellectual labour • Engaging in communicative action • Feeling engaged
Acting to change society	Learning social justice	• Engaging with others including 'the other' • Engaging constructively in cultural and political life • Recognizing and critiquing repressive tolerance • Challenging hegemonic discourses • Understanding and engaging with cultural politics • Recognizing and combating abuses of power • Acting constructively in the world • Acting as a catalyst for auctioning ideas

engagement. These are drawn from both mainstream and critical literature and practice. The second column summarizes how these tasks may be applied in mainstream engagement. Items in column 3 repeat the applications that first appeared in column 3 of Table 12.2. They are intended to act as an organic catalyst: one that "stays attuned to the best of what the mainstream has to offer … yet maintains a grounding for affirming and enabling sub cultures of criticism" (West 1993, p. 27). This column offers a holistic socio-cultural ecological view of engagement grounded in developing a critical consciousness that encourages an appetite for social and ecological justice.

Table 12.3 Combining mainstream and critical engagement practices

Tasks for student engagement	Practical examples from the mainstream	Practical examples from critical practice
Learner agency	• Experiencing self-belief • Working autonomously • Building relationships • Feeling competent	• Engaging in critical reflection • Asking questions • Taking personal control over learning • Speaking back to injustice • Sharing intellectual labour
Learner success	• Rising to academic challenge • Engaging in deep learning experiences • Being active learners • Engaging in constructive learning interactions • Having constructive peer relationships • Using social skills • Using learning support services • Experiencing social and academic integration • Having success—e.g. completion • Participating in governance • Experiencing service learning • Working in learning communities	• Participating in planning learning processes including assessment of learning • Conducting discourse analyses and acting on results • Developing multiple frameworks of analysis • Learning in a critical learning community • Understanding that the world is fluid and uncertain • Engaging with troubling ideas • Uncoupling from the stream of cultural givens
Learner well-being	• Trusting in self and others • Belonging with others • Understanding emotions	• Building social, cultural and political capital for self and others • Engaging in consensual decision-making • Understanding own and others' positions in the world • Sharing in intellectual labour • Engaging in communicative action • Feeling engaged
Learning fairness	• Accepting that rules apply to everyone • Being honest with self and others • Treating others as self wants to be treated • Affording and receiving equal learning opportunities in class	• Engaging with others including 'the other' • Engaging constructively in cultural and political life • Recognizing and critiquing repressive tolerance • Challenging hegemonic discourses • Understanding and engaging with cultural politics • Recognizing and combating abuses of power • Acting constructively in the world • Acting as a catalyst for actioning ideas

The focus in this concluding chapter (and indeed the whole book) is to show why a change in approach to student engagement is needed. In short, because mainstream engagement is narrowly conceived, instrumental and aligned with the demands of a particular ideology, it must be broadened to engage students in the workings of the world as critical and active citizens who engage in more than learning to be employable and manageable. Table 12.3 pictures a student engagement framework that makes that change by merging the mainstream into what I call critical student engagement. Two important points need to be made here. The first is that Table 12.3 is **not** intended as a generic recipe to be followed. It is more a palette from which teachers select curriculum, pedagogy and evaluation processes that engage their students in ways that suit their discipline, the context and the prior experiences of their students. This leads to the second point. Because the framework focuses squarely on what students think, feel and do, the work of teachers fades into the background. This obscures the important point that teachers implement the framework. So at the forefront of the student engagement framework in Table 12.3 is the hidden engagement of the teacher. I suggest that it is vital that teachers engage with the critical practices in the table as well as the mainstream ones. Here some actual examples of how the overarching meanings embedded in Table 12.3 have already been actioned by university teachers over a lengthy period of time could be of value.

Stories of Critical Engagement in Practice

The stories I share in this section I have adapted from examples of critical student engagement practices I found in existing publications. The stories come from the United Kingdom and the United States and are 'take outs' from the work of Brookfield (2013), Deeley (2015), Scandrett (2008) and Shor (1996). Their stories do not attempt to cover each and all practices in Table 12.3. Rather, they relate ways in which important assumptions about critical engagement feature in their work. The stories tell how ideals of a democratic classroom built around dialogue, power sharing, critical thinking and learning social and environmental justice may be used to critically engage students in learning in the classroom and the wider world. Each story is told in two parts. The first backgrounds the stories; the second tells how they are implemented. I share these stories not in the expectation that they can ever be replicated, but as inspiration to develop your own critical practice.

Towards a Democratic Classroom

From my perspective, critical engagement can only develop in a democratic classroom in which students participate in making decisions about their learning. Stephen Brookfield has written at length (e.g. 2013) about his goal to work towards more democratic engagement in learning. He admits that this is not easy to achieve and is always a moving target. Difficulties are to be expected in a mainstream climate in which teachers are expected to be in charge of planning, teaching and evaluation while under the control of government and institutional policies that define useful knowledge, the performances expected and accountability scores. Brookfield nevertheless considers three core elements are required to achieve a democratic classroom. First, democratic practice provides opportunities for the widest possible range of voices to be heard in learning situations. Second, decisions about learning activities are made by those most affected by them—usually the students. Third, a democratic classroom does not shy away from examining unfamiliar perspectives, particularly dominant ideologies. These core elements must be handled carefully as each raises complications. For example, external authorities may overrule democratic practice, students may not have the necessary knowledge to contribute a great deal and a cacophony of diverse voices may impede learning. Brookfield tries to address these concerns by outlining his practice.

Brookfield tells his students that control in his classroom is shared in three ways. One third of what happens in classrooms is controlled by him. This third includes his specialist knowledge, the objectives of the learning experiences to be on offer and the means he has to overcome resistance. One third of the control is held by students. Typically they use this to decide what activities to engage in, what texts to read and what contributions to classroom management to make. The final third is negotiated. He is transparent about his objectives. This enables students to respond to them and for the two parties to negotiate the way forward. Brookfield describes a number of practices that fit the final, the negotiated third. As already stated, he values transparency so that students understand what he is trying to achieve. He encourages student governance by establishing a decision-making body out of the whole class which can respond to his suggestions and expectations. This can be a messy business, as students whose confidence in his practice has been awakened often disagree with his and peers' proposals. This is where negotiation skills enter the picture as Brookfield uses consensus in the negotiated third of control, not majority voting, to make decisions. To avoid time wasting debate he uses a number of engaging activities to make progress. He takes great care to ensure that all students are aware of what others think about issues in order to reach a consensus. In a critical incident questionnaire, individuals and small groups answer critical questions. Brookfield publishes responses, and in turn answers them. Such activities progress decision-making to a point where a consensus can emerge.

Dialogue and Power in the Classroom

Brookfield's way towards achieving a learning consensus in a more democratic classroom is through dialogue. One of the best examples of a dialogic classroom is provided by Ira Shor in his book *When students have power* (1996). The book is about an experiment in sharing power with students through dialogue and negotiation. The context is a windowless basement room in a crumbling New York university campus where Shor is tasked to teach a compulsory course on Utopia. Most of the students do not want to be there and choose to sit as far away from Shor as they can get—into a kind of self-selected exile. Shor labelled this seating pattern the Siberian Syndrome. He considers it a repetitive pattern of behaviour that develops over time in the education system. Shor attributes the retreat of students to the margins of the classroom as students enacting their agency as a form of rebellion against an authoritarian culture in which the teacher is placed into a position of unilateral authority over curriculum content and processes. As a result of this rebellion they expect Shor to teach from the front of the room in a traditional manner. Shor is determined to change this culture of separation. He chooses to be unpredictable in how he works with the students by using a critical pedagogy centred on dialogue. This was not an easy path for him to take as students were at first resistant to his methods and not all were ever won over.

An example of how Shor used dialogue in his teaching is provided by Lewis Dimmick, a former student in an *Afterword* to the book. Right at the beginning of the course Shor invited students to enter a contract with him. In it students nominated their goals, for example grades they wanted to achieve. Contracts also spelt out what Shor would do to facilitate learning and what students would do to achieve their goals. The contract was designed to discuss, to motivate, to be an ongoing check on progress and to sell the course to students as a learning partnership. Classes were built around readings about utopian themes. Students were invited to nominate titles to be read and discussed in class. At one point in the course, the theme was about short utopian stories. Each student was invited to bring a short story to class. In small groups each story was read aloud; questions were asked about it and answered in discussion by the group. Each group selected one story to be analyzed by the whole class. Dimmick reflected on this process (p. 223):

> As a student I was inspired….I looked forward to reading and discussing the stories. I had never felt so good about school. Upon reflection, the beautiful simplicity of it all stuns me: we decided what the class talked about. We asked the questions. And we discussed them for hours. We shaped the class. We codeveloped the curriculum.

To be sure, not all students responded like this and you will have to read the book to find out how Shor handled difficulties.

Critical Thinking and Critical Incidents

Brookfield and Shor engaged their students critically by sharing power and using dialogic methods. These required students to reflect, think and act critically on their own and others' experiences. In neoliberal times this is not so easy to do. Susan Deeley uses critical incidents in learning situations to encourage her students to learn how to think critically about themselves, their actions and how they affect the world around them. For Deeley critical incidents are experiences that stop us in our tracks. They are not necessarily earth shaking as they often take the form of being puzzling, perhaps disorientating. But a critical incident is an experience resulting in major or minor change. Deeley suggests that critical incidents have to be sought out. How to make use of them as part of critical engagement has to be taught deliberately. From a student's point of view the effect of a critical incident is akin to a 'light bulb moment', but one that requires critical reflection to turn it on. Critical reflection on an experience identifies the critical incident and also provides ways to analyze and use it in learning. Deeley suggests the use of journal writing to enable critical incidents to be identified. In my view minor critical incidents benefit from being written down in case they are missed, but major ones often do not need this treatment as it is difficult for them to escape our notice. I have already used one example of the effects of critical incidents on critical engagement in Chap. 9. I now relate another.

This example is based on the experiences and critical reflection of a first year student on placement in a community serving elderly people. The incident was major. In attempting to help shift a table in a common room used by the elderly residents, the student attracted verbal abuse from one of the residents. The student was shocked, standing frozen holding the table. Despite requests to shift the table by a charge carer, she was not able to move. To learn from the critical incident the student was asked to examine alternatives actions she could have taken, to identify a best response, to examine underlying issues and how the learning she has done will affect her future actions. She identified an appropriate response. This involved her unfreezing by putting the table down, engaging in a discussion with the enraged resident and attempting to reassure her. Further engagement with the critical incident revealed a number of underlying problems. The resident had Alzheimer's and was confused by the student's action. She learnt that talking to the resident would probably have mitigated the distress. Critical reflection also revealed that she lacked confidence to deal with this situation and that this made the situation worse. She decided that in future she must learn to be more proactive, to build up rapport with residents and to learn something about their dispositions and afflictions. Other learning, not found in her journal, might be to find ways to encourage residents to engage in decisions about such matters as placement of furniture.

Engagement in the World

This example of critical engagement in practice was written by Scandrett (2008) at a university in the United Kingdom. It is a story of how a university partnered with an environmentally focused social movement. The partnership aimed to provide sustained learning that was both academically rigorous and practically useful. Its dynamics centred on strongly reflective interactions between the two. This higher education certificate course also sought to be democratic, involve students and teachers in ongoing dialogue about what to include and what not, employ critical reflection and thinking as feature in the curriculum. In short, it builds on the ideas about critical engagement already canvassed through the work of Brookfield, Shor and Deeley. It was initially delivered through residential weekend courses but these were discontinued in favour of distance learning using interactive software. The pedagogy was based on the methods of Paulo Freire that used students' own experiences to tackle human and environmental problems. Students learnt ways to tackle them in a dialogic process linking two different forms of knowledge—the action orientated experience of the environmental movement and the academic knowledge base of the university. The knowledge taught followed Freire's advice that educators take a partisan position on the side of those who are oppressed, in order to build a curriculum through dialogue conjointly using the knowledge of student and teacher. Together, these approaches proved fruitful in encouraging progressive social change and greater social justice.

The course is organized as a project around environmental campaigns students are involved in. At the beginning of the course students present their project to the rest of the class. Teachers guide a discussion about each project. This leads to the group asking ever more analytical and critical questions about it. Topics and questions enable the class to identify themes that enable students to gain an appreciation for and understanding about the nature of environmental justice. The themes are then linked in further discussion to relevant parts of the formal curriculum underpinning the course. The group may also identify extra themes from their reading of course material. The themes, along with linked parts of the formal curriculum, become the focus for course learning and evaluation. The way topics, questions and themes are developed, breeds a pedagogy that is democratic, power sharing, dialogic and critical; a mirror for Brookfield's, Shor's and Deeley's narratives. Moreover, it is concerned with environmental and social justice. Because each project is different, students learn from each other by discussing emerging themes. New knowledge gained from discussions is passed through the filter of the formal curriculum to ensure that course requirements are met. With the focus on personal projects the course offers a high level of flexibility. It is highly dialogic and students have a big part in designing the curriculum and influencing pedagogy and evaluation. Students' learning is supported by university teachers and members of the social movement running the campaign.

Challenges and Limitations

But can engagement in its critical theory guise replace the neoliberal hegemony? Any discussion about the possibility of such change in learning and teaching in higher education is heavily dependent on the future of neoliberalism. Key aspects of such a discussion must focus on whether a critical form of student engagement can escape its elective affinity with neoliberalism and whether researchers, teachers and students actually want to escape its shadow. Such questions highlight challenges facing a general expansion of critical student engagement. They also point out the potential limits of such change.

Since the 2008 financial crisis, economic and political analysts increasingly question the sustainability of neoliberal ideas and policies. The recovery from the crisis has been fragile and there is an increasing fear that a new crisis may loom on the horizon. As a consequence, intellectual voices have forecast a severe decline in the influence of neoliberalism. Critique is nourished by the mediocre performance of the neoliberal economy throughout the western world brought about, according to Summers (2016), by secular stagnation. This results from a severe drag on demand due to an increase in savings and a decrease in investment. Piketty (2014) has also commented on the lack of success of neoliberal policies and practices to improve the economy and the lives of the vast majority of people. He argues that the most growth in western economies was in the era of welfare capitalism between 1945 and the 1970s. Jacques (2016) sees neoliberalism in its death throes as populist movements have joined intellectuals in rebelling against growing inequality, free trade and subsequently the loss of jobs this entails. At the time of writing the outcome of insipient voter rebellions in countries like France, Germany, the United Kingdom and the United States against the political classes which champion neoliberalism over issues such as immigration, inequality and globalization is uncertain. But it is probably safe to say that the future of neoliberalism is in the balance. Even International Monetary Fund staffers, previously prophets of neoliberalism, are asking whether neoliberalism is oversold (Ostry et al. 2016).

But to announce the death of neoliberalism and its affinity with student engagement is premature. As mentioned in Chap. 4, neoliberalism has a resilience that enables it to change and re-emerge in new guises without departing from its original ideological commitments (Collier 2005). Collier recognizes three stages in neoliberal ideology: first, an intellectual movement that envisages the restoration of free markets; second, a stage where state power is mobilized to establish free markets and to deregulate state involvement in society; third, a stage to fix the perverse consequences and tensions produced by the second stage. This involves using state power to ease social stress without departing from its original mission. Collier (2005) also notes that neoliberalism is rarely found in its pure form. Although, it is a global presence, it is a hybrid that acts in slightly different ways in different jurisdictions. Consequently, the fate of neoliberalism is tied to local conditions and cannot be generalized. This resilience offers both opportunities and restrictions for change. Opportunities for a critical form of engagement are offered at the local level. The examples provided in the book show that committed teachers can change to a more critical practice if they want to. Shor (1996) for example demonstrates that students also can be motivated to engage critically. But neoliberalism's resilience also signals limits on what students and teachers can do to change the performativity and accountability cultures in higher education. But again, the book has shown that where there is a will, there is a way, if not to ignore such restrictions, but to adjust them in ways that suits critical work.

We know that individual teachers have embarked on and inspired students to join them in a critical form of student engagement. Despite this, a major challenge remains. Will teachers and students be prepared in big numbers to embark on a critical path? Here some limits on the spread of critical student engagement should be noted. Foucault's (2008) explanation of how the conduct of conduct results in *governmentality* shows why teachers and students could be reluctant to engage with critical engagement. Even if the influence of neoliberalism wanes or changes direction, revolutionary change will be unlikely. Foucault alerts us that the conduct of conduct is not just decreed by governments but is embedded in peoples' daily lives. Students, teachers and the public at large discipline themselves to live their lives according to the norms of a dominant ideology. They have for many years incorporated neoliberal conduct of conduct into their ways of being (Dean 1999). Most people find that neoliberal values and behaviours in their own lives to be compelling and natural and so can be reluctant to abandon them. Brookfield and Shor alert us to potential student resistance. For similar reasons teachers are also often resistant to change.

But, recognizing that there may be some inertia does not mean that changing mainstream engagement into a more critical form is a remote prospect. This optimism can be justified by reference to the uncertain future of neoliberalism and to the work of individual teachers like Neary et al. (2014) and institutions like Elon University (see Bovill et al. 2008) which is gaining increasing publicity and support for their critical practice in books, journals and social media, and the recurring critique that neoliberal higher education is in many ways not fit for use. It is true that critical student engagement will not flood into higher education on an irresistible tide, but it is an increasingly attractive option to be adapted in a variety of contexts.

References

Bernstein, B. (1996). *Pedagogy, symbolic control and identity: Theory, research, critique*. London, UK: Taylor and Francis.

Brameld, T. (1965/2000). *Education as power: A re-issue by the Society of Educational Reconstruction*. New York, NY: Holt, Rinehart & Wilson.

Brookfield, S. (2013). *Powerful techniques for teaching adults*. San Francisco, CA: Jossey Bass.

Collier, S. (2005). *The spatial forms and social norms of 'actually existing neoliberalism': Toward a substantive analytics. New School University International Affairs Working Paper 2005-04*. Retrieved from New York, NY: https://stephenjcollier.files.wordpress.com/2012/07/spatial-forms.pdf

Dean, M. (1999). *Governmentality: Power and rule in modern society*. London: UK: Sage.

Deeley, S. (2015). *Critical perspectives on service-learning in higher education*. London, UK: Palgrave Macmillan.

Elon University. (2016). General academic regulations: 2015–2016 academic catalogue. Retrieved from http://www.elon.edu/docs/e-web/academics/catalog/09academicregs10.pdf

Foucault, M. (2008). *The birth of biopolitics: Lectures at the College de France 1978–1979*. New York, NY: Picador.

Fredricks, J., Blumenfeld, P., & Paris, A. (2004). School engagement: Potential of the concept, state of the evidence. *Review of Educational Research, 74*(1), 59–109.

Freire, P. (1972). *Pedagogy of the oppressed*. Harmondsworth, UK: Penguin Books.

Habermas, J. (1984). *The theory of communicative action, Volume 1: Reason and the rationalization of society*. Boston, MA: Beacon Press.

Hartley, D. (2010). Paradigms: How far does research in distributed leadership 'stretch'? *Educational Management Administration & Leadership, 38*(3), 271–285.

hooks, B. (1994). *Teaching to transgress: Education as the practice of freedom*. New York, NY: Routledge.

Jacques, M. (21 August 2016). The death of neoliberalism and the crisis in western politics. *The Guardian*. Retrieved from https://www.theguardian.com/commentisfree/2016/death-of-neoliberalism-crisis-in-western-politics

Neary, M., Saunders, G., Hagyard, A., & Derricot, D. (2014). *Student as producer: Research-engaged teaching, an institutional approach.* Project report. Retrieved from http://www.heacademy.ac.uk/sites/default/files/projects/lincoln_ntfs_2010_project_final_report_fv.pdf

Ostry, J., Loungani, P., & Furceri, D. (2016). Neoliberalism: Oversold? *Finance and Development, 53*(2), 38–41. Retrieved from http://www.imf.org/external/pubs/ft/fandd/2016/06/ostry.htm

Piketty, T. (2014). *Capital in the 21st century.* (A. Goldhammer, Trans.). Cambridge, MA: The Bellknap Press of Harvard University Press.

Scandrett, E. (2008). Case study 3. *Curriculum design for the first year. First year enhancement theme report.* Retrieved from http://www.enhancementthemes.ac.uk/docs/publications/the-first-year-experience-curriculum-design-for-the-first-year.pdf?sfvrsn=18

Shor, I. (1996). *When students have power: Negotiating authority in a critical pedagogy.* Chicago, ILL: University of Chicago Press.

Smith, L. (1999). *Decolonizing methodologies: Research and indigenous peoples.* London, UK; Dunedin, New Zealand: Zed Books and University of Otago Press.

Summers, L. (2016). The age of secular stagnation: What it is and what to do about it. *Foreign Affairs*(March/April). Retrieved from https://www.foreignaffairs.com/articles/united-states/2016-02-15/age-secular-stagnati

West, C. (1993). *Keeping faith: Philosophy and race in America.* New York, NY: Routledge.

Appendix A
What Students Say About
the 10 Propositions in Chap. 3

Appendix A explores how students in Aotearoa New Zealand relate to the 10 propositions in Chap. 3.

Chapter 3 used the rich and diverse mainstream student engagement research literature to develop 10 propositions for practice. I was keen to discover whether these propositions were in any way grounded in the reality of student opinion. To get a feel for student views, I used results from a Teaching and Learning Research Initiative (TLRI) conducted in Aotearoa New Zealand (Zepke et al. 2008) to confirm (or not) whether the propositions found any support in student views. Appendix A demonstrated to me anyway, that there was such support and that I could offer these propositions for further discussion. After a brief introduction to the research design, student views about each of the propositions are reported.

Research Design

Two objectives underpinned the research design for the TLRI project. The first was to gather student and teacher views to discover the relative importance of motivation, pedagogy, and external influences to student engagement. The project focused on identifying student and teacher perception data about engagement. The use of such subjective data was justified by Hu and Kuh (2003) who argued that perception research is valid and valuable provided students are asked about their actual experiences. The second objective for the TLRI project was to drill down into how teachers and students perceived engagement in different kinds of institutions. To achieve this objective the researchers decided to use case studies to better understand engagement in different contexts. This followed Fenwick's (2005, p. 9)

© Springer Nature Singapore Pte Ltd. 2017
N. Zepke, *Student Engagement in Neoliberal Times*,
DOI 10.1007/978-981-10-3200-4

view that education is situated practice, performed "in the habitual practices of a particular site or community". The findings from cases did not differ significantly between cases and the decision was made to combine the results and present a national response picture in addition to results from the case studies. The data presented here follows this decision and combines results from all nine participating institutions operating in the postsecondary (tertiary) space in New Zealand.

The nine higher education institutions included two universities, four institutes of technology, one wānanga (an institution dedicated to serve Māori, New Zealand's indigenous people), one private training provider and one community education provider. The research team sought a good geographic spread, different types and sizes of institutions, at least one offering distance delivery, at least one with a rural hinterland, and at least one with a significant Māori and Pasifika (people from the islands of the Pacific) student population. The project used a mixed-method quantitative dominant approach to investigate the research question: how do institutional and non-institutional learning environments influence student engagement with learning in diverse tertiary settings?

The project used a survey of first-year students enrolled in the case study institutions (1246 responses), follow-up interviews with 72 students and a survey of teachers in these institutions (376 responses). Student and teacher surveys contained the same questions arranged in three scales—motivation, pedagogy and external influences. The student survey was distributed in each of the case study institutions to a sample of first-time enrolled students, representative of gender, age and ethnicity in each institution. The teacher survey went to teachers of first-year students. Sample sizes were determined by institution size. Response rates were uneven and did not allow generalization across all institutions to be made. We used means to analyse these responses. Means reveal the central tendencies of responses to the four points on a Likert scale ranging from 1 (strongly affirmative) to 4 (strongly negative), with the smallest means (between 1 and 2) indicating strongest affirmation. Interviews were conducted in every case study institution. They were recorded, transcribed and analysed by researchers there (Zepke et al. 2008) and, like survey results, are combined for presentation in this chapter.

Student Support for the 10 Propositions

To gauge whether there is support for the 10 propositions emerging in Chap. 3 I looked for evidence in both the quantitative survey and qualitative interview data generated by the TLRI project. Items addressing the propositions in the questionnaire were identified. Not all items in the questionnaire were suitable for inclusion in Appendix A because they predated the propositions developed for this book from the literature and therefore did not address the propositions. Consequently only survey items that directly addressed the propositions were selected. As it turned out, at least three survey items addressed each proposition and the most important are used in this chapter. In the TLRI project respondents could choose from a 4 point

Likert scale ranging from very important to not important at all. The percentage of students rating each selected question very important and important was computed and is presented in the tables. All qualitative interview data generated in the case studies were used to assess the suitability of the propositions. The section first presents the quantitative data for each proposition with brief commentary before presenting student comments.

Student self-belief is vital for success	Very important %	Important %
Taking responsibility for my learning	63.5	33.6
Knowing how to achieve my goals	59.3	37.1
Knowing how to apply what I learn	60.8	34.8

More than 90% of respondents thought that these items were either very important or important for engagement. Around 60% deemed each item to be very important, the most for any proposition. Each item involved students believing in their own strengths, the overarching theme for this proposition.

Student interview responses reinforced the impression that engaged and successful students were self-believers. They were assertive in taking control of their learning: "I make sure I go and do what I have to do ... I don't allow interruptions ... we actually moved so I wouldn't be interrupted" (D2); "everything is under my control ... everything is up to me, I'm not going to get hounded for something I am not doing, and in a way it motivates me" (D6); and "maybe it's a bit arrogant of me to think I don't need support but part of me thinks if I needed it I would be quite confident asking for it" (E4). They were goal orientated: Keeping an eye on my ultimate goal ... taking things one step at a time rather than getting overwhelmed by the course as a whole (E6); and "I'm fairly methodical. I like to have a long-term plan with stages ... with areas I have achieved and not achieved on my own" (F4). An assertion of independence was another indicator of self-belief: "I'm pretty independent ... I've done it myself" (H2); "I tried to get through it myself" (F7); and "I am a high achiever, I am a capable student, I have significant strategies" (D2).

Student motivation grows self-confidence	Very important %	Important %
Making social contacts with other students	20.7	41.0
Finding my own resources to help me learn	38.2	48.8
Knowing how to draw attention to what needs changing	24.5	48.0

These items probed students' self-determination, the underlying assumption for this proposition. Responses were not as strong as for the first proposition. Nevertheless each item was regarded as very important or important by more than 60% of respondents.

Three ingredients for motivation in self-determination theory (Ryan and Deci 2000)—competence, autonomy and relatedness—were repeatedly mentioned in interviews. But contrary to their research the wish for relational learning was stronger than the others: "student interaction was great" (I5); "that's why I came to [polytech], to be in a classroom and be surrounded by other students" (I3); "working together on a task is … up there on a 9.9 out of 10 scale (I4); and "just having someone there to bounce ideas off, just another example of a way to do something, so you are not just looking at yourself and your ideas" (D7). A number of students also sought sound relationships with teachers: "…just having a chat online (with her) has been good, it makes you feel like you belong" (E8). Some were not so fussed about this "I'm not really worried about having a close student/teacher relationship. I guess as a learner I can work things out for myself." (E3). Other respondents also believed in their own capability and autonomy: "I'm pretty sussed" (H3); "I don't really like team work because other people frustrate me and I tend to think I can do it faster myself" (C11); and "I'm thinking I may be able to influence the content somehow … to challenge the teachers" (E9).

Social and cultural capital enhance engagement	Very important %	Important %
Feeling I belong here	35.4	47.0
Having my cultural background respected	35.1	33.9
Feeling I am valued as a person	36.0	45.5

These three items support the proposition only indirectly. They do not enable us to affirm that social and cultural capital is enhanced by engagement. They do suggest though that the three items—belonging, respect and being valued—have considerable support among students. Belonging and being valued are considered by around 82% to be very important and important. It is surprising though that only 69% feel that cultural respect is very important and important. Even though taking these caveats into account it seems that having social and cultural capital are supportive of engagement.

The qualitative data supports the importance of social and cultural capital more directly than the survey results. Some respondents felt that social and cultural understanding broadened them as people: "it broadened my horizons" (F2): "I've learnt stuff that I was pretty cynical about really and now I feel much more open minded about that sort of thing" (I5). Others felt it introduced them to think in new directions: "every corner you turn there is something. It's interesting, something valid, something controversial—it gets you thinking" (D3); "I'm learning stuff that I just didn't think about" (D1); and "we are all cut from a different cloth and my point of view can be totally different than someone else's … it kind of broadens my thinking" (H4). Some felt closely connected to the institution: "I feel very much part of [the university. I tell people I go to … [this university] and the lecturers have been really good … I get emails from [the university] telling me what is going on" (C6). Not all students felt valued or that they belonged: "Feeling terribly disconnected to be honest" (C7); "everyone likes to feel valued. I'm just a number. I don't feel particularly well engaged" (E9).

Engaged learners are deep learners	Very important %	Important %
Setting high standards for myself	50.7	42.2
Teachers challenging me in helpful ways	44.3	47.1
Knowing how to use the library to support my learning	36.4	41.7

Most students thought that setting high standards for themselves, meeting challenges and knowing how to use learning resources were very important or important. Results for these indicators of deep learning were high, ranging from 78.1 to 92.9%. This suggests that most students were aware that to succeed they needed to invest more in their learning than token effort. While these results do suggest that students engage in deep learning, they do not imply that students always learn in this way.

Students told interviewers about how they engaged in deep learning. A number enjoyed challenges: "they (teachers) push you … its really good … if you are about to give up she gets persuasive" (I4). There were numerous examples of excitement generated by new learning: "I'm learning stuff that I just didn't think about. You just do stuff day to day and don't realise why you are doing it" (C1). Some shared deep learning strategies: "I will read it a few times just to make sure my brain is working and then I will carry on reading past it and come back with fresh eyes and then if I'm thinking I can't get this I will go on the internet and Google it" (E4); and "I learn by reading and writing notes in my own words. I do that a lot, especially with things I'm not so strong at, so I understand them" (C11). According to many respondents learning involved using many different resources to solve problems or get scarce information: "I've googled a lot and [used] wikipedia' (I8); "I use the Internet quite a lot … a lot of more up-to-date information is available on the Internet … the library frustrates me" (C7). Many also accessed information and interacted with others through learning management systems: "we have 'Blackboard' and 'Moodle'. If you happen to miss a lecture or haven't taken notes, you can get them off 'Blackboard', so I use those" (A10); "and e-mails from the tutors and support from the other students, just having a chat on-line has been good, makes you feel like you get it" (F8).

Quality teaching and institutional support enhance engagement	Very important %	Important %
Teachers provide feedback to improve my learning	73.0	24.6
Teachers teaching in ways that enable me to learn	68.7	26.8
Being given information on how systems work	42.1	42.5

Teaching and institutional support was very important or important to most students—responses for the selected items ranged from 84.6 to 97.6%. The provision of learning enhancing feedback was the most important thing teachers do according to survey respondents. But even the more administrative item of enabling students to navigate institutional settings was considered to be important by 84.6% of respondents.

Interview responses mirrored the statistical results as the most transcript pages related to this proposition. But opinion was quite divided how well teachers and teaching engaged these learners. There was extensive praise of teachers and teaching: "to me the lecturers are the best part, being able to relate to them and not feel excluded" (A3); "to feel able to approach them and talk to them, particularly when they don't talk down to you" (I5); "some of the lecturers make it fun, joke here and there, so we get to know them better" (C10); "they make me feel comfortable" (D4); and, "when they show us respect it makes us want to learn" (I6). Students also appreciated teachers who were supportive and positive: "the two tutors I went to were great … they were 100% supportive … they are good to talk to" (E7), "it was the one time I had to ask for help and it was positive and supportive" (C9); "she doesn't mind people asking these questions" (D6). There were many examples of teachers going beyond the call of duty: "In my previous course I didn't understand how differentials in a car worked and my tutor took me over to a differential in a workshop that was cut away and showed me all the workings and explained how it works" (S4).

There were positive responses about the quality of feedback received—"the markers are awesome. They give me the best feedback" (C6), "some of them give you very good feedback" (F2). However, the greatest number of responses on what prevented engagement also related to feedback: "It took us 3 months to get assignments back and that was our first academic writing. Our first big assignment and we handed it in 3 months ago. If the tutors are overworked and underpaid and short staffed it's not our fault. So we started asking when we could get them back … until eventually we got—don't ask. That is not OK since it was handed in when it was supposed to be and in order to better yourself you need to know where you are going wrong. And that didn't happen. It's not acceptable; we're not allowed to hand stuff in 3 months late" (F3); and "I've been a bit disappointed over how long it has been taking to get them (assignments) back. You put all this work in and you are thinking how you have done and it kind of impacts on the next assignment. If I've made some huge mistakes I want to know now so I can think about the next assignment" (E8).

Over a third of the students interviewed had never used support services provided by their institution, most because they hadn't needed them: "I don't need academic assistance and there isn't a lot of external research required in my course and what there is I manage to do" (E9); some because they used non-institutional support: "if I know about a group out in the community that might be able to assist with say childcare, I will contact them" (G2); a few because "I haven't been bothered, because in my mind I perceive it as a bit of a hassle" (F3); although some recognized that they "should have" (A3, E6); and a few because of lack of awareness—"there is one that helps you when someone has died, like a counsellor or something. Can't think of any others" (D3).

Disciplinary knowledge engages students	Very important %	Important %
Teachers making the subject really interesting	60.8	32.6
Being challenged by the subject I am learning	46.0	45.8
Teachers are enthusiastic about their subject	63.5	30.8

More than 90% mentioned the importance to engagement of learning their chosen discipline/subject/profession. The role of teachers in this is particularly important but so is the interest bearing nature of the discipline itself. These results support findings from various meta analyses reported by Pascarella and Terenzini (2005) about the importance of disciplines to student learning and engagement.

The interview data also support survey results. When asked about the things that engaged their interest in the subjects they were studying, two themes dominated. One was interest in the subject: "it's all about a passion what I'm doing … always had an interest in [subject]" (A6); "[the subject] that's my passion" (A10); and "if the assignment relates to a real world scenario then I really enjoy that … the theoretical side and the real world and linking the two together I find very interesting" (E8). Passion and personal readiness were other themes associated with the discipline: "for me personally it was just a level of being ready, and maturity and having that element of passion involved. It has to be something I'm interested in … because when you do have such a busy life, if it's something that you're not into, and something that you're not passionate about you really almost become resentful having to do it, so the interest in it is pretty important to me. It really is. That way it's motivating. If not I won't be motivated at all" (B3).

The other theme focused on the teacher: "to have good teachers definitely helps" (A2); "I found the tutor very good. It makes a big difference" (D3). Even when interest in the subject was low, a good teacher was able to engage the students. One student commented that they had never liked a particular subject, but that they "had a really friendly teacher [who] made it easier to learn" (A2). Another was worried that a subject would be boring but found that the teacher "was good and made it easy to understand" (I1). Passion and extensive knowledge were important for engaging in a discipline: "enthusiastic lecturers who have a broad knowledge of the subject not just that little bit they are teaching. It's important to not only have that key aspect but often when they can see the bigger picture that helps a lot and also having tutors who are passionate too and that generally results in people around you being enthusiastic, they want to do it and you want to do it" (B8); and "when a tutor gets up there you can tell there is a passion for a subject and that is contagious. I have had two tutors in both courses that you could tell they were so passionate about it and you know if you are not grasping a particular subject they will take extra time to explain it another way" (F5).

Quality teaching adapts to changing student expectations	Very important %	Important %
Receiving helpful guidance and advice about my study	57.4	35.5
Support services are available at the times I need them	42.0	38.9
Having access to the learning resources I need to succeed	61.2	33.9

The items selected to check out support for this proposition were all backed heavily as important for engagement. Support ranged from 80.9 to 95.1% for the selected items, among the strongest affirmation for any item in the survey. However, the TLRI project survey did not ask specifically about adaptability of the institution and teachers to respond to changing students' needs. The information about this came out in the interviews.

A number of students observed that their institution went to great lengths to support their learning needs. One student had an example of this: "I have tried the support staff, the support through the department, support through 'learning services' which has been beneficial to a certain degree but because I'm part Māori, I went through the Māori support services and they were much more helpful" (C2). A few mentioned that they could influence how the content of a course was delivered: "there is one teacher … you can criticize him for various things and that's good" (D3), "so I'm thinking I may be able to influence the content somehow … being able to challenge the teachers" (E9). However, it emerged that institutions were not incredibly flexible and that impeded engagement: "twice now when I've asked them to be a bit flexible the answer was no. The whole idea of doing a distance learning course for me was so that I could manage and organise my own time, not for them to say right you will do this when we want you to do it … they should be making it a bit easier because life is stressful as it is" (E2).

Engagement occurs across the lifespan	Very important %	Important %
Recognition that I have family and community responsibilities	36.0	31.4
Teachers valuing my prior knowledge	29.6	43.8
Recognition that I am employed	25.5	26.7

Most students were aware that engagement and learning did not stop at the classroom door. While not as great as for other propositions, support for the idea that engagement is impacted by external factors was still considered to be very important or important by 67.4, 73.4 and 52.2% of respondents. It is noteworthy though that fewer students thought that these items were very important compared to other propositions.

Most respondents reported facing major challenges outside the classroom. Responsibility to family, work and social networks were frequently mentioned, as were money problems, time poverty generally and tiredness after completing competing tasks. But stories of support for their studies by family members, friends and employers were also frequent. Support from family was most frequent: "my mum is very good, she helps out and has the kids once a week" (C6); "I tell my parents what food I need and so on and so I don't have to worry about meals" (I1); "I try to work things out with my husband and even my extended family have had the kids to stay or get someone to have the kids so I can get things done" (D5). Sometimes family support comes in unusual ways: "my daughter does the course with me. Two minds are better than one" (G3); "I actually still use the teen parent centre" (C6). Peer support outside the learning institution is also mentioned: "I've relied a lot on peer support" (D6); "I sort of utilize other friends to peer review some of my stuff" (C5). The support of employers is sometimes mentioned: "the support that my employer has given me has definitely encouraged me ... and it's made it easier to get started, and also time to do things on my various assessments that need to be done during work time" (H3).

Learning from outside the classroom also impacted learning inside it: "I talk to my employer because he is qualified and he is really helpful ... pretty much all my questions he has been able to answer" (E3); "a lot of people I'm talking to are grandparents ... you can see how they have been learning for the last twenty years and you get tips from them and how they approach their learning" (C3); and "I have ... a great flat mate who's been to University, she's been there and done that and she's given me tips about time management and my mum has been pretty good" (F5). One respondent learnt from the cleaner: 'I have a great relationship with the cleaner. I talk to her everyday ... she is quite a clued up woman ..." (D6).

Engagement is supported by subjective well-being	Very important %	Important %
Receiving helpful guidance and advice about my study	57.4	35.5
Knowing how to contact people to get help	49.0	42.5
Learning in a pleasant working environment	51.4	35.3

Subjective well-being focuses on how peoples' emotions support or detract from their learning. In a number of cases students were quite open about their subjective well-being and how this impacts their engagement in learning. Having guidance about study was very important or important to 92.9% of respondents; working in a pleasant working environment was very important or important to 84.7% and knowing how to contact people when in need to 91.5%. These responses, while only representative of subjective well-being suggest its importance for engagement.

Students mentioned a number of factors that contributed to their feelings of well-being: "I'm lucky I've got quite a lot of support from my husband and my family and they give me the time that I need" (E6); "I've got lots of support from my employer ... he is giving me four hours study time a week (paid) at work. I have to do at least four hours study at home too. But the support my employer has given me has definitely encouraged me to put in the effort myself and also made it easier to get started" (F3); "just having someone there to bounce ideas off, just another example of a way to do something, so you are not just looking at yourself and your ideas" (C7); and teachers "being really welcoming with my questions, making time, little things like that" (S6).

On the other hand, there were numerous negatives impacting well-being: "probably the number one thing that turns me off learning is that I finish my day at work then I feel I have more work to do" (E3); it's all the social commitments, family commitments, just being busy at work and coming home feeling really tired and not feeling like it" (D4); and "because I am a solo mum now and finding time to study and juggle work and it's very hard" (F2); "I broke up with my partner three months ago and study has hit a brick wall" (E1); and "I've actually had to put it on hold at the moment because my youngest is disabled and she uses up a lot of my time" (E7). Also coming through at times is a feeling of distrust: "I would always have at the back of my mind that you couldn't speak frankly because of the effect at the end of the day when you are having assessments" (C1).

Active citizenship is important for engagement	Very important %	Important %
Taking a leadership role in student affairs	8.0	23.6
Learning to affect change in the community/society	27.8	36.9
Learning to question teachers' practices	23.8	38.1

Judging by survey results, active citizenship, however defined, was not a priority for these students.

Nevertheless a third of these students made comments that suggest they do engage in active citizenship in various ways. They engage effectively with other students: "we have some students in our class who are racist. They don't like dark people … either way they are going to have to communicate with other people. In the end they have to get over it and realize we are all in one class" (D4); and "we must help each other" (D3). They like to develop their own views: "like I thought we were supposed to think critically, demand the answers, to try to dispute the theory and engage with it" (A10). A few challenge teachers and the content of their courses: "there is one teacher … you can criticize him for various things and that's good" (D3), "so I'm thinking I may be able to influence the content somehow … being able to challenge the teachers" (E9).

Interpretation

The empirical evidence from the TLRI project offered here suggests that there is support for the 10 propositions emergent from the literature. This evidence implies that these propositions can act as reference frames for discussions of engagement for students, teachers and their significant others. It also reveals further evidence for the inclusion of external environments as factors in student engagement. Student engagement is multifaceted, holistic and lifewide and is not confined to classrooms or formal curricula.

However, the evidence offered here falls short of validating the propositions in a formal positivist way. The propositions are derived from diverse literature and the items supporting each proposition were not originally created for the TLRI project. Consequently the propositions belong in an interpretative research domain. They offer valuable reference frames for thinking about indicators of engagement, but the evidence assembled in their support is suggestive rather than absolute.

Appendix B
Published Work Informing the Argument in the Book

My own published work has significantly informed the chapters in the book. To avoid overloading individual book chapters with references from my previous publications, I record them here.

Chapter 1

Zepke, N., & Leach, L. (2010). Improving student engagement: Ten proposals for action. *Active Learning in Higher Education, 11*(3), 167–179. doi:10.1177/1469787410379680

Chapter 2

Leach, L., & Zepke, N. (2011). Engaging students in learning: A review of a conceptual organiser. *Higher Education Research & Development, 30*(2), 193–204. doi:10.1080/07294360.2010.509761

Leach, L., & Zepke, N. (2012). Student engagement in learning: Facets of a complex interaction. In I. Solomonides, A. Reid, & P. Petocz (Eds.), *Engaging with learning in higher education* (pp. 231–256). Faringdon, UK: Libri Publishing.

Zepke, N. (2011). Understanding teaching, motivation and external influences in student engagement: How can complexity thinking help? *Research in Post-compulsory education, 16*(1), 1–24. doi:10.1080/13596748.2011.549721

Zepke, N. (2013). Lifelong education for subjective well-being: How do engagement and active citizenship contribute? *International Journal of Lifelong Education, 32*(5), 639–651. doi:10.1080/02601370.2012.753125

Zepke, N. (2013). Threshold concepts and student engagement: Revisiting pedagogical content knowledge. *Active Learning in Higher Education, 14*(2), 97–107. doi:10.1177/1469787413481127

Zepke, N., & Leach, L. (2010). Improving student engagement: Ten proposals for action. *Active Learning in Higher Education, 11*(3), 167–179. doi:10.1177/1469787410379680

© Springer Nature Singapore Pte Ltd. 2017
N. Zepke, *Student Engagement in Neoliberal Times*,
DOI 10.1007/978-981-10-3200-4

Zepke, N., Leach, L., & Butler, P. (2011). Non-institutional influences and student perceptions of success. *Studies in Higher Education, 36*(2), 227–242. doi:10.1080/03075070903545074

Chapter 3

Leach, L., & Zepke, N. (2011). Engaging students in learning: A review of a conceptual organiser. *Higher Education Research & Development, 30*(2), 193–204. doi:10.1080/07294360.2010.509761

Leach, L., Zepke, N., & Butler, P. (2014). Further and higher education teachers' perspectives on their role in student engagement: A snapshot from Aotearoa New Zealand. *Journal of Further and Higher Education, 38*(1), 19–36. doi:10.1080/0309877X.2012.699513

Zepke, N. (2011). Understanding teaching, motivation and external influences in student engagement: How can complexity thinking help? *Research in Post-compulsory education, 16*(1), 1–24. doi:10.1080/13596748.2011.549721

Zepke, N. (2013). Student engagement: A complex business supporting the first year experience in tertiary education. *International Journal of the First year in Higher Education, 4*(2), 1–14. doi:10.5204/intjfyhe.v4i1.183

Zepke, N., & Leach, L. (2010). Beyond hard outcomes: 'Soft' outcomes and engagement as student success. *Teaching in Higher Education, 15*(6), 661–673. doi:10.1080/13562517.2010.522084

Zepke, N., Leach, L., & Butler, P. (2009). The role of teacher student interactions in tertiary student engagement. *New Zealand Journal of Educational Studies, 44*(1), 69–82.

Zepke, N., Leach, L., & Butler, P. (2010). Engagement in post-compulsory education: Students' motivation and action. *Research in Post-compulsory education, 15*(1), 1–17. doi:10.1080/13596740903565269

Zepke, N., Leach, L., & Butler, P. (2010). Student engagement: What is it and what influences it? Retrieved from http://www.tlri.org.nz/sites/default/files/projects/9261-Introduction.pdf

Zepke, N., Leach, L., & Butler, P. (2011). Non-institutional influences and student perceptions of success. *Studies in Higher Education, 36*(2), 227–242. doi:10.1080/03075070903545074

Zepke, N., Leach, L., & Butler, P. (2014). Student engagement: Students' and teachers' perceptions. *Higher Education Research & Development, 33*(2), 386–398. doi:10.1080/07294360.2013.832160

Chapter 4

Zepke, N. (2001). In the net of economic rationalism. *New Zealand Journal of Adult Learning, 29*(2), 7–24.

Zepke, N. (2013). Lifelong education for subjective well-being: How do engagement and active citizenship contribute? *International Journal of Lifelong Education, 32*(5), 639–651. doi:10.1080/02601370.2012.753125

Zepke, N. (2014). What future for student engagement? *Higher Education, 69*(4), 693–704. doi:10.1997/s10734-014-9797-y

Zepke, N., & Leach, L. (2006). Improving tertiary student outcomes in an evidence-based accountability policy framework. *New Zealand Review of Education, 15:2005*, 23–43.

Chapter 5

Zepke, N. (2014). Student engagement research in higher education: Questioning an academic orthodoxy. *Teaching in Higher Education, 19*(6), 697–708. doi:10.1080/13562517.2014.901956

Zepke, N. (2015). Student engagement and neo-liberalism: Mapping and elective affinity. *International Journal of Lifelong Education, 34*(6), 696–709. doi:10.1080/02601370.2015.1096312

Zepke, N., & Leach, L. (2012). *The contribution of the Teaching and Learning Research Initiative to building knowledge about teaching and learning: A review of tertiary sector projects 2003–2011*. Retrieved from Wellington, New Zealand: http://www.tlri.org.nz/sites/default/files/pages/A%20review%20of%20tertiary%20sector%20projects%202003%E2%80%932011.pdf

Chapter 6

Zepke, N. (2014). What future for student engagement? *Higher Education, 69*(4), 693–704. doi:10.1997/s10734-014-9797-y

Zepke, N. (2015). Student engagement research: Thinking beyond the mainstream. *Higher Education Research & Development, 34*(6), 1311–1323. doi:10.1080/07294360.2015.1024635

Zepke, N., & Leach, L. (2010). Improving student engagement: Ten proposals for action. *Active Learning in Higher Education, 11*(3), 167–179. doi:10.1177/1469787410379680

Chapter 7

Zepke, N. (2011). Inclusive teaching: Making space for difference. In N. Zepke, D. Nugent, & L. Leach (Eds.), *Reflection to transformation: A self help book for teachers* (2nd ed., pp. 99–115). Wellington, New Zealand: Dunmore Publications.

Zepke, N. (2011). Navigating between Maori particularism and economic universalism in adult literacy provision in Aotearoa New Zealand: The case of a Wananga. *Discourse: Studies in the Cultural Politics of Education, 32*(3), 431–442. doi:10.1080/01596306.2011.573259

Zepke, N. (2015). Student engagement research: Thinking beyond the mainstream. *Higher Education Research & Development, 34*(6), 1311–1323. doi:10.1080/07294360.2015.1024635

Zepke, N., & Leach, L. (2011). Planning to engage. In N. Zepke, D. Nugent, & L. Leach (Eds.), *Reflection to transformation: A self help book for teachers* (2nd ed., pp. 195–218). Wellington, New Zealand: Dunmore Publications.

Chapter 9

Jordens, Z., & Zepke, N. (2009). A network approach to curriculum quality assessment. *Quality in Higher Education, 15*(3), 79–289. doi:10.1080/13538320903399125

Chapter 10

Leach, L., Neutze, G., & Zepke, N. (2001). Assessment and empowerment: Some critical questions. *Assessment and Evaluation in Higher Education, 26*(4), 293–306.

Chapter 11

Zepke, N. (2007). Leadership, power and activity systems in a higher education context: Will distributive leadership serve in an accountability driven world? *International Journal of Leadership in Education, 10*(3), 301–314. doi:10.1080/13603120601181514

Appendix A

Zepke, N., Leach, L., Anderson, H., Ayrton, A., Butler, P., Henderson, J., . . . Wiseley, A. (2008). *Improving student engagement in post-school settings: Nine case studies.* Retrieved from https://www.tlri.org.nz/tlri-research/research-completed/post-school-sector/learning-environments-and-student-engagement

Index

CPI Antony Rowe
Eastbourne, UK
April 07, 2020